WASHINGTON CONSUMERS' CHECKBOOK

GUIDE

to
Washington
Area

RESTAURANTS

by Jean Shirhall
and the
Editors of
Washington Consumers'
CHECKBOOK magazine

More copies may be ordered at $7.95 per copy from:

CHECKBOOK's Restaurant Guide
806 15th Street, N.W., Suite 925
Washington, D.C. 20005
(202) 347-7283

Make check payable to "Checkbook." Quantity prices available upon request.

CONTENTS

This book is a special publication of the Center for the Study of Services, a nonprofit organization dedicated to helping consumers get the most for their money when they buy services. Founded in 1974 with the help of funding from Consumers Union and the U.S. Office of Consumer Affairs, the Center is now supported primarily by subscribers to the two magazines it publishes in the Washington, D.C., and the San Francisco Bay areas. The magazines, entitled ***Washington Consumers' CHECKBOOK*** and ***Bay Area Consumers' CHECKBOOK***, rate the quality and prices of local service firms of various kinds, ranging from auto repair shops to hospitals to banks.

Book and Cover Design: DRPollard & Associates Inc.
Typesetting: Unicorn Graphics

Our sincere thanks to the thousands of *CHECKBOOK* magazine and ***Consumer Reports*** subscribers whose ratings made this book possible.

ISBN 0-9611432-3-1 $7.95

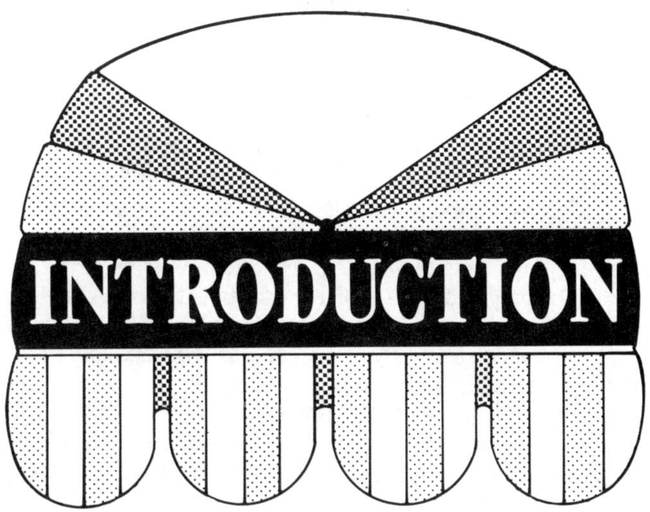

In this guide, we've pulled together in as brief a form as possible a broad range of information to help you find genuine dining pleasure at a fair price.

Many readers will know our nonprofit organization, the Center for the Study of Services, and our magazine, ***Washington Consumers' CHECKBOOK***, for in-depth evaluations of hospitals, insurance companies, auto repair services, home maintenance firms, and other types of local services. The basic approach is the same here: our research is careful, thorough, and unbiased; we accept no advertising nor other fees (nor free meals) from the firms we rate; and ***we*** decide which service firms to rate, whether they want to be included or not.

But restaurants are different in some respects. In most of our other reports, we try to steer you away from trouble; in this guide, we're trying to steer you to a good time. Also, what's good in a restaurant is literally a matter of taste; so there is, and should be, a lot more subjectivity and opinion in this guide than in our other reports.

For each restaurant, you'll find numerical scores showing how the restaurant was evaluated by consumer raters. These raters are *CHECKBOOK* magazine and ***Consumer Reports*** magazine subscribers who returned our questionnaires with ratings of restaurants they had recently visited. They rated the "food," "service," "ambience," and "value for your money." Possible scores run from 25 ("unacceptable") to 100 ("perfect"), but most restaurants scored between 60 and 90. So that you can understand what's behind the scores, we tell you how many ratings each restaurant received and how consistent the ratings were.

The raters are not master chefs nor professional critics. Rather, they are "real people," from all walks of life. They do, however, have characteristics in common—an ability to form (and explain) opinions, an interest in dining out, and a strong interest in getting what they pay for. As we reviewed the thousands of ratings and comments these raters submitted, we were struck by their keen appreciation for—indeed, excitement about—fine food. But we were equally struck by their ability to look at quality and price separately. As you will see, many restaurants received top marks for food, service, and ambience but weren't, in the opinion of our raters, worth the price. On the other hand, some restaurants were rated lower for the quality of their offerings had such good prices or generous portions that they were rated very high for "value."

While we think the opinions of "real people" are an excellent guide to restaurants you're likely to enjoy, it is interesting to have another perspective for comparison. So we've collected professionals' reviews from the ***Washington Post***, the ***Washingtonian***, the ***Washington Times***, the suburban ***Journal*** papers, and the ***Washington Business Journal***—as well as such guides as Phyllis Richman's ***Best Restaurants & Others***, and ***Frommer's 1987-1988 Guide to Washington, D.C.*** And we've included in our write-ups highlights of those comments, judgments, and recommendations. In addition, the write-ups note any recent honors a restaurant has received—such as a ***Travel-Holiday*** award, selection among the ***Washingtonian's*** "50 Best," or a high rating in the ***Mobil Travel Guide***."

Still another perspective on restaurants is health and sanitation. We tell you which of the restaurants have been closed for health code violations over a 21-month period, and the reasons for the closings, as reported in the ***Washington Post***. Fortunately, only a very few of the restaurants in this guide have suffered this fate—and for those that have the closing was only for a few days or less.

To help you find the right place for your budget, each restaurant has been categorized by price level, based on the range of prices on its menu and a sampling of the prices of the most popular items. And to help you satisfy your taste at the moment, the restaurants have been categorized by type of cuisine.

You'll also find the practical details on location, dress and reservation requirements, credit card acceptance, parking, Metrorail access, handicapped access, nonsmoking areas, entertainment, and hours.

The full facts on each restaurant, including a write-up of comments, are included in an alphabetized listing, which makes up the bulk of the guide. But we've pulled out information in a number of ways to make the guide easier to use.

Most important is the "Quick Check" table, beginning on page 9, which lists all the restaurants, separated into the District, Maryland, and Virginia, and into price categories within these three geographic areas. Within each location-price category, the restaurants are listed in order of the "food" score they received from our raters, and the type of cuisine is given for each. You can easily go to a location-price category and run your finger down the list until you find a top-rated, conveniently located restaurant serving a type of cuisine that suits your fancy.

To help you locate the restaurants, there are maps. Both in the alphabetical listing and on the Quick Check table you'll find map references—a letter and a number, such as "J-12"—that steer you to a section of the grid on one of the maps beginning on page 18.

We've also included a "Best for Food" list and a "Best for Value" list on page 8. And at the back of the guide, beginning on page 155, there's a list of the highest rated (for "food") restaurants grouped by type of cuisine.

Finally, beginning on page 157, you'll find listings of restaurants with such selected special features as Saturday or Sunday brunch, dim sum, sushi, scenic view, and outdoor dining.

The guide covers 422 restaurants—131 in the District of Columbia, 130 in Maryland, and 161 in Virginia. We included any restaurant (except a number of fast-food/mass-food chains) that received 10 or more ratings from our consumer raters. These are, in other words, the places where our raters eat. Virtually all of our raters live in the District, Alexandria, and Montgomery, Prince George's, Howard, Arlington, Fairfax, Loudoun, and Prince William counties. And these places were convenient enough that at least 10 raters had tried them.

Most of the best-known restaurants in the area are included. But so are many little-known places that our "real people" have discovered.

Read, eat, and enjoy.

BEST FOR FOOD

Inn at Little Washington
Ruth's Chris Steak House
L'Auberge Chez Francois
Le Lion d'Or
Morton's of Chicago
Le Pavillon
Le Chardon d'Or
Tachibana
The Prime Rib
Maison Blanche
Hunan East–Baileys Crossroads
Nora
Jean Louis
La Bergerie
Calvert House Inn
Iron Skillet
Mamma Regina
Terrazza
La Maree
Buon Giorno
Kazan
The Restaurant in Bethesda
Mandarin Inn
Bangkok Gourmet
House of Kao
Le Rivage
Artie's

BEST FOR VALUE

Thai Derm
Hunan East–Burke
Ambrosia
Panjshir
Hunan East–Baileys Crossroads
P. J. Skidoos
Peking & Hunan Gourmet
L'Auberge Chez Francois
Meadowlark Inn
El Bandito
Pasta Plus
Calvert House Inn
Hunan Village
Mandarin Inn
My An
Ivy's Place
Ledo
Parkway Deli
House of Mandarin
Meskerem
Zio's
Hsian Foong
Tachibana
Venice
La Maree
Tortilla Factory
Le Gaulois
Chef Theo's
Hunan Dynasty
Csiko's
House of Dynasty
Thai Kingdom

QUICK-CHECK TABLE

District of Columbia

		Food	Service	Value
$				
Geppetto–*Georgetown (J-11)*	Italian	84	71	75
Ivy's Place–*Cleveland Park (I-11)*	Indonesian	82	74	84
Szechuan Gallery–*Chinatown (J-12)*	Chinese	81	76	82
Meskerem–*Adams Morgan (J-12)*	Ethiopian	78	74	84
Vietnam Georgetown–*Georgetown (J-11)*	Vietnamese	78	73	79
Mixtec–*Adams Morgan (J-12)*	Mexican	76	65	71
Red Sea–*Adams Morgan (J-12)*	Ethiopian	75	69	81
Thai Room–*Van Ness (I-11)*	Thai	75	67	78
Fio's–*Mount Pleasant (I-12)*	Italian	74	61	81
Cafe Petitto–*Dupont Circle (J-12)*	Italian	73	67	68
Colonel Brook's Tavern–*Brookland (J-13)*	American	72	66	72
Hamburger Hamlet–*Friendship Heights (H-11)*	American	72	67	70
La Fonda–*Dupont Circle (J-12)*	Mexican	72	67	76
A.V. Ristorante Italiano–*Mount Vernon Square (J-13)*	Italian	71	49	70
Cafe Splendide–*Dupont Circle (J-12)*	Continental	71	63	79
Machiavelli's–*Capitol Hill (K-13)*	Italian	70	72	72
Mr. L's and Sun–*Van Ness (I-11)*	Chinese-Jewish	70	68	75
Reeves–*Downtown (J-12)*	American	70	71	73
Chadwicks–*Friendship Heights (H-11)*	American	69	69	70
$$				
Nora–*Dupont Circle (J-12)*	New American	88	79	75
Le Rivage–*S.W. Waterfront (K-12)*	French	87	82	82
Bacchus–*Dupont Circle (J-12)*	Lebanese	86	80	81
Le Gaulois–*West End (J-11)*	French	86	74	83
New Orleans Emporium–*Adams Morgan (J-12)*	Seafood	85	76	69
Thai Kingdom–*Downtown (J-12)*	Thai	85	84	83
Thai Taste–*Woodley Park (I-11)*	Thai	85	75	81
Helen's–*Dupont Circle (J-12)*	New American	84	76	76
Hunan Chinatown–*Chinatown (J-12)*	Chinese	83	77	82

District of Columbia *continued*

$$ *continued*

		Food	Service	Value
La Fourchette–*Adams Morgan (J-12)*	French	83	78	82
Bombay Palace–*Downtown (J-12)*	Indian	82	79	72
Floriana–*Friendship Heights (H-11)*	Italian	82	81	79
Hunan Dynasty–*Capitol Hill (K-13)*	Chinese	82	80	83
La Colline–*Capitol Hill (J-13)*	French	82	77	78
Mikado–*Tenleytown (I-11)*	Japanese	81	81	77
Occidental Grill–*Downtown (J-12)*	New American	81	79	72
Sarinah Satay House–*Georgetown (J-11)*	Indonesian	81	80	80
Csiko's–*Cleveland Park (I-11)*	Hungarian	80	84	83
Houston's–*Georgetown (J-11)*	American	80	76	82
Khyber Pass–*Woodley Park (I-11)*	Afghan	80	74	80
La Chaumiere–*Georgetown (J-11)*	French	80	75	77
Mrs. Simpson's–*Woodley Park (I-11)*	New American	80	76	74
Primi Piatti–*Downtown (J-12)*	Italian	80	73	70
Tout Va Bien–*Georgetown (J-11)*	French	80	78	75
Trattu–*Dupont Circle (J-12)*	Italian	80	73	77
Bistro Francais–*Georgetown (J-11)*	French	79	77	80
The Broker–*Capitol Hill (K-13)*	Swiss	79	79	73
Golden Palace–*Chinatown (J-12)*	Chinese	79	73	79
Le Caprice–*Upper Georgetown (J-11)*	French	79	70	73
New Heights–*Woodley Park (I-11)*	New American	79	78	69
Omega–*Adams Morgan (J-12)*	Cuban	79	75	80
Sushi-Ko–*Upper Georgetown (J-11)*	Japanese	79	79	69
City Cafe–*West End (J-11)*	New American	78	73	70
Japan Inn–*Upper Georgetown (J-11)*	Japanese	78	74	68
Katmandu–*Dupont Circle (J-12)*	Indian	78	68	72
Perry's–*Adams Morgan (J-12)*	Japanese	78	68	69
Pleasant Peasant–*Friendship Heights (H-11)*	American	78	77	75
700 Water Street Grill–*S.W. Waterfront (K-12)*	American	78	78	75
Tony Cheng's–*Chinatown (J-12)*	Mongolian	78	74	76
West End Cafe–*West End (J-11)*	New American	78	74	73
Caffe Italiano–*Cleveland Park (I-11)*	Italian	77	79	77
China Inn–*Chinatown (J-12)*	Chinese	77	65	77
Enriqueta's–*Georgetown (J-11)*	Mexican	77	72	71
Bamiyan I–*Georgetown (J-11)*	Afghan	76	72	79
Cafe La Ruche–*Georgetown (J-11)*	French	76	71	74
El Caribe–*Georgetown (J-11)*	Latin American	76	73	76
Lauriol Plaza–*Dupont Circle (J-12)*	Mexican	76	69	76
L'Escargot–*Cleveland Park (I-11)*	French	76	73	79
Petitto's–*Woodley Park (I-11)*	Italian	76	69	69
American Cafe–*Capitol Hill (J-13)*	American	75	64	67
Foggy Bottom Cafe–*Foggy Bottom (J-11)*	American	75	75	71
Le Jardin–*West End (J-11)*	French	75	71	74
Marrocco's–*Downtown (J-12)*	Italian	75	80	76
Odeon Cafe–*Dupont Circle (J-12)*	Italian	75	69	69
Otello–*Dupont Circle (J-12)*	Italian	75	70	79
Iron Gate Inn–*Dupont Circle (J-12)*	Lebanese	74	70	74
Luigi's–*Downtown (J-12)*	Italian	74	65	70
New Orleans Cafe–*Adams Morgan (J-12)*	New Orleans	74	69	72
2 Quail–*Capitol Hill (J-13)*	New American	74	70	72
Annie's Paramount Steak House–*Dupont Circle (J-12)*	Steak	73	72	78
Caspian Tea Room–*Spring Valley Center (I-10)*	Persian	73	73	71

District of Columbia *continued*

		Food	Service	Value
$$ *continued*				
Dar Es Salam–*Georgetown (J-11)*	Moroccan	73	82	70
Dona Flor–*Tenleytown (I-11)*	Brazilian	73	71	67
Hunan Gourmet–*Chinatown (J-12)*	Chinese	73	68	72
Market Inn–*Federal Center SW (K-12)*	Seafood	73	70	69
Suzanne's–*Dupont Circle (J-12)*	American	73	66	65
Szechuan–*Chinatown (J-12)*	Chinese	73	67	74
Yenching Palace–*Cleveland Park (I-11)*	Chinese	73	71	72
American Cafe–*Friendship Heights (H-11)*	American	72	68	70
Armand's Chicago Pizzeria–*Tenleytown (I-11)*	Pizza	72	61	68
Cafe Mozart–*Downtown (J-12)*	Viennese	72	69	75
House of Hunan–*Downtown (J-12)*	Chinese	72	71	69
Marrakesh–*Mount Vernon Square (J-12)*	Moroccan	72	78	74
Pier 7–*S.W. Waterfront (K-12)*	Seafood	72	70	71
Tandoor–*Georgetown (J-11)*	Indian	72	67	68
Old Ebbitt Grill–*Downtown (J-12)*	American	71	70	66
Swiss Cafe–*Chevy Chase, DC (H-11)*	Swiss	71	70	68
Jenny's–*Waterside Mall (K-12)*	Chinese	70	74	74
Wolensky's–*Foggy Bottom (J-11)*	American	70	64	68
Devon Bar & Grill–*Downtown (J-12)*	Seafood	69	67	65
Blackie's House of Beef–*West End (J-11)*	Steak House	66	66	66
Gangplank–*S.W. Waterfront (K-12)*	Seafood	66	66	62
Les Champs–*Foggy Bottom (J-11)*	Continental	64	71	68
Au Pied de Cochon–*Georgetown (J-11)*	French	63	65	74
Roma–*Cleveland Park (I-11)*	Italian	63	60	65
$$$				
Ruth's Chris Steak House–*Dupont Circle (J-12)*	Steak House	94	84	79
Morton's of Chicago–*Georgetown (J-11)*	Steak House	90	83	73
La Maree–*Downtown (J-12)*	Seafood	87	83	83
Filomena–*Georgetown (J-11)*	Italian	84	71	70
Prime Plus–*Downtown (J-12)*	New American	83	78	72
Dominique's–*Downtown (J-12)*	French	82	80	76
Germaine's–*Upper Georgetown (J-11)*	Asian	82	77	73
La Brasserie–*Capitol Hill (J-13)*	French	81	75	72
Vincenzo–*Dupont Circle (J-12)*	Seafood	81	72	61
Cantina D'Italia–*Downtown (J-12)*	Italian	80	77	59
Charley's Crab–*Downtown (J-12)*	Seafood	80	74	69
Harvey's–*Downtown (J-12)*	Seafood	79	74	70
Tabard Inn–*Dupont Circle (J-12)*	New American	78	66	70
Galileo–*Dupont Circle (J-12)*	Italian	77	72	58
Duke Ziebert's–*Downtown (J-12)*	American	72	70	63
The Fishery–*Chevy Chase, DC (G-11)*	Seafood	70	64	59
Phillips Flagship–*S.W. Waterfront (K-12)*	Seafood	67	66	63
Hogate's–*S.W. Waterfront (K-12)*	Seafood	64	62	59
$$$$				
Le Lion d'Or–*Downtown (J-12)*	French	90	84	72
Le Pavillon–*Downtown (J-12)*	French	90	87	65
Maison Blanche–*Downtown (J-12)*	French	89	86	80
The Prime Rib–*Downtown (J-12)*	Steak House	89	87	75
Jean Louis–*Foggy Bottom (J-11)*	French	88	84	67
Mr. K's–*Downtown (J-12)*	Chinese	85	88	67
Tiberio–*Downtown (J-12)*	Italian	85	80	60

District of Columbia *continued*

		Food	Service	Value
$$$$ *continued*				
Willard Room–*Downtown (J-12)*	New American	79	85	64
Mel Krupin's–*Downtown (J-12)*	American	73	73	64

Maryland

		Food	Service	Value
$				
Ledo–*Hyattsville (H-14)*	Italian	84	73	84
Thai Derm–*Silver Spring (G-12)*	Thai	84	75	92
Zio's–*Gaithersburg (B-3)*	Italian	83	73	84
Hunan Village–*Greenbelt (D-6)*	Chinese	82	77	85
Ambrosia–*Rockville (C-4)*	Greek	81	75	88
Bangkok Garden–*Bethesda (G-10)*	Thai	81	78	81
Chi-Chi's–*Gaithersburg (B-3)*	Mexican	81	77	81
China D'Lite–*Laurel (C-6)*	Chinese	81	81	80
Alamo–*Riverdale (H-15)*	Mexican	80	76	81
Hunan Inn–*Silver Spring (G-12)*	Chinese	80	73	78
La Posada–*Bethesda (G-10)*	Mexican	80	78	80
Maharaja–*Greenbelt (D-6)*	Indian	80	80	75
Parkway Deli–*Silver Spring (G-12)*	Delicatessen	80	78	84
Thai Place–*Bethesda (G-10)*	Thai	80	75	82
O'Brien's Pit Barbecue–*Rockville (C-4)*	Barbecue	78	67	74
Amalfi–*Rockville (C-4)*	Italian	77	68	79
Roy's Place–*Gaithersburg (B-3)*	American	77	70	71
Olney Ale House–*Olney (B-4)*	American	76	68	78
Tony Lin's Kitchen–*Rockville (C-4)*	Chinese	76	82	78
O'Brien's Pit Barbecue–*Bethesda (G-10)*	Barbecue	75	68	77
Ruby Tuesday–*Gaithersburg (B-3)*	American	75	69	77
El Torito–*Greenbelt (D-6)*	Mexican	74	70	77
Houlihan's–*Chevy Chase (H-11)*	American	74	72	75
Siddhartha–*Silver Spring (G-12)*	Indian	74	58	82
Geppetto–*Bethesda (G-10)*	Italian	72	67	68
Hamburger Hamlet–*Bethesda (G-10)*	American	70	65	70
Hard Times Cafe–*Rockville (C-4)*	Chili	68	72	76
Chi-Chi's–*Rockville (C-4)*	Mexican	67	65	69
El Torito–*Rockville (C-4)*	Mexican	62	64	65
$$				
Buon Giorno–*Bethesda (G-10)*	Italian	87	84	78
House of Kao–*Bethesda (G-10)*	Chinese	87	86	77
Mamma Regina–*Silver Spring (G-12)*	Italian	87	84	77
Mandarin Inn–*Rockville (C-4)*	Chinese	87	80	84
Le Vieux Logis–*Bethesda (G-10)*	French	85	77	74
Pasta Plus–*Laurel (C-6)*	Italian	85	77	85
Chez Nous–*Bethesda (G-10)*	French	84	82	76
J. J. Muldoon's–*Gaithersburg (B-3)*	Continental	84	81	80
Pancho Villa–*Rockville (C-4)*	Mexican	84	76	81
Chef's Secret–*Greenbelt (D-6)*	Continental	83	72	74
Hunan–*Rockville (C-4)*	Chinese	83	74	75
Le Manouche–*Rockville (C-4)*	French	83	84	79
Ocean Garden–*Silver Spring (G-12)*	Japanese-Chinese	83	77	80
Sakura Palace–*Silver Spring (G-12)*	Japanese	83	78	74
Bare Bones–*Gaithersburg (B-3)*	Barbecue	82	74	78
Flaming Pit–*Gaithersburg (B-3)*	American	82	86	80

Maryland *continued*		Food	Service	Value
$$ *continued*				
Golden Bull–*Adelphi (G-14)*	Steak House	82	76	77
Houston's–*Rockville (C-4)*	American	82	78	77
Dynasty–*Wheaton (C-4)*	Chinese	81	73	80
Embassy–*Wheaton (C-4)*	French	81	82	77
Far East–*Rockville (C-4)*	Chinese	81	75	79
Kabul West–*Bethesda (G-10)*	Afghan	81	71	79
Matuba–*Bethesda (G-10)*	Japanese	81	77	79
O'Donnell's–*Bethesda (G-10)*	Seafood	81	77	78
Meadowlark Inn–*Poolesville (B-2)*	American	80	79	86
North China–*Bethesda (G-10)*	Chinese	80	69	77
Peking & Hunan Gourmet–*Bethesda (G-10)*	Chinese	80	78	87
Pines of Rome–*Bethesda (G-10)*	Italian	80	72	82
Positano–*Bethesda (G-10)*	Italian	80	76	71
Cafe Royal–*Potomac (C-4)*	French	79	70	70
Frascati–*Bethesda (G-10)*	Italian	79	77	77
House of Chinese Gourmet–*Rockville (C-4)*	Chinese	79	73	76
Red Lobster–*Gaithersburg (B-3)*	Seafood	79	70	77
Bish Thompson's–*Bethesda (G-10)*	Seafood	78	74	73
China Coral–*Bethesda (G-10)*	Chinese	78	72	77
Four Rivers–*Rockville (C-4)*	Chinese	78	72	76
Golden Bull–*Gaithersburg (B-3)*	Steak House	78	73	74
Sylvia's–*Rockville (C-4)*	Italian	78	74	76
Tung Bor–*Wheaton (C-4)*	Chinese	78	66	75
Chef Theo's–*Silver Spring (G-12)*	Continental	77	74	83
China Harbor–*Rockville (C-4)*	Chinese	77	71	80
Claude's–*Gaithersburg (B-3)*	French	77	73	76
Fritzbe's–*Rockville (C-4)*	American	77	76	77
Mrs. K's Toll House–*Silver Spring (G-12)*	American	77	78	77
Oscar Taylor's–*Rockville (C-4)*	American	77	71	67
Red Lobster–*Lanham (D-6)*	Seafood	77	74	75
Sir Walter Raleigh–*Bethesda (G-10)*	American	77	74	77
Venice–*Wheaton (C-5)*	Italian	77	80	83
China Village–*Bethesda (G-10)*	Chinese	76	78	79
Cracked Claw–*Gaithersburg (B-3)*	Seafood	76	71	75
El Caribe–*Bethesda (G-10)*	Latin American	76	71	72
Jasper's–*Greenbelt (D-6)*	American	76	72	73
Plata Grande–*Beltsville (C-6)*	Mexican	76	75	73
Rips Country Inn–*Mitchellville (D-6)*	American	76	76	77
Sir Walter Raleigh–*College Park (G-15)*	American	76	76	74
Tia Queta–*Bethesda (G-10)*	Mexican	76	73	76
Vagabond–*Bethesda (G-10)*	Central European	76	69	75
Anchor Inn–*Wheaton (C-5)*	Seafood	75	74	73
Clyde's–*Columbia (B-6)*	American	75	77	75
Ferdinand's–*Wheaton (C-4)*	Continental	75	73	79
Fred & Harry's–*Silver Spring (G-12)*	Seafood	75	72	72
La Luna–*Bethesda (G-10)*	Italian	75	71	68
La Panetteria–*Bethesda (G-10)*	Italian	75	71	75
94th Aero Squadron–*College Park (G-15)*	Continental	75	71	69
Phineas–*Rockville (C-4)*	American	75	71	74
Raindancer–*Rockville (C-4)*	Seafood	75	75	76
Sir Walter Raleigh–*Gaithersburg (B-3)*	American	75	72	73
Sir Walter Raleigh–*Wheaton (C-4)*	American	73	75	74

Maryland *continued*		Food	Service	Value
$$ *continued*				
Asti-Roseto–*Bethesda (G-10)*	Italian	72	71	74
Jake's on the Pike–*Rockville (C-4)*	Italian	72	68	72
Michel's–*Bethesda (G-10)*	French	72	74	82
Schooner Bay Cafe–*Langley Park (G-13)*	Seafood	72	72	73
Wellington's–*Silver Spring (G-12)*	American	72	77	80
Misty Harbor–*Rockville (C-4)*	Seafood	71	66	69
New York, New York–*Rockville (C-4)*	American	71	67	67
Oscar's–*Rockville (C-4)*	American	71	65	70
Fireside Beef House–*Berwyn Heights (G-15)*	American	70	75	69
Marie Callendar's–*Rockville (C-4)*	American	70	64	69
Plata Grande–*Columbia (B-6)*	Mexican	70	67	72
Glen Echo Station–*Glen Echo (H-9)*	American	69	65	64
Kangaroo Katie's–*Greenbelt (D-6)*	American	69	70	68
The Rib–*Rockville (C-4)*	American	69	68	60
Sandpiper–*Olney (B-4)*	Seafood	69	69	63
Partners–*Bethesda (G-10)*	American	68	67	68
Carmack's–*Chevy Chase (G-11)*	American	67	72	68
Golden Flame–*Silver Spring (G-12)*	Continental	67	70	73
Blair Mansion Inn–*Silver Spring (G-12)*	American	61	64	64
$$$				
Calvert House Inn–*Riverdale (H-15)*	Seafood	87	81	85
The Restaurant in Bethesda–*Bethesda (G-10)*	French	87	81	79
King's Contrivance–*Columbia (B-6)*	French	86	76	73
La Ferme–*Chevy Chase (G-11)*	French	86	80	79
Le Marmiton–*Bethesda (G-10)*	French	86	82	73
La Miche–*Bethesda (G-10)*	French	85	79	75
Bello Mondo–*Bethesda (G-10)*	Italian	84	83	68
Crisfield's–*Silver Spring (G-12)*	Seafood	84	73	70
Harvey's–*Rockville (B-3)*	Seafood	83	80	69
Kona Kai–*Bethesda (G-10)*	Polynesian	82	74	75
Nova Europa–*Wheaton (C-5)*	Continental	82	81	77
Old Angler's Inn–*Potomac (D-3)*	French	77	71	62
Normandie Farm Inn–*Potomac (C-3)*	French	75	76	71
Comus Inn–*Comus (A-2)*	American	66	71	67

Virginia

$				
Hsian Foong–*Arlington (K-10)*	Chinese	86	79	84
Charlie Chiang's–*Alexandria (M-10)*	Chinese	84	77	79
Fantasy Garden–*Springfield (F-3)*	Chinese	84	82	80
Panjshir–*Falls Church (K-8)*	Afghan	84	74	88
Bar J–*Lorton (F-4)*	Tex-Mex	83	73	81
Fuddruckers–*Annandale (E-3)*	American	81	71	79
House of Mandarin–*Vienna (D-3)*	Chinese	81	76	84
My An–*Arlington (K-10)*	Vietnamese	81	72	84
Pines of Italy–*Arlington (K-10)*	Italian	81	68	79
Thai House–*Arlington (K-10)*	Thai	81	68	81
Duck Chang's–*Annandale (E-3)*	Chinese	79	71	72
El Bandito–*Alexandria (F-4)*	Mexican	79	74	85
T.G.I. Friday's–*Tysons Corner (D-3)*	American	79	73	74
Hard Times Cafe–*Alexandria (N-11)*	Chili	78	70	82
Nam Viet–*Arlington (K-10)*	Vietnamese	78	75	80

Virginia *continued*		Food	Service	Value
$ *continued*				
Ruby Tuesday–*Fairfax (E-2)*	American	78	72	75
Tortilla Factory–*Herndon (D-2)*	Mexican	78	76	83
H. I. Ribster's–*Annandale (E-3)*	American	77	74	75
Anita's–*Vienna (D-3)*	Mexican	76	70	76
Cafe Dalat–*Arlington (K-10)*	Vietnamese	76	67	79
Chadwicks–*Alexandria (N-12)*	American	76	76	76
Hunan West–*Springfield (F-3)*	Chinese	75	75	76
Joe's Place Pizza & Pasta–*Arlington (J-9)*	Italian	74	72	80
Casa Maria–*Alexandria (M-10)*	Mexican	73	68	73
Bennigan's–*Falls Church (K-8)*	American	72	66	71
Carlos O'Kelly's–*Fairfax City (E-3)*	Mexican	72	69	76
Chi-Chi's–*Baileys Crossroads (L-9)*	Mexican	72	70	74
Chili's–*Baileys Crossroads (L-9)*	American	72	70	73
PoFolks–*Fairfax City (E-3)*	Southern	72	69	77
Dalt's–*Baileys Crossroads (L-9)*	American	71	72	72
Rick Walker's Scoreboard–*Herndon (D-2)*	American	70	67	68
Anita's–*Burke (E-3)*	Mexican	68	70	71
Chili's–*Springfield (F-3)*	American	68	73	71
O'Brien's Pit Barbecue–*Springfield (F-3)*	Barbecue	68	64	69
Bombay Bicycle Club–*Alexandria (M-10)*	American	67	62	63
Casa Maria–*Tysons Corner (D-3)*	Mexican	67	66	65
Chi-Chi's–*Fairfax (E-2)*	Mexican	67	61	69
Chi-Chi's–*Springfield (F-3)*	Mexican	67	67	70
Chi-Chi's–*Alexandria (F-4)*	Mexican	65	61	70
Amphora–*Vienna (D-3)*	American	63	67	67
Anita's–*Herndon (D-2)*	Mexican	63	59	65
$$				
Tachibana–*Arlington (J-10)*	Japanese	89	80	84
Hunan East–*Baileys Crossroads (L-9)*	Chinese	88	87	88
Artie's–*Fairfax City (E-3)*	American	87	82	78
Bangkok Gourmet–*Arlington (L-11)*	Thai	87	81	74
Kazan–*McLean (I-9)*	Turkish	87	86	79
Hunan East–*Burke (E-3)*	Chinese	86	83	89
Matuba–*Arlington (K-11)*	Japanese	86	78	81
Peking Gourmet Inn–*Baileys Crossroads (L-9)*	Chinese	86	82	81
East Wind–*Alexandria (N-11)*	Vietnamese	85	83	77
Nizam's–*Vienna (D-3)*	Turkish	85	83	81
RT's–*Alexandria (L-11)*	Seafood	85	77	76
Hunan Lion–*Tysons Corner (D-3)*	Chinese	84	87	75
J. R.'s Steak House–*Fairfax (E-3)*	Steak House	84	80	71
L'Alouette–*Arlington (K-10)*	French	84	81	82
Mike's Italian Restaurant–*Alexandria (F-4)*	Italian	84	75	75
Alpine–*Arlington (J-10)*	Italian	83	80	80
Heart in Hand–*Clifton (F-2)*	American	83	79	81
House of Dynasty–*Alexandria (F-4)*	Chinese	83	79	83
Italia Bella–*Arlington (K-9)*	Italian	83	80	80
Mountain Jack's–*Falls Church (K-8)*	Steak House	83	84	80
Pierre et Madeline–*Vienna (D-3)*	French	83	85	75
Black Orchid–*Annandale (E-3)*	Continental	82	84	78
Da Domenico–*McLean (D-3)*	Italian	82	76	75
Espositos Pizza 'n Pasta–*Fairfax City (E-3)*	Italian	82	76	81
Gadsby's Tavern–*Alexandria (N-12)*	American	82	82	80

Virginia *continued*

$$ *continued*

Restaurant	Cuisine	Food	Service	Value
Geranio–*Alexandria (N-11)*	Italian	82	79	73
J. R.'s Stockyards Inn–*McLean (D-3)*	Steak House	82	78	76
Lebanese Taverna–*Arlington (K-10)*	Lebanese	82	71	79
Old Peking–*Oakton (E-3)*	Chinese	82	76	77
Bamiyan II–*Alexandria (N-12)*	Afghan	81	71	79
Bonaroti–*Vienna (D-3)*	Italian	81	82	76
Jacques' Cafe–*Arlington (K-10)*	French	81	73	79
Kabul Caravan–*Arlington (K-10)*	Afghan	81	77	81
Landini Brothers–*Alexandria (N-12)*	Italian	81	78	74
Le Refuge–*Alexandria (N-12)*	French	81	79	77
Marco Polo–*Vienna (D-3)*	Italian	81	78	76
Piatti Pizza & Pasta–*Alexandria (F-4)*	Italian	81	77	77
Taverna Cretekou–*Alexandria (N-11)*	Greek	81	78	79
Bilbo Baggins Cafe–*Alexandria (M-12)*	American	80	79	76
Helga's Cafe–*McLean (I-9)*	German	80	79	68
Il Porto–*Alexandria (N-12)*	Italian	80	76	78
Kohinoor–*Alexandria (M-10)*	Indian	80	69	78
Mount Vernon Inn–*Mt Vernon (F-4)*	American	80	84	72
P. J. Skidoos–*Fairfax (E-3)*	American	80	74	87
Phoenix–*Arlington (K-10)*	Greek	80	77	79
Sir Walter Raleigh–*Alexandria (F-4)*	American	80	79	75
Wu's Garden–*Vienna (D-3)*	Chinese	80	74	78
Eastport Raw Bar–*Alexandria (M-10)*	Seafood	79	72	76
House of Fortune–*McLean (I-9)*	Chinese	79	67	77
Kilroy's–*Springfield (F-3)*	American	79	75	82
Peking Imperial–*McLean (I-9)*	Chinese	79	76	82
Red Lobster–*Falls Church (K-8)*	Seafood	79	72	79
Squire Rockwell's–*Annandale (E-3)*	American	79	73	77
Cafe Tatti–*McLean (I-9)*	European	78	76	80
Carlyle Grand Cafe–*Arlington (L-11)*	American	78	77	73
Carnegie's–*Alexandria (M-10)*	American	78	72	73
Chesapeake Bay Seafood House–*Springfield (F-3)*	Seafood	78	75	80
Fedora Cafe–*Vienna (D-3)*	Italian	78	71	68
Fritzbe's–*Reston (D-2)*	American	78	71	77
Mustache Cafe–*Alexandria (N-11)*	American	78	87	77
Portner's–*Alexandria (M-12)*	American	78	76	74
Woo Lae Oak–*Arlington (K-11)*	Korean	78	67	78
Devon Seafood Grill–*Vienna (D-3)*	Seafood	77	72	70
Mama's Italian–*Fairfax City (E-3)*	Italian	77	75	78
Fritzbe's–*Annandale (E-3)*	American	76	74	75
Kaiserhof–*Fairfax City (E-3)*	German	76	74	72
Sir Walter Raleigh–*Falls Church (K-8)*	American	76	76	76
5 and Dime Cafe–*Herndon (D-2)*	American	75	68	69
Four Seasons–*Alexandria (M-10)*	Continental	75	71	75
La Mirabelle–*McLean (I-9)*	French	75	77	70
Tom Sarris' Orleans House–*Rosslyn (K-11)*	American	75	69	81
Joe Theismann's–*Alexandria (N-11)*	American	74	71	75
Red Lobster–*Fairfax City (E-3)*	Seafood	74	68	69
Rusty Scupper–*Vienna (D-3)*	Seafood	74	72	69
Shooter McGee's–*Alexandria (M-10)*	American	74	73	71
Tom Weston's–*Annandale (E-3)*	American	74	74	76
Cafe Italia II–*Fairfax City (E-3)*	Italian	73	71	74

Virginia *continued*

		Food	Service	Value
$$ *continued*				
Ecco Cafe–*Arlington (K-10)*	New American	73	68	66
American Cafe–*Vienna (D-3)*	American	72	63	61
Fish Market–*Alexandria (N-12)*	Seafood	72	68	70
Blackie's House Of Beef–*Springfield (F-3)*	Steak House	71	70	71
Caldwell's–*Annandale (E-3)*	American	71	70	70
Grand Wok–*McLean (I-8)*	Chinese	71	70	71
Potowmack Landing–*Alexandria (F-4)*	American	71	67	67
Charley's Place–*Springfield (F-3)*	American	70	68	70
Italian Oven–*McLean (I-9)*	Italian	70	71	73
Charley's Place–*McLean (I-9)*	American	69	68	67
Chesapeake Bay Seafood House–*Herndon (D-2)*	Seafood	69	77	77
Joe Theismann's–*Baileys Crossroads (L-9)*	American	69	69	69
Blue Channel Inn–*Reston (D-2)*	Seafood	68	64	65
New York, New York–*Rosslyn (K-11)*	American	68	68	69
Rhiannon's–*Springfield (F-3)*	American	68	68	65
Union Street Public House–*Alexandria (N-12)*	American	68	70	66
Amelia's–*Arlington (L-11)*	American	67	63	64
Joe Theismann's–*Vienna (D-3)*	American	67	68	67
Evans Farm Inn–*McLean (I-8)*	American	66	72	63
Heidelberg–*Alexandria (N-12)*	German	58	63	53
$$$				
La Bergerie–*Alexandria (M-12)*	French	88	83	79
Iron Skillet–*Baileys Crossroads (L-9)*	French	87	85	80
Terrazza–*Alexandria (N-11)*	Italian	87	78	76
Falls Landing–*Great Falls (D-3)*	Seafood	83	82	76
Le Couvert–*Springfield (F-3)*	French	83	83	74
La Guinguette–*Merrifield (E-3)*	French	82	82	71
Portofino–*Arlington (L-11)*	Italian	82	78	77
Tivoli–*Rosslyn (K-11)*	Italian	82	81	78
Alibi–*Fairfax City (E-3)*	French	81	81	70
Laporta's–*Alexandria (N-11)*	New American	81	78	73
Le Canard–*Vienna (D-3)*	French	81	82	74
Vinnie's–*Springfield (F-3)*	American	81	77	80
Johnny's–*McLean (D-3)*	New American	80	76	65
219–*Alexandria (N-12)*	French Creole	80	73	71
Clyde's–*McLean (D-3)*	American	79	76	72
Henry Africa–*Alexandria (N-11)*	French	78	79	72
Ice House Cafe–*Herndon (D-2)*	New American	77	75	67
Wayfarers–*Alexandria (N-12)*	Continental	65	63	58
$$$$				
Inn at Little Washington–*Washington (Off map)*	New American	96	92	81
L'Auberge Chez Francois–*Great Falls (D-3)*	French	93	89	86
Le Chardon d'Or–*Alexandria (N-12)*	French	90	84	70
Windows–*Rosslyn (K-11)*	New American	85	80	66
Serbian Crown–*Great Falls (D-3)*	Russian	78	76	64

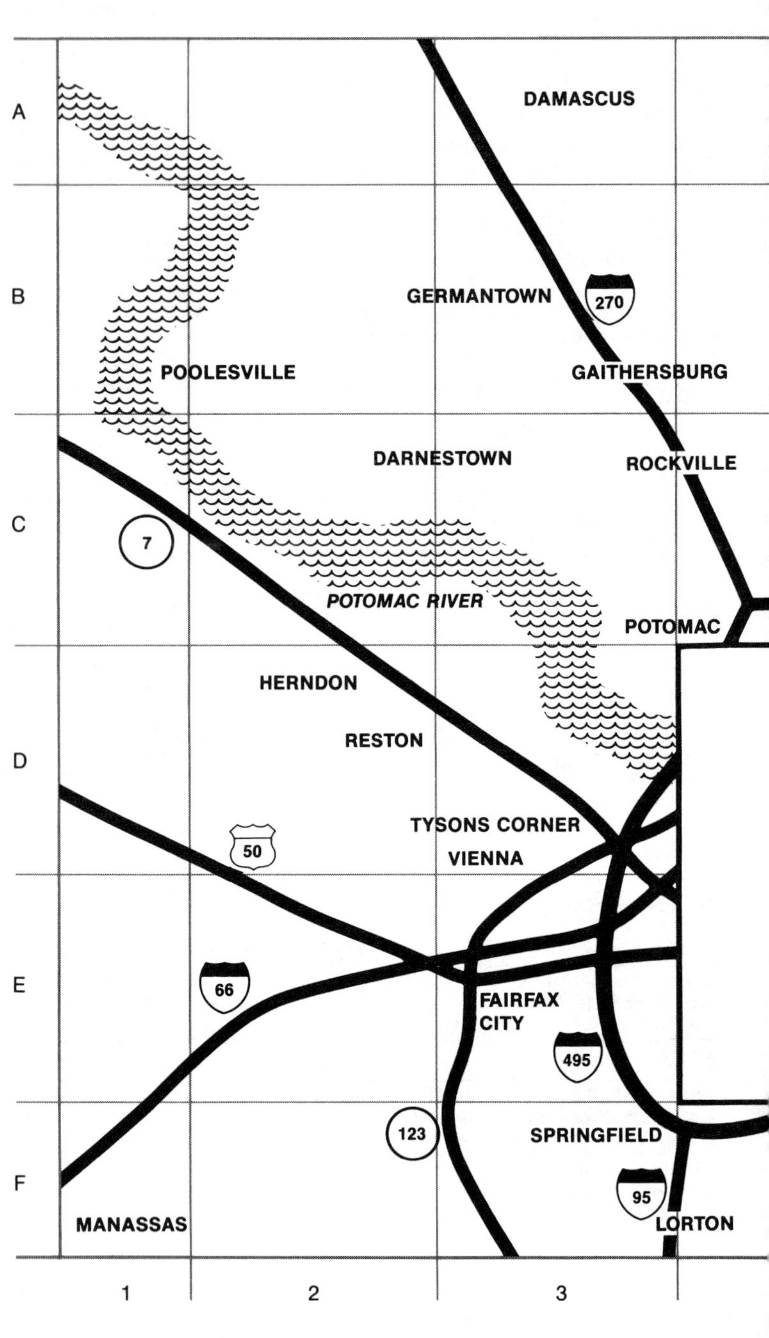

A
B
C
D
E
F
1
2
3
DAMASCUS
GERMANTOWN
270
POOLESVILLE
GAITHERSBURG
DARNESTOWN
ROCKVILLE
7
POTOMAC RIVER
POTOMAC
HERNDON
RESTON
TYSONS CORNER
VIENNA
50
66
FAIRFAX
CITY
495
123
SPRINGFIELD
95
MANASSAS
LORTON

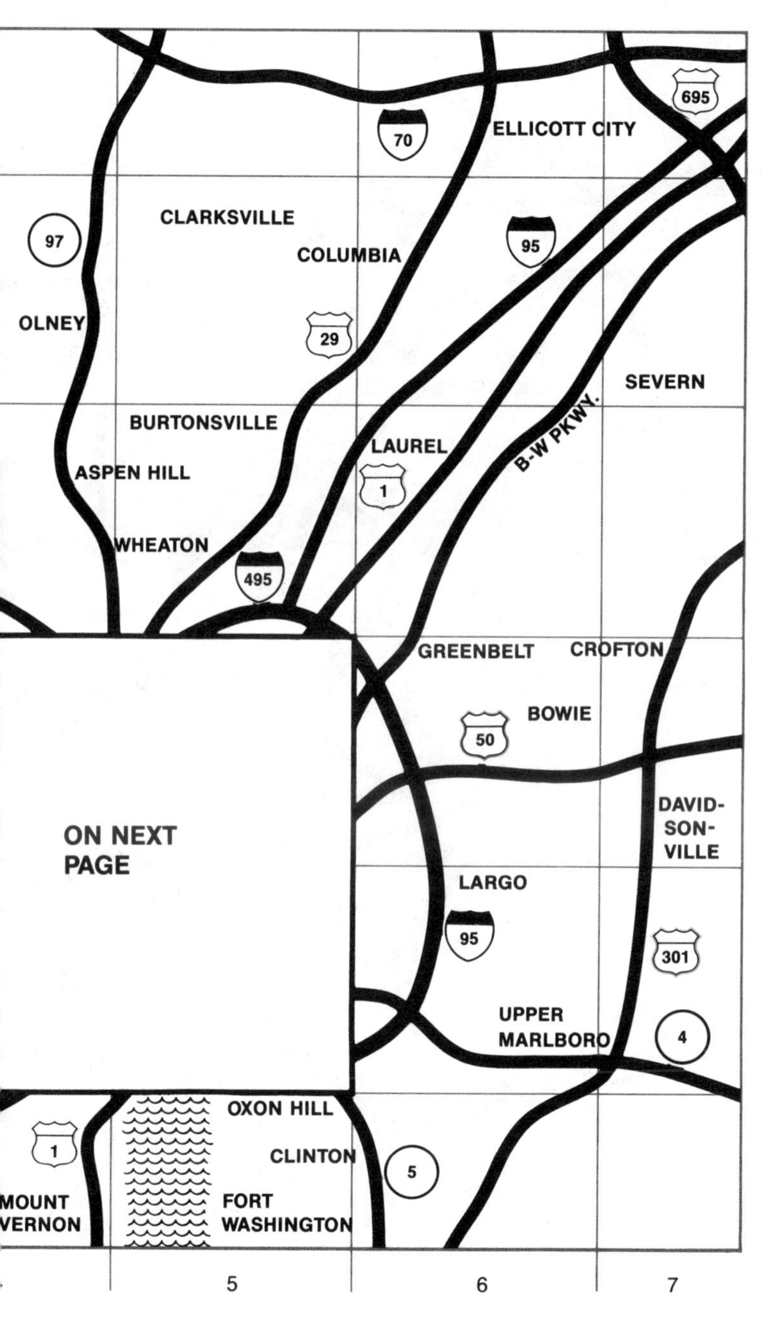
695
70
ELLICOTT CITY
CLARKSVILLE
97
COLUMBIA
95
OLNEY
29
SEVERN
B-W PKWY.
BURTONSVILLE
LAUREL
ASPEN HILL
1
WHEATON
495
GREENBELT
CROFTON
BOWIE
50
DAVID-
SON-
VILLE
ON NEXT
PAGE
LARGO
95
301
UPPER
MARLBORO
4
OXON HILL
1
CLINTON
5
MOUNT
VERNON
FORT
WASHINGTON
5
6
7

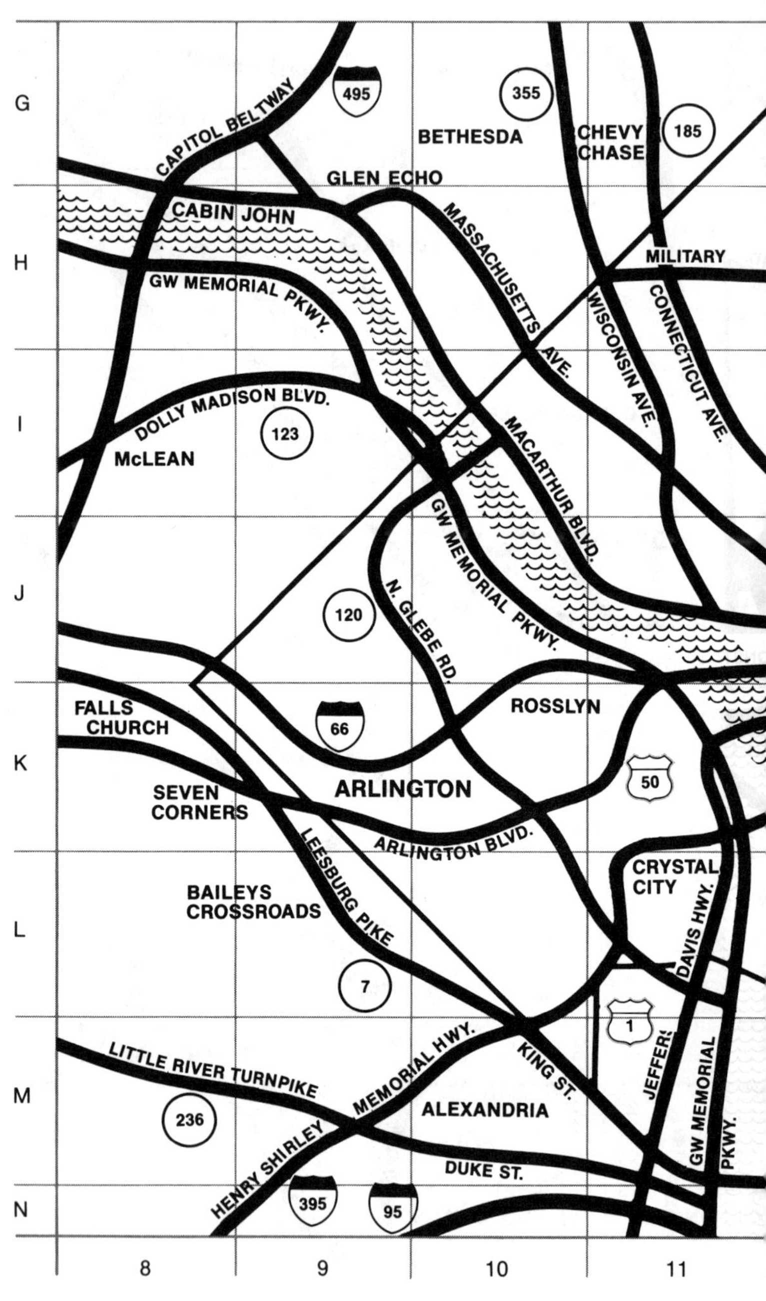
G
H
I
J
K
L
M
N
8
9
10
11
495
CAPITOL BELTWAY
355
BETHESDA
CHEVY CHASE
185
GLEN ECHO
CABIN JOHN
MASSACHUSETTS AVE.
MILITARY
GW MEMORIAL PKWY.
WISCONSIN AVE.
CONNECTICUT AVE.
DOLLY MADISON BLVD.
123
McLEAN
MACARTHUR BLVD.
GW MEMORIAL PKWY.
120
N. GLEBE RD.
FALLS CHURCH
66
ROSSLYN
50
SEVEN CORNERS
ARLINGTON
ARLINGTON BLVD.
LEESBURG PIKE
CRYSTAL CITY
BAILEYS CROSSROADS
DAVIS HWY.
7
1
MEMORIAL HWY.
LITTLE RIVER TURNPIKE
KING ST.
JEFFER
236
ALEXANDRIA
GW MEMORIAL PKWY.
HENRY SHIRLEY
DUKE ST.
395
95

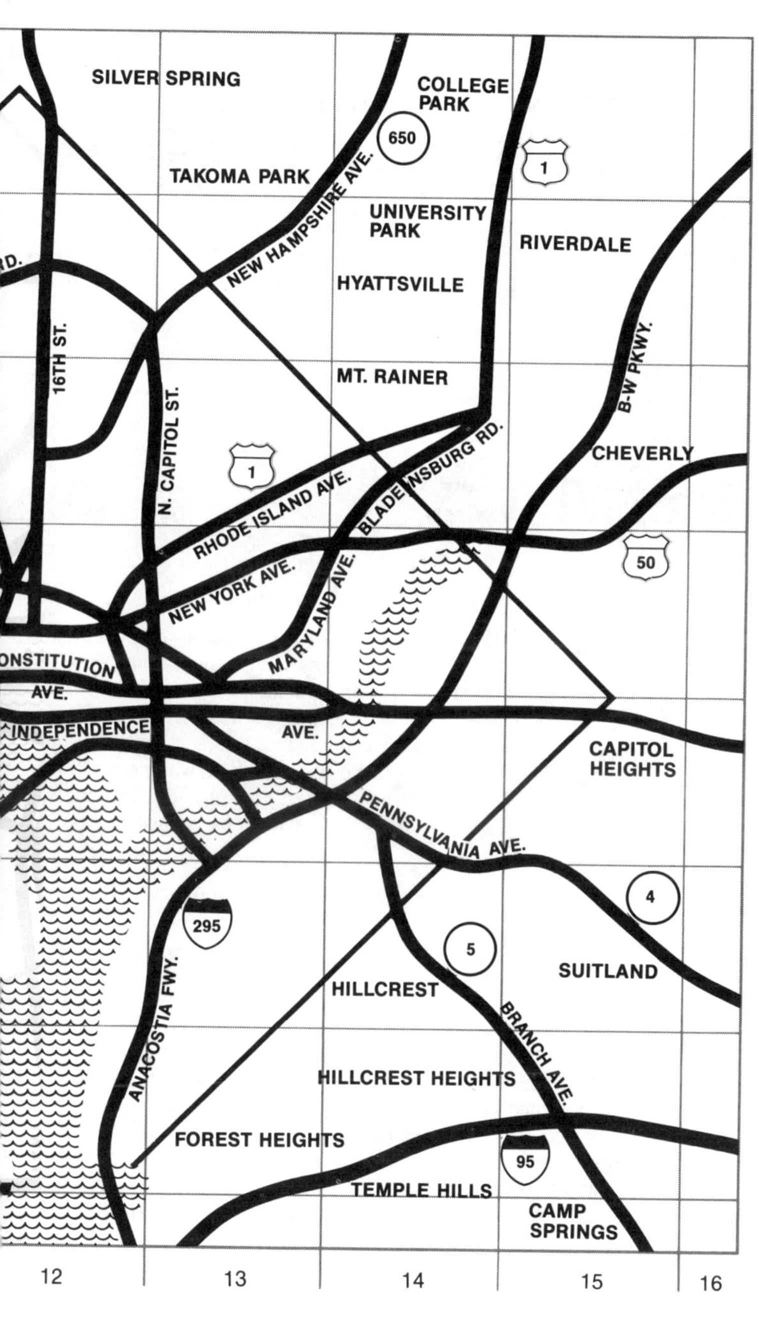

SILVER SPRING
COLLEGE PARK
650
TAKOMA PARK
NEW HAMPSHIRE AVE.
1
UNIVERSITY PARK
RIVERDALE
HYATTSVILLE
16TH ST.
N. CAPITOL ST.
MT. RAINER
B-W PKWY.
BLADENSBURG RD.
CHEVERLY
1
RHODE ISLAND AVE.
NEW YORK AVE.
50
MARYLAND AVE.
CONSTITUTION AVE.
INDEPENDENCE AVE.
CAPITOL HEIGHTS
PENNSYLVANIA AVE.
4
295
5
SUITLAND
ANACOSTIA FWY.
HILLCREST
BRANCH AVE.
HILLCREST HEIGHTS
FOREST HEIGHTS
95
TEMPLE HILLS
CAMP SPRINGS
12
13
14
15
16

HOW TO USE THE RESTAURANT WRITE-UPS

Beginning on page 29, you'll find an alphabetical listing of restaurants, with information on each. Below is a single restaurant's write-up, keyed to an explanation of each piece of information.

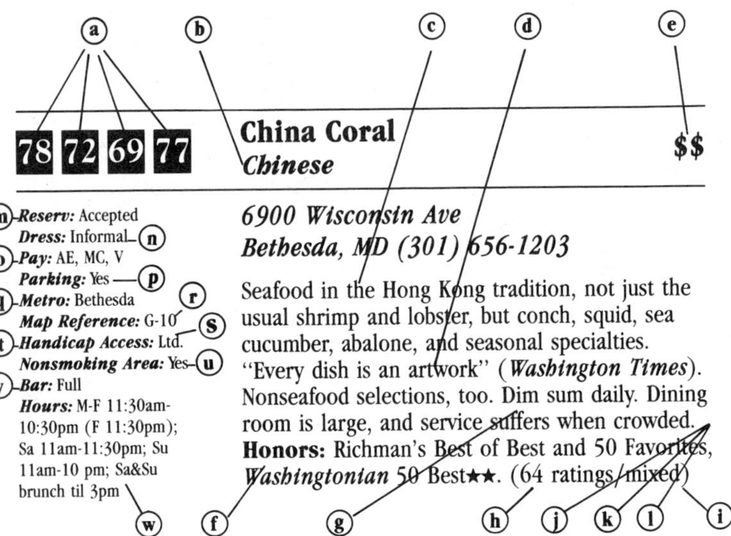

(a) **Consumer ratings.** These are the average scores each restaurant received from subscribers to *CHECKBOOK* and *Consumer Reports* magazines who returned our questionnaire (from mid-1987 through early 1988) and reported having eaten there. The scores are for the quality of "food," "service," and "ambience" and for "value for your money." The ratings were converted to a scale that runs from 25 to 100. A score of 25 would mean that every rater considered the restaurant "unacceptable"; 100 would mean that every rater considered it "perfect." As a practical matter, the scores for food, for example, range from 58 to 96, with an average score of about 78. The key in using these ratings is to *compare* restaurants. The figure below shows how restaurants' food scores were distributed among various categories.

Number of Restaurants by "Food" Ratings Score

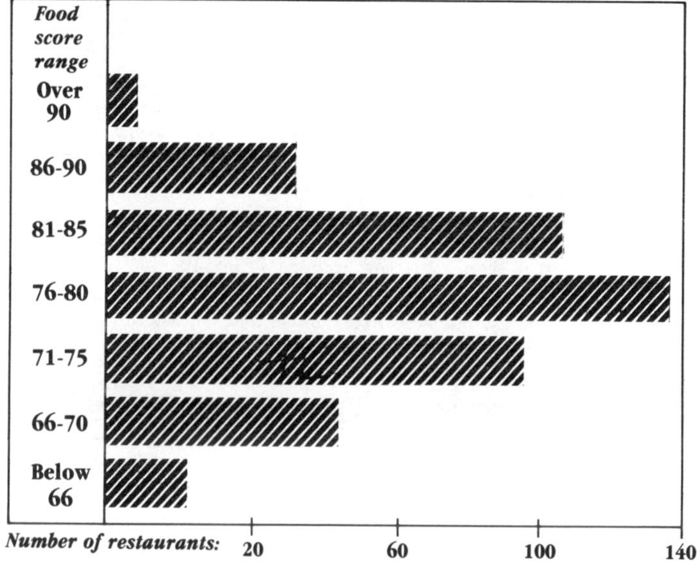

(b) **Cuisine.** We've categorized a restaurant's cuisine based on management's own claims and our review of menus. Many restaurants offer a variety of types of cooking and so aren't easily categorized, but our description should give you a rough idea of what to expect.

(c) **Description.** One element of each restaurant's write-up is a few comments on the type of food served, the nature of the service, and the ambience. We also mention especially popular or appealing menu items. This information is based on our own knowledge of the restaurants, questionnaires and interviews completed by restaurant management, menus and other written materials supplied by the restaurants, published reviews, and most important, thousands of comments made by our consumer raters.

(d) **Professional reviewers' comments.** For comparison, we've tried to pull out key phrases that highlight the insights, judgments, or recommendations of professionals who have reviewed the restaurant. Many of the restaurants, however, have not been reviewed, and even for those that have our selected phrases capture only a fragment of the entire review, although we've tried to retain the reviewer's intent.

To obtain this information, we monitored selected local newspapers and magazines. We refer to the following sources: the *Journal* papers *(Arlington Journal, Montgomery Journal,* etc.) (January 1987–May 1988), the *Washington Business Journal* (December 1986–December

1987), the ***Washington Post*** (January 1986–May 1988), the ***Washington Times*** (September 1987–May 1988), the ***Washingtonian*** magazine (January 1986–May 1988), ***Frommer's 1987-1988 Guide to Washington, D.C.*** (Prentice Hall Press, New York), and Phyllis Richman. Reviews by Ms. Richman, the ***Washington Post***'s restaurant editor, are referred to by her name, to distinguish them from the opinions of other reviewers who write for the ***Post***. Ms. Richman's reviews are cited as "Richman" whether they appeared in the ***Washington Post*** or in her book, ***Best Restaurants & Others***, published by 101 Productions, San Francisco.

(e) **Price category.** We've categorized restaurants on the basis of the average cost of dinner ***entrees***, exclusive of tax, tip, and such items as appetizers, beverages, and desserts. The figure below shows what the categories are and the number of restaurants that fell within each.

Number of Restaurants in Different Price Categories

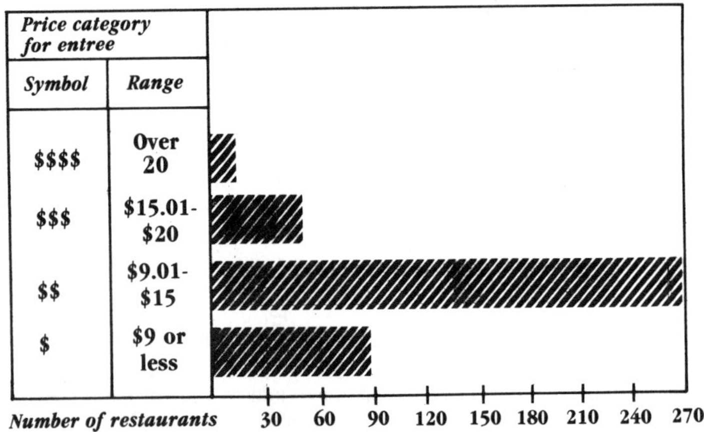

These categories are rough guides at best. For example, a restaurant in the "$$" category ($9.01 to $15) might well offer a few entrees for well below $9 and others costing considerably more than $15. Also, remember that your total ***meal*** will cost more than these ***entree*** price ranges. Tax and tip alone will add about 20 percent, and you are very likely to have drinks, an appetizer, a dessert, or some other item that adds to the cost. Often the extras are relatively more expensive than the basic entree. There has to be an element of judgment in our price groupings—for example, we had to adjust figures for restaurants that charge by the several-course dinner and don't price by entree alone.

(f) **Honors.** We've reported the following honors for the restaurants that earned them so that you can compare them to our raters' score.

From the American Automobile Association's *Tour Book, Mid-Atlantic (1987-88)*, restaurants receiving three or four "diamonds" (up to five are awarded, but none in this area received five) are indicated by "AAA◆◆◆" or "AAA◆◆◆◆."

From the *Journal* papers, restaurants receiving more than two stars (out of four) during the period from April 1987 through May 1988 are so indicated.

From the *Mobil Travel Guide*, Middle Atlantic States (1988), restaurants receiving three or four stars (up to five are awarded, but none in this area received five) are indicated by "Mobil★★★" or "Mobil★★★★." "Mobil specialty spots" are also noted.

From reviews by Phyllis Richman, we've indicated those restaurants that were singled out as being the "best" in Ms. Richman's book (1985 edition) of *Best Restaurants & Others* or selected for her September 20, 1987, *Washington Post* article entitled "My 50 Favorite Restaurants." These honors are noted as "Richman's Best of Best" and "Richman's 50 Favorites."

From *Travel-Holiday* magazine, any restaurant included in the magazine's "1988 Guide to Fine Dining in North American Restaurants" (December 1987) as an "award" winner or "selection" is so identified.

From the *Washington Times*, restaurants receiving three or four stars (the maximum is four) from September 1987 through May 1988 are so identified.

From the *Washingtonian* magazine, restaurants included on the magazine's January 1988 list of "The 50 Very Best Restaurants" are identified as "50 Best" restaurants and the number of stars awarded (maximum of four) is indicated; restaurants included on the magazine's May 1988 list of "50 Best Bargain Restaurants" are identified as "Cheap Eats" restaurants.

(g) **Special Features.** Where space allows, we've noted such special features as lunch buffets, happy hours, and early bird dinners.

(h) **Number of ratings.** This is the number of survey responses upon which our consumer ratings scores are based.

(i) **Consistency of ratings.** This information tells you the degree to which different raters agreed on the quality of the restaurant (the degree of consistency we've reported relates to "food" ratings). If you're considering two restaurants, each with a "food" score of 75, and the first received "very mixed" ratings while the second received "very consistent" ratings, you'll know that the first was loved by some raters and disliked by others while the second received about an average rating from almost everyone who ate there. This tells you that there's more risk *and* more chance of a real treat in going to the first restaurant rather than the second.

The consistency information, when combined with information on the number of consumer ratings, also bears on a second point: the confidence you can put in the ratings.

The consumer ratings are obviously an imperfect measure. For example, some restaurants may have scored low just because they were rated by unusually critical consumers or because the raters hit them on a bad day or ordered the worst items on the menu. The risk of such distortions is lower if there are a large number of raters and consistent ratings than if the opposite is true. The table below gives you an idea of the size of the differences in score you should look for in deciding whether the difference between two restaurants is important. For example, if both restaurants were rated by 30 raters and both received "consistent" ratings, you wouldn't want to put much weight on a difference in the two restaurants' scores unless one restaurant's score was at least five points higher than the other's.

Remember that even consistent large differences in the ratings two restaurants receive from large numbers of raters won't mean much if different types of individuals, with different standards or biases, rated the different restaurants. And remember that even if all of our raters loved a restaurant, that's no assurance that your tastes will run along the same lines.

How Many Points Difference in Ratings Score Should You Look for in Comparing Two Restaurants

Consistency category	***Number of ratings for each of two restaurants you are comparing***			
	10	***30***	***60***	***100***
Very consistent	**6**	**3**	**2**	**2**
Consistent	**9**	**5**	**3**	**3**
Mixed	**12**	**7**	**5**	**4**
Very mixed	**15**	**9**	**6**	**5**

(j) **Entertainment** *(not offered by sample restaurant)*. We note whether a restaurant offers entertainment and very briefly describe it. In many cases, this entertainment is quite modest—an occasional passthrough by a guitarist, for example. Moreover, entertainment arrangements change constantly. If you're interested, call before going and find out what's on schedule, when it will occur, and whether there is a cover charge.

(k) **Health department closings** *(none for sample restaurant)*. We report at this point in a restaurant's write-up instances in which the restaurant was required to close as a result of deficiencies found by local health department inspectors. This information is drawn from the *Washington Post* for the period September 1986 through May 1988. We indicate the reasons for the closing and the dates, as reported in the *Post*. We have not included closings caused by fire, power failures, or other problems that seemed to us beyond the restaurant's control.

(l) **Cross references to other restaurant locations** *(none for sample restaurant)*. If a restaurant has other locations, we tell you here. If we have consumer ratings for any of those locations, we give you the telephone number. You can find those ratings on the Quick Check table beginning on page 9. We've included a write-up in the alphabetical listing only for the location with the largest number of ratings.

(m) **Reservations.** We've reported the restaurant's most stringent policy regarding reservations at dinner for small parties (up to four people) and the days it applies if not every day. The policy for lunch is reported if it is more stringent than the policy for dinner. Many restaurants require reservations at lunch and dinner for parties of six or more. Our categories are "Required," "Accepted," "Suggested," "Not Accepted."

(n) **Dress.** This is the restaurant's most stringent dress requirement for male patrons at dinner and the days it applies if not every day. The dress code for lunch is reported if it is more stringent than the one for dinner. Our categories are "Coat [and/or] Tie Required," "Coat [and/or] Tie Suggested," "Informal."

(o) **Payment.** Accepted forms of payment are reported here: cash only, personal checks, and the following credit cards—AE (American Express), CB (Carte Blanche), DC (Diners Club), Disc (Discover), M (MasterCard), V (Visa). Those restaurants that accept personal checks often require one or more major credit cards for identification. U.S. traveler's checks are assumed to be acceptable everywhere.

(p) **Parking.** This refers to the availability of free parking in a restaurant lot or a public lot. Categories are "Yes," "No," "Valet" (includes "Yes"). For some restaurants, parking conditions apply only at certain times, and we have included that information when available. For example, "Yes (after 6pm)" indicates that free or validated parking is available in a public lot or parking garage after 6pm. Of course, at some restaurants that don't offer lot parking, parking will be no problem for you—if there is ample parking on the street.

(q) **Metro.** Metrorail information is reported only for those restaurants that are within easy walking distance (approximately three-eighths of a mile) of a subway station.

(r) **Map Reference.** The location of each restaurant is keyed to one of the two maps on pages 18 to 21. Sections A through F are located on the area-wide map and sections G through N are located on the enlarged map of the District of Columbia and close-in suburbs. "Off map" identifies those restaurants that are outside the area covered by the maps.

(s) **Area** *(not reported in sample)*. Commonly used area or neighborhood names are reported to help you locate the restaurant. An area name is not reported if it is the same as the name of the Metro station reported.

(t) **Handicap Access.** The information on access for handicapped persons was obtained largely from the restaurants themselves. We did not inspect the restaurants to determine the extent to which they met established standards for handicapped access. Secondary sources that report accessibility based on on-site inspections were used to verify the restaurants' reports to the maximum extent possible. One of our restaurant raters who uses a wheelchair also provided access information on the restaurants he had visited. The categories used are "Yes," "No," and "Limited." If a restaurant said it was not accessible, we took its word on the matter. "Limited" usually indicates that the parking or restroom facilities do not meet the standards for handicapped access. Handicapped persons should interpret the information reported here only as a general indicator of accessibility, not as a guarantee. We hope it will be helpful, but we suggest you call the restaurant before going.

(u) **Nonsmoking area.** Regulations regarding nonsmoking areas and definitions of what constitutes a nonsmoking area differ from one jurisdiction to another. Restaurants were asked if they had "separate smoking and nonsmoking areas," and their yes or no response is reported.

(v) **Bar.** We indicate here what type of alcoholic beverages are served—"Wine," "Beer," "Full" (meaning cocktails in addition to wine and beer), or "None." We also include the word "Separate" when you can get drinks not just at your table but also at a separate bar.

(w) **Hours.** Approximate opening and closing times are reported. But keep in mind that this information is hard to pin down and changes frequently. The hours reported are the approximate hours during which food is served; many restaurants have lounge areas that remain open after the dining room is closed, but we have not reported those variations. Again, if this information is of particular importance to you, we suggest you call and verify the hours for the day in question.

Food	Service	Ambience	Value

A.V. Ristorante Italiano
Italian $

71	49	55	70

Reserv: Not accepted
Dress: Informal
Pay: AE, MC, V, DC
Parking: Yes
Metro: Gallery Place
Map Reference: J-13
Area: Mount Vernon Square
Handicap Access: Yes
Nonsmoking Area: No
Bar: Full/separate
Hours: M-F 11:30am-11pm (F midnight); Sa 1pm-midnight

607 New York Ave, NW
Washington, DC (202) 737-0550

Going to this "cross between crazy and cozy" for great pizza or large platters of hearty Italian food is a tradition for many Washingtonians. Some dishes are better than others, so choose carefully. Don't be put off by the service; it's a tradition, too. Phyllis Richman says the place has "mellowed," and the *Washington Times* found it "better than ever." The old jukebox is still there. (14 ratings/mixed)

Alamo
Mexican $

80	76	65	81

Reserv: Not accepted
Dress: Informal
Pay: AE, MC, V, DC, CB
Parking: Yes
Map Reference: H-15
Handicap Access: Yes
Nonsmoking Area: Yes
Bar: Full/separate
Hours: M-Sa 11am-11pm; Su noon-10pm

5510 Kenilworth Ave
Riverdale, MD (301) 927-8787

An oldtimer (1954) of a Mexican restaurant, though ownership has changed several times. Known for generous portions and reasonable prices. Chef on premises prepares "authentic" versions of popular Mexican dishes—fajitas, burritos, tacos, and more. TV-equipped lounge; strolling guitarists Fri. and Sat. nights. "An oasis of 'la cuicina Mejicana' " (*Journal* papers). (10 ratings/consistent)

Alibi
French $$$

81	81	76	70

Reserv: Suggested
Dress: Coat req. F&Sa
Pay: AE, MC, V, DC, CB
Parking: Valet (eves)
Map Reference: E-3
Handicap Access: No
Nonsmoking Area: No
Bar: Full/separate
Hours: M-F 11am-2:30pm, 6-10pm (F 10:30pm); Sa 6-10:30pm; Su 5-10pm

10418 Main St
Fairfax City, VA (703) 591-6319

French food prepared with a deft hand. Veal Alibi and beef (or lamb) Wellington recommended by raters; seafood dishes are the chef's favorites. Prices a bit high for Fairfax City, but fixed priced dinners available. Noise level at busy times can mar otherwise intimate atmosphere. "Generally meets expectations for a good French restaurant" (*Journal* papers). (18 ratings/consistent)

83 80 77 80

Alpine
Italian

$$

Reserv: Suggested
Dress: Informal
Pay: AE, MC, V, DC, CB
Parking: Yes
Map Reference: J-10
Handicap Access: No
Nonsmoking Area: Yes
Bar: Full
Hours: M-Sa 11:30am-11pm; Su noon-10pm

4770 Lee Hwy
Arlington, VA (703) 528-7600

The two owner-chefs are a winning combination of long standing. Northern Italian menu features very good homemade pasta, seafood, and a variety of veal dishes. Professional European service. Rustic dining rooms are a bit dark. Guitarist/singer Fri. and Sat. Parking space is limited. (46 ratings/mixed)

77 68 62 79

Amalfi
Italian

$

Reserv: Not accepted
Dress: Informal
Pay: AE, MC, V, DC, CB
Parking: Yes
Metro: Twinbrook
Map Reference: C-4
Handicap Access: Ltd.
Nonsmoking Area: Yes
Bar: Full
Hours: T-F 11:30am-10pm (F 11pm); Sa 1:30-11pm; Su 1:30-9pm

12307 Wilkins Ave
Rockville, MD (301) 770-7888

Cozy neighborhood restaurant serving "the true cooking of Italy" (***Washington Business Journal***)—and at reasonable prices. Menu includes deep-fried mozzarella, Italian soups, white pizza, and veal, chicken, and seafood entrees. Raters really liked white pizza and homemade bread. Good place for families, but may have long wait for table at popular times. (34 ratings/mixed)

81 75 57 88

Ambrosia
Greek

$

Reserv: Not accepted
Dress: Informal
Pay: Cash only
Parking: Yes
Metro: Twinbrook
Map Reference: C-4
Handicap Access: Yes
Nonsmoking Area: Yes
Bar: Beer/wine/separate
Hours: M-Sa 7am-2am

1765 Rockville Pike
Rockville, MD (301) 881-3636

Still a great bargain—ample portions of Greek dishes (plus some Italian) at very reasonable prices. The Ambrosia Special (souvlaki and gyros on pita) and the moussaka got good marks from ***Washington Post*** and ***Washingtonian***. Small, friendly, family-type place; makes no pretenses about providing atmosphere. Good spot for breakfast and late-night snacks. (27 ratings/consistent)

Food	Service	Ambience	Value

Amelia's
American $$

1725 Jefferson Davis Hwy
Arlington, VA (703) 920-6650

Reserv: Suggested
Dress: Informal
Pay: AE, MC, V, DC
Parking: Yes (2 hrs)
Metro: Crystal City
Map Reference: L-11
Area: Crystal City Underground
Handicap Access: Yes
Nonsmoking Area: Yes
Bar: Full/separate
Hours: M-Sa 11am-10pm

Pleasant, informal cafe and formal dining room. Has a ready clientele of Crystal City office and apartment dwellers, but food and service can be erratic. Menu of American favorites, some with a different twist, such as the crab-stuffed chicken Amelia. Singer in cafe evenings. (21 ratings/mixed)

72 68 71 70

American Cafe
American $$

5252 Wisconsin Ave, NW
Washington, DC (202) 363-5400

Reserv: Accepted; sugg. lunch
Dress: Informal
Pay: AE, MC, V, DC
Parking: Yes (2 hrs)
Metro: Friendship Heights
Map Reference: H-11
Handicap Access: Yes
Nonsmoking Area: Yes
Bar: Full/separate
Hours: M-Th 11am-11pm; F&Sa 11am-1am; Su 10:30am-11pm, brunch til 3pm

The many fans of the American Cafes still enjoy the trendy cafe lunches and dinners, the late night snacks, the Sun. brunches. Others say they're overrated and are bothered by the erratic service, noise, and unpredictable kitchen. *Washington Times* found some "favorites are back on the mark." Seven other locations; see ratings for Mass. Ave., NE (547-8500) and Vienna, Va. (848-9476) locations. (48 ratings/mixed)

63 

67

Amphora
American $

377 Maple Ave, W
Vienna, VA (703) 938-7877

Reserv: Not accepted
Dress: Informal
Pay: AE, MC, V, DC, CB
Parking: Yes
Map Reference: D-3
Handicap Access: Yes
Nonsmoking Area: Yes
Bar: Full/separate
Hours: Daily, 24 hrs

Family-style restaurant and diner providing full-menu service around the clock. Large menu, which has been changed as part of tenth anniversary celebration, includes many homemade Greek dishes and a long list of pastries from bakery on premises. Suburban stop for breakfast or a late-night snack. Food preparation uneven. Same ownership as the Knossos restaurants in the area. (47 ratings/very mixed)

Food	Service	Ambience	Value

75	74	71	73

Anchor Inn $$
Seafood

Reserv: Suggested
Dress: Informal
Pay: AE, MC, V
Parking: Yes
Map Reference: C-5
Handicap Access: Yes
Nonsmoking Area: Yes
Bar: Full/separate
Hours: M-Sa 11am-midnight; Su noon-midnight

2509 University Blvd, W
Wheaton, MD (301) 933-8111

The Scaggs have been serving a variety of fresh Chesapeake Bay seafood, such as their fisherman's platter, shrimp and crab Norfolk, and surf and turf platter, for over 25 years. But in Phyllis Richman's opinion, "if one dish can make a restaurant, it is the Anchor Inn's crab imperial." Daily lunch and dinner specials. Also own the Raindancer (see below) and Cuckoo's Nest. (64 ratings/mixed)

76	70	51	76

Anita's $
Mexican

Reserv: Not accepted
Dress: Informal
Pay: Checks
Parking: Yes
Map Reference: D-3
Handicap Access: Ltd.
Nonsmoking Area: No
Bar: Beer/wine
Hours: M-Th 7am-9:30pm; F&Sa 7am-10:30pm; Su 7am-9pm

147 Maple Ave, W
Vienna, VA (703) 938-0888

Real New Mexico chili and other authentic dishes from the Southwest. Food is good and plentiful. Critics agree with raters who say Anita's has the best New Mexican food. Four other locations; see ratings for Burke, Va. (455-3466) and Herndon, Va. (481-1441) locations. Food gets higher ratings at this headquarters location, which will be moving. Some locations serve brunch. **Honors:** Richman's 50 Favorites. (40 ratings/consistent)

73	72	75	78

Annie's Paramount Steak House $$
Steak House

Reserv: Accepted
Dress: Informal
Pay: AE, MC, V, DC
Parking: No
Metro: Dupont Circle
Map Reference: J-12
Handicap Access: No
Nonsmoking Area: No
Bar: Full/separate
Hours: M-Th 11am-11:30pm; F 11am-1am; Sa 10:30am-1am; Su 10:30am-11:30pm; Sa&Su brunch til 3:45pm

1609 17th St, NW
Washington, DC (202) 232-0395

Annie's has been serving moderately priced steaks to Washington area diners for 40 years. Crab cakes, other seafood, chicken, and salads also on menu. Gets crowded on weekends; popular with gay community. Other location is "one of few venerable spots left in historic Georgetown" (Phyllis Richman). (15 ratings/consistent)

Food	Service	Ambience	Value

72	61	60	68

Armand's Chicago Pizzeria $$
Pizza

Reserv: Not accepted
Dress: Informal
Pay: AE, MC, V, DC, CB, Disc.
Parking: No
Metro: Tenleytown
Map Reference: I-11
Handicap Access: Ltd.
Nonsmoking Area: No
Bar: Full
Hours: Su-Th 11:30am-midnight; F&Sa 11:30am-2am

4231 Wisconsin Ave, NW
Washington, DC (202) 686-9450

Well-known for popularizing Chicago-style pizza in this area. Fans say it has best pizza in town. Appeals to youngish set. Long wait to be seated and noisy when busy. Pizza and all-you-can-eat salad bar at lunch. Sidewalk cafe. Numerous other locations, but some are only carryouts. **Honors:** Mobil specialty spot. (27 ratings/mixed)

87	82	80	78

Artie's $$
American

Reserv: Not accepted
Dress: Informal
Pay: AE, MC, V
Parking: Yes
Map Reference: E-3
Area: Off Fairfax Circle
Handicap Access: Yes
Nonsmoking Area: Yes
Bar: Full/separate
Hours: M-Th 11:30am-1am; F&Sa 11:30am-2am; Su 10:30am-midnight, brunch til 3pm

3260 Old Lee Hwy
Fairfax City, VA (703) 273-7600

Attractive fern bar with an air of vitality. Expanded menu features grilled meats and seafood, fresh pasta, some Cajun dishes, and very good desserts. Food is well prepared; service is cheerful. "Enough tasty creations to bring you back again" (***Washington Post***). Piano music Wed.-Sat. and during Sun. brunch. (49 ratings/consistent)

72	71	76	74

Asti-Roseto $$
Italian

Reserv: Accepted
Dress: Informal
Pay: AE, MC, V, DC, CB
Parking: No
Metro: Bethesda
Map Reference: G-10
Handicap Access: No
Nonsmoking Area: No
Bar: Full
Hours: M-Sa 11:30am-2:30pm, 5-10pm (F&Sa 11pm); Su 5-10:30pm

7940 Wisconsin Ave
Bethesda, MD (301) 652-1300

Some of the ratings were in before the owners lowered prices, expanded the menu, and redid the dining room. The menu of northern and southern Italian dishes still includes pasta, veal, chicken, and seafood. Some patrons will be disappointed that the live opera performances now occur only on the first Sunday of the month. Piano music Fri. and Sat. evenings. (26 ratings/mixed)

Food	Service	Ambience	Value
63	65	65	74

Au Pied de Cochon $$
French

Reserv: Not accepted
Dress: Informal
Pay: AE, MC, V, DC, CB
Parking: No
Map Reference: J-11
Area: Georgetown
Handicap Access: Ltd.
Nonsmoking Area: No
Bar: Full/separate
Hours: Daily, 24 hrs, except M 2:30-11:30am

1335 Wisconsin Ave, NW
Washington, DC (202) 333-5440

The "Pig's Foot" is a lively, all-night cafe/dining room. Light fare—omelets, quiches, and onion soup—and more substantial dishes—ratatouille, coq au vin, seafood—on menu. Portions are generous. The Georgetown bustle and being open at odd hours are primary ingredients of its staying power. "Perfect post-movie or post-party destination" (***Frommer's***). (18 ratings/consistent)

Food	Service	Ambience	Value
86	80	79	81

Bacchus $$
Lebanese

Reserv: Suggested
Dress: Informal
Pay: AE, MC, V
Parking: No
Metro: Dupont Circle
Map Reference: J-12
Handicap Access: No
Nonsmoking Area: No
Bar: Full
Hours: M-F 11:30am-2pm, 6-10pm (F 10:30pm); Sa 6-10:30pm

1827 Jefferson Pl, NW
Washington, DC (202) 785-0734

Excellent Lebanese food, beautifully presented in a small, casually elegant setting. Known for its array of delicious appetizers, a selection of which can be a meal in itself or a tantalizing introduction to Middle Eastern food. Homemade desserts. Branch in Bethesda is larger, but it has the same menu. **Honors:** Richman's Best of Best and 50 Favorites, *Washingtonian* 50 Best★★. (35 ratings/consistent)

Food	Service	Ambience	Value
81	71	71	79

Bamiyan II $$
Afghan

Reserv: Suggested
Dress: Informal
Pay: AE, MC, V
Parking: No
Map Reference: N-12
Area: Old Town
Handicap Access: Ltd.
Nonsmoking Area: No
Bar: Full
Hours: M-F 11:30am-2:30pm, 5-10:30pm; Sa&Su 5-10:30pm

300 King St
Alexandria, VA (703) 548-9006

The lamb or chicken kebabs served here and dishes that include aushak (similar to scallion-filled ravioli) provide good introductions to Afghan food. Pleasant, often crowded surroundings. This and other location, Georgetown (338-1896), were called "Washington's best Afghan restaurants" by ***Washingtonian***, but several raters thought service marred evening. **Honors:** ***Washingtonian*** 50 Best★. (31 ratings/consistent)

Food	Service	Ambience	Value

81	78	71	81

Bangkok Garden $
Thai

4906 St. Elmo Ave
Bethesda, MD (301) 951-0670

Reserv: Required
Dress: Informal
Pay: AE, MC, V
Parking: Yes (after 6pm)
Metro: Bethesda
Map Reference: G-10
Area: Woodmont Triangle
Handicap Access: No
Nonsmoking Area: Yes
Bar: Full
Hours: M-Th 11am-10:30pm; F&Sa 11am-11pm; Su 4-10pm

Attractive, reasonably priced restaurant. Menu of Thai standards includes beef or pork saute, chicken with crab meat and mushrooms, pat tai noodles, and a selection of vegetarian dishes. The chef, previously at the Thai Room in D.C., recommends the crispy hot and sour whitefish filet with onions. Daily specials. (22 ratings/consistent)

87	81	73	74

Bangkok Gourmet $$
Thai

523 S. 23rd St
Arlington, VA (703) 521-1305

Reserv: Req. weekends
Dress: Informal
Pay: MC, V, DC, CB
Parking: No
Metro: Crystal City
Map Reference: L-11
Handicap Access: No
Nonsmoking Area: No
Bar: Full
Hours: M-F 11am-10:30pm; Sa&Su 3-11pm

Menu of traditional Thai dishes and Thai nouvelle selections changes weekly. The pork with chili and garlic upholds restaurant's "reputation as hottest hot in town" (***Washingtonian***), but those who can't stand the heat won't lack for interesting choices. Homemade desserts. **Honors:** Richman's 50 Favorites, ***Washingtonian*** 50 Best★★ and Cheap Eats. (15 ratings/consistent)

83	73	55	81

Bar J $
Tex-Mex

9377 Richmond Hwy
Lorton, VA (703) 339-9686

Reserv: Not accepted
Dress: Informal
Pay: AE, MC, V, Checks
Parking: Yes
Map Reference: F-4
Handicap Access: No
Nonsmoking Area: No
Bar: Beer
Hours: Daily, 11am-10pm (Su 9pm)

The first of the Bar J's, this one is a hole-in-the-wall in a nice sense. Local people know it as a fun place for Texas and Cincinnati chili, green chili burritos, and fajitas. "In an area with few good places to eat, it stands out" (*Journal* papers). Also in Stafford and Woodbridge, Va. (12 ratings/very mixed)

Food | Service | Ambience | Value

82 74 67 78

Bare Bones $$

Barbecue

617 S. Frederick Ave
Gaithersburg, MD (301) 948-4344

Reserv: Not accepted
Dress: Informal
Pay: AE, MC, V, DC, CB
Parking: Yes
Metro: Shady Grove
Map Reference: B-3
Handicap Access: Ltd.
Nonsmoking Area: Yes
Bar: Full/separate
Hours: M-Th 11:30am-10:30pm; F&Sa 11:30am-11:30pm; Su noon-10:30pm

Family-type rib joint. "Out of this world" baby back ribs (beef and pork); bigger (and fattier) ribs, barbecued chicken, and chili also popular. The onion-ring loaf, fried chicken wings, and nacho salad make good shared appetizers. Generous portions of everything, but it's the "excellent" (***Washington Post***) baby back ribs that are the "star of the show" (***Washingtonian***). (23 ratings/consistent)

84 83 87 68

Bello Mondo $$$

Italian

5151 Pooks Hill Rd
Bethesda, MD (301) 897-9400

Reserv: Suggested
Dress: Coat req.
Pay: AE, MC, V, DC, CB, Disc.
Parking: Valet
Map Reference: G-10
Area: Pooks Hill Marriott
Handicap Access: Yes
Nonsmoking Area: Yes
Bar: Full/separate
Hours: M-F 11:30am-2pm; dinner daily 6-10pm; Su brunch 10:30am-2:30pm

A la carte dining in beautiful surroundings. Tables near the fountain in the main dining room are particularly attractive. Menu of familiar Italian-Continental dishes; food is well prepared and nicely served. "Shining lights here tend to be the seafoods and tomato-based sauces" (***Washington Post***). A nice place for a special occasion. **Honors:** Mobil★★★. (15 ratings/mixed)

72 66 71 71

Bennigan's $

American

6290 Arlington Blvd
Falls Church, VA (703) 237-6288

Reserv: Accepted
Dress: Informal
Pay: AE, MC, V
Parking: Yes
Map Reference: K-8
Area: Seven Corners
Handicap Access: Yes
Nonsmoking Area: Yes
Bar: Full/separate
Hours: Daily, 11am-2am; Sa&Su brunch til 3pm

National chain of contemporary restaurants that is quick to pick up on latest trends. Good for a group with varied tastes—baby back ribs, fajitas, stir fries, pasta, and the like. Service can be slow when busy. Loud background music and overall noise bothered a number of raters. Several other locations in area. (28 ratings/mixed)

Food	Service	Ambience	Value

Food	Service	Ambience	Value
80	79	76	76

Bilbo Baggins Cafe $$

American

Reserv: Suggested; none at lunch
Dress: Informal
Pay: AE, MC, V
Parking: No
Map Reference: M-12
Area: Old Town
Handicap Access: No
Nonsmoking Area: No
Bar: Full/separate
Hours: Tu-Su 11:30am-2:30pm, 5:30-10:30pm; Su brunch til 2:30pm

208 Queen St
Alexandria, VA (703) 683-0300

Small, intimate cafe named after the hero of Tolkien's ***The Hobbit***. Eclectic menu of American dishes, including seafood. The raves were for the extensive wine list, the selection of wines by the glass at upstairs wine bar, and the homemade breads and desserts. May have to wait for table at lunch. (36 ratings/very mixed)

Food	Service	Ambience	Value
78	74	69	73

Bish Thompson's $$

Seafood

Reserv: Sugg. weekends
Dress: Informal
Pay: AE, MC, V, DC, CB
Parking: Yes
Metro: Bethesda
Map Reference: G-10
Handicap Access: No
Nonsmoking Area: Yes
Bar: Full/separate
Hours: M-F 11:30am-11pm; Sa noon-11pm; Su noon-10pm

7935 Wisconsin Ave
Bethesda, MD (301) 656-2400

This oldtimer seems to have good days and bad days. You can depend on the seafood being fresh every day, but the execution in kitchen and service are off some days. Crab cakes placed among best in a ***Washingtonian*** review. Seafaring theme. Good place for children. Some nonseafood items on menu. (42 ratings/very mixed)

Food	Service	Ambience	Value
79	77	78	80

Bistro Francais $$

French

Reserv: Suggested
Dress: Coat/tie sugg.
Pay: AE, MC, V, DC, CB
Parking: No
Map Reference: J-11
Area: Georgetown
Handicap Access: No
Nonsmoking Area: No
Bar: Full
Hours: Su-Th 11am-3am; F&Sa 11am-4am; Sa&Su brunch til 4pm

3128 M St, NW
Washington, DC (202) 338-3830

Lively cafe and dining room. Regular menu and daily specials include a variety of fresh seafood, tarragon chicken from the rotisserie, chicken in red wine sauce, and veal chops with dates and juniper berry sauce. The chef's favorites are the Dover sole with lemon butter and the swordfish. "Captures the air of excitement we associate with Parisian bistros" (***Frommer's***). (18 ratings/very consistent)

82 84 76 78

Black Orchid $$

Continental

7410 Little River Tpke
Annandale, VA (703) 941-4400

Reserv: Required
Dress: Coat/tie sugg.
Pay: AE, MC, V, DC, CB, Checks
Parking: Yes
Map Reference: E-3
Area: Little River Shopping Center
Handicap Access: Yes
Nonsmoking Area: Yes
Bar: Full/separate
Hours: Daily, 11am-1:30am

Good food and nightly entertainment make this a popular neighborhood spot. Seafood, steak, veal, and daily specials, all done with a Continental flair. The lighting, tableside flambes, piano bar (5:30-8:30pm), and dancing contribute to a romantic atmosphere. (29 ratings/mixed)

66 66 69 66

Blackie's House of Beef $$

Steak House

22nd & M Sts, NW
Washington, DC (202) 333-1100

Reserv: Suggested
Dress: Informal
Pay: AE, MC, V, DC, CB, Disc., Checks
Parking: Yes
Metro: Foggy Bottom
Map Reference: J-11
Area: West End
Handicap Access: No
Nonsmoking Area: No
Bar: Full/separate
Hours: M-Sa 11am-10:30pm; Su 4-10:30pm

This traditional American beef house is another Washington institution for beef eaters, business people, and tourists. If you don't fancy a large portion of beef, there's seafood, omelets, and other choices. Serves "lots of decent food for the money" (Phyllis Richman). Can top evening off next door at Blackie's disco, Deja Vu. See ratings for Springfield, Va. (971-4200) location. (35 ratings/very mixed)

61 64 70 64

Blair Mansion Inn $$

American

7711 Eastern Ave
Silver Spring, MD (301) 588-1688

Reserv: Suggested
Dress: Informal
Pay: AE, MC, V, DC
Parking: Yes
Map Reference: G-12
Handicap Access: Ltd.
Nonsmoking Area: Yes
Bar: Full
Hours: M-F 11:30am-3pm, 5-9pm; Sa 5-9pm; Su noon-9pm

The Victorian mansion is primarily given over to private parties now. Public dining is available, but call ahead to make sure space hasn't been taken over by private function. Menu features regional American dishes, like Maryland crab imperial and roast duck Chesapeake, with some Continental influences. (12 ratings/very mixed)

Blue Channel Inn

68 64 70 65

Seafood **$$**

Reserv: Suggested
Dress: Informal
Pay: AE, MC, V
Parking: Valet
Map Reference: D-2
Area: South Lakes Shopping Center
Handicap Access: Yes
Nonsmoking Area: Yes
Bar: Full/separate
Hours: Su-F 11:30am-11pm (F 11:30pm); Sa 4-11:30pm; Su brunch til 3pm

11150 South Lakes Dr
Reston, VA (703) 620-6570

Casual dining overlooking Lake Thoreau (for those lucky enough to be seated on glassed-in porch). Fresh seafood selections, particularly crab, can be outstanding, but order carefully and make sure what you order is fresh not frozen. Two fireplaces. Make reservations for Fri. nights. (19 ratings/mixed)

Bombay Bicycle Club

67 62 70 63

American **$**

Reserv: Not accepted
Dress: Informal
Pay: AE, MC, V, DC
Parking: Yes
Map Reference: M-9
Handicap Access: No
Nonsmoking Area: Yes
Bar: Full/separate
Hours: M-Sa 11am-2am; Su 11am-11:30pm; Sa&Su brunch til 3pm

4580 Duke St
Alexandria, VA (703) 370-3800

Spacious fern bar and restaurant with a bicycle motif. One of few alternatives to fast food along this stretch of Duke Street. Menu of trendy light fare and heartier dishes is ample for lunch but less so for dinner. Backgammon and TVs in lounge area. Greenhouse area is bright and airy. Local crowd gathers in evenings. (19 ratings/mixed)

Bombay Palace

82 79 77 72

Indian **$$**

Reserv: Required
Dress: Informal
Pay: AE, MC, V, DC
Parking: Yes (eves)
Metro: Farragut North/West
Map Reference: J-12
Area: Downtown
Handicap Access: No
Nonsmoking Area: No
Bar: Full
Hours: Su-Th noon-3pm, 5:30-10pm; F&Sa noon-10:30pm; Sa&Su brunch til 2:30pm

1835 K St, NW
Washington, DC (202) 331-0111

"The most upscale of Washington's Indian restaurants" (***Frommer's***). Tandoori-cooked foods (like the prawns and butter chicken), the curries, and the hot Indian sauces will awaken your taste buds. Service and prices are not as good as they used to be, however. You can visit other Bombay Palaces on your world travels. **Honors:** *Washingtonian* 50 Best★★. (23 ratings/mixed)

Food	Service	Ambience	Value

81	82	77	76

Bonaroti
Italian $$

Reserv: Required
Dress: Informal
Pay: AE, MC, V, DC, CB
Parking: Yes
Map Reference: D-3
Area: Wolf Trap Shopping Center
Handicap Access: No
Nonsmoking Area: No
Bar: Full
Hours: M-Th 11:30am-3pm, 5:30-10:30pm; F 11:30am-3pm, 5-11pm; Sa 5-11pm

428 E. Maple Ave
Vienna, VA (703) 281-7550

The gracious surroundings and northern Italian cuisine add up to more than just another neighborhood Italian restaurant. The homemade pasta, fried calamari, and veal dishes were raters' favorites. Both appetizers and entrees include a number of daily specials. Convenient to Wolf Trap Farm Park and Tysons Corner. (16 ratings/consistent)

79	79	82	73

The Broker
Swiss $$

Reserv: Suggested
Dress: Coat/tie sugg.
Pay: AE, MC, V
Parking: Valet
Metro: Eastern Market
Map Reference: K-13
Area: Capitol Hill
Handicap Access: Ltd.
Nonsmoking Area: No
Bar: Full/separate
Hours: M-F 11:30am-2:30pm, 5:30-10pm (F 11pm); Sa 5:30-11pm

713 8th St, SE
Washington, DC (202) 546-8300

Small, airy restaurant in Capitol Hill townhouse. Menu includes raclette, fondue, lamb chops gorgonzola, veal cordon bleu, and homemade breads and desserts. Daily specials feature seasonal ingredients. A bit expensive for some, but the pre-theater specials can help to keep price down. "Occasionally it soars much higher" than good (Phyllis Richman). **Honors:** Mobil★★★. (26 ratings/consistent)

87	84	85	78

Buon Giorno
Italian $$

Reserv: Suggested
Dress: Coat/tie sugg.
Pay: AE, MC, V, DC, Checks
Parking: No
Metro: Bethesda
Map Reference: G-10
Area: Woodmont Tri.
Handicap Access: Ltd.
Nonsmoking Area: Yes
Bar: Full
Hours: Tu-Fr 11:30am-2:30pm, 5:30-10pm (F 10:30pm); Sa 5:30-10:30pm; Su 5:30-10pm

8003 Norfolk Ave
Bethesda, MD (301) 652-1400

The family members who operate the kitchen and dining room are an "unbeatable" combination in this relaxing neighborhood restaurant. Pasta, fresh seafood, veal, and other dishes "heartfully" prepared and presented. The chefs recommend the ravioli. Good place for families. (21 ratings/consistent)

Food	Service	Ambience	Value

76	67	55	79

Cafe Dalat
Vietnamese

$

Reserv: Not accepted
Dress: Informal
Pay: Cash only
Parking: No
Metro: Clarendon
Map Reference: K-10
Handicap Access: Ltd.
Nonsmoking Area: Yes
Bar: Full
Hours: M-Th 11am-9:30pm; F&Sa 11am-10:30pm; Su noon-9:30pm

3143 Wilson Blvd
Arlington, VA (703) 276-0935

One of several restaurants in close proximity that have earned Arlington's Little Saigon a reputation for authentic Vietnamese food at reasonable prices. No pretenses here about providing atmosphere or smart service. The energy goes into the kitchen and the results are popular with Vietnamese and Occidentals alike. **Honors:** *Journal* papers★★★, *Washingtonian* Cheap Eats. (16 ratings/mixed)

73	71	70	74

Cafe Italia II
Italian

$$

Reserv: Not accepted
Dress: Informal
Pay: AE, MC, V, DC, CB
Parking: Yes
Map Reference: E-3
Handicap Access: Ltd.
Nonsmoking Area: Yes
Bar: Full
Hours: M-F 11am-10:30pm (F 11pm); Sa 5-11pm; Su 5-9:30pm

10515 Main St
Fairfax City, VA (703) 385-6767

The double-decker salad bar is a major attraction here; can definitely be a meal in itself (all you can eat). Pizza, pasta, and an array of entrees available, too. Make-your-own sandwich bar added recently. Comfortable surroundings; outdoor patio for dining in good weather. Another location in Crystal City, Va. (19 ratings/very mixed)

76	71	69	74

Cafe La Ruche
French

$$

Reserv: Sugg. weekends
Dress: Informal
Pay: MC, V
Parking: No
Map Reference: J-11
Area: Georgetown
Handicap Access: No
Nonsmoking Area: No
Bar: Full
Hours: M-F 11:30am-11pm (F 2am); Sa 10am-2am; Su 10am-11pm; Sa&Su brunch til 3pm

1039 31st St, NW
Washington, DC (202) 965-2684

Busy bistro known for its great pastries. Basic menu of soups, sandwiches, quiches, and interesting salad platters is augmented with daily meat and seafood specials. Nice place for an afternoon break. Early bird specials weekdays, 5-7pm. In warm weather you can escape bustle inside by retreating to the attractive courtyard cafe. Branch at White Flint Mall, Md. (18 ratings/mixed)

Food | Service | Ambience | Value

Cafe Mozart **$$**
Viennese

Reserv: Suggested
Dress: Coat/tie sugg.
Pay: AE, MC, V, DC, CB
Parking: No
Metro: McPherson Square
Map Reference: J-12
Area: Downtown
Handicap Access: Yes
Nonsmoking Area: Yes
Bar: Full/separate
Hours: M-F 7:30am-10pm; Sa 9am-10pm; Su 11am-10pm

1331 H St, NW
Washington, DC (202) 347-5732

Up front it's a German deli; in back it's a cafe and bar where you can linger in the evenings and enjoy Viennese music. Classic, hearty Viennese and German cafe food—boiled beef, Wiener schnitzel, goulash, sauerbraten—plus daily specials, lighter fare, and homemade pastries. "As close to a genuine Viennese cafe as you will encounter" in D.C. (***Washington Business Journal***). (41 ratings/mixed)

Cafe Petitto **$**
Italian

Reserv: Not accepted
Dress: Informal
Pay: AE, MC, V, DC, CB
Parking: No
Metro: Dupont Circle
Map Reference: J-12
Handicap Access: Ltd.
Nonsmoking Area: No
Bar: Full/separate
Hours: Daily, 11:30am-midnight

1724 Connecticut Ave, NW
Washington, DC (202) 462-8771

Casual cafe featuring Calabrian pizza fritta (fried) and a large, serve-yourself antipasto table. Pasta dishes, hoagies, and desserts also available. Location and prices make this a popular spot, which can mean long waits and noise. Might want to save this for a late lunch or other off-hour visit. **Honors:** Mobil specialty spot, ***Washingtonian*** Cheap Eats. (34 ratings/consistent)

Cafe Roval **$$**
French

Reserv: Not accepted
Dress: Informal
Pay: MC, V, DC, Checks
Parking: Yes
Map Reference: C-4
Area: Potomac Promenade
Handicap Access: Yes
Nonsmoking Area: Yes
Bar: Beer/wine
Hours: Daily, 11:30am-10pm

9812 Falls Rd
Potomac, MD (301) 299-3000

Small, pleasant, neighborhood bistro featuring seasonally available foods and homemade pastries. Entrees include salmon filet, chicken with Dijon mustard sauce, shrimp and pasta, and the chef's favorite, fruits de mer. "Has fast become the place to meet one's neighbors or pause for refreshment" (***Washington Business Journal***). (10 ratings/very consistent)

Food | Service | Ambience | Value

Cafe Splendide

Continental $

Reserv: Accepted
Dress: Informal
Pay: Cash only
Parking: No
Metro: Dupont Circle
Map Reference: J-12
Handicap Access: Ltd.
Nonsmoking Area: No
Bar: Full
Hours: T-F 9am-11:30pm (F 1am); Sa 8am-1am; Su 8am-11pm

1521 Connecticut Ave, NW
Washington, DC (202) 328-1503

Tiny cafe with reputation for value. Menu, the same for lunch and dinner, is limited but includes such favorites as Hungarian goulash, chicken parmigiana, paprika schnitzel, broiled lamb chops, and great homemade pastries. Good spot for an afternoon break, late night dessert, or leisurely weekend breakfast. Outdoor garden in rear. **Honors:** *Washingtonian* Cheap Eats. (17 ratings/very consistent)

Cafe Tatti

European $$

Reserv: Required
Dress: Informal
Pay: AE, MC, V, DC, CB
Parking: Yes
Map Reference: I-9
Area: McLean Square Mall
Handicap Access: Yes
Nonsmoking Area: No
Bar: Full
Hours: M-Sa 11am-10pm

6627 Old Dominion Dr
McLean, VA (703) 790-5148

Tiny neighborhood restaurant with atmosphere of European cafe. Draws a regular clientele from area. One of owners greets all who enter. Menu has a decided French accent; chef's favorites are the fresh seafood and lamb dishes. Quiche, caesar salad, and other light fare available at lunch. "Easy to like once you know what kitchen does best" (*Washington Post*). (24 ratings/mixed)

Caffe Italiano

Italian $$

Reserv: Accepted
Dress: Informal
Pay: AE, MC, V
Parking: No
Metro: Cleveland Park
Map Reference: I-11
Handicap Access: Ltd.
Nonsmoking Area: No
Bar: Full
Hours: M-F 11:30am-3pm, 4-11pm; Sa&Su 4-11pm

3516 Connecticut Ave, NW
Washington, DC (202) 966-2172

Cozy neighborhood spot; close to Circle Uptown Theater. Popular dishes include veal Ivana (named after owner), osso buco, and pollo Lombardo. Crowded at times, but food and friendly staff can make it all worthwhile. Branch on Capitol Hill. (16 ratings/consistent)

71 70 70 70

Caldwell's
American

$$

Reserv: Not accepted
Dress: Informal
Pay: AE, MC, V, DC
Parking: Yes
Map Reference: E-3
Handicap Access: Yes
Nonsmoking Area: Yes
Bar: Full/separate
Hours: M-Sa 11:30am-1:30am; Su 10am-1:30am, brunch til 3pm

7131 Little River Tpke
Annandale, VA (703) 750-0777

A neighborhood gathering place where the baby back ribs, prime ribs, seafood, and other foods are cooked over a mesquite grill. ***Journal*** papers found it "better than most" restaurants of its type. A deejay plays the Top 40 tunes and oldies Tues.-Sat. in the lounge. Noise from the lounge can be bothersome if that's not your scene. (24 ratings/consistent)

87 81 72 85

Calvert House Inn
Seafood

$$$

Reserv: Required
Dress: Informal
Pay: AE, MC, V
Parking: Yes
Map Reference: H-15
Handicap Access: No
Nonsmoking Area: Yes
Bar: Full
Hours: M-F 11am-10pm; Sa&Su 5-10pm

6211 Baltimore Ave
Riverdale, MD (301) 864-5220

The broiled fish and crab dishes top the list of things to try at this down-home type inn. A crab cake here is "a jewel" (***Journal*** papers) and a "first-rate . . . refreshing change" (***Washington Times***). Among the nonseafood items, the spinach pie and cucumber salad were recommended by raters. Now in Annapolis, too. **Honors:** ***Journal*** papers★★★. (35 ratings/consistent)

80 77 69 59

Cantina D'Italia
Italian

$$$

Reserv: Required
Dress: Coat req./tie sugg.
Pay: AE, MC, V, DC, CB
Parking: No
Metro: Farragut North
Map Reference: J-12
Area: Downtown
Handicap Access: No
Nonsmoking Area: No
Bar: Full
Hours: M-F noon-2:30pm, 6-10:30pm; Sa 6-10:30pm

1214-A 18th St, NW
Washington, DC (202) 659-1830

The undisputed champion of northern Italian cuisine for close to 20 years, the Cantina has had its ups and downs the past few years. Some thought it had become overpriced and less exciting than it once was. Under new management since our survey, Phyllis Richman said it has become "serenely excellent, less frantic, and more consistent." **Honors:** ***Travel-Holiday*** Award. (17 ratings/very mixed)

Food	Service	Ambience	Value

72	69	71	76

Carlos O'Kelly's $
Mexican

Reserv: Not accepted
Dress: Informal
Pay: AE, MC, V, DC, CB, Checks
Parking: Yes
Map Reference: E-3
Handicap Access: Yes
Nonsmoking Area: Yes
Bar: Full/separate
Hours: M-Th 11am-11pm; F&Sa 11am-midnight; Su noon-midnight

9959 Main St
Fairfax City, VA (703) 591-7113

Despite the unusual name, this is another place for tacos, fajitas, enchiladas, and other Mexican (Arizona style) fast foods. The food is basically okay, but it strikes some raters as "plastic." Portions are generous. *Washington Post* found it "a warm and inviting spot." Lots of families; can get very crowded. (34 ratings/mixed)

78	77	79	73

Carlyle Grand Cafe $$
American

Reserv: Suggested
Dress: Informal
Pay: AE, MC, V
Parking: Yes
Map Reference: L-11
Area: Shirlington Village
Handicap Access: Yes
Nonsmoking Area: Yes
Bar: Full/separate
Hours: M-Sa 11:30am-2am; Su 10am-midnight, brunch til 3pm

4000 S. 28th St
Arlington, VA (703) 931-0777

Trendy cafe/bar and art deco dining rooms. One rater called it overpriced, overrated yuppiedom. The critics' opinions varied: "interesting throughout" (*Washington Times*), "frequently praiseworthy" (*Washingtonian*), and "not competition for serious kitchens" (Phyllis Richman). For fun and atmosphere, if not serious food, this could be a good choice. (45 ratings/mixed)

67	72	73	68

Carmack's $$
American

Reserv: Suggested
Dress: Coat/tie sugg.
Pay: AE, MC, V, DC, CB
Parking: Yes
Map Reference: G-11
Area: Chevy Chase Lake Bldg
Handicap Access: Ltd.
Nonsmoking Area: Yes
Bar: Full/separate
Hours: M-F 11:30am-10pm; Sa 5-10pm; Su noon-8pm, brunch til 3pm

8401 Connecticut Ave
Chevy Chase, MD (301) 652-6400

The menu reflects recent changes back to basic American dishes, but the word from our raters is that it still needs work. Several dining rooms and tavern. Daily specials, including fresh seafood, and early bird dinners. Very pleasant, relaxed atmosphere, which makes the food even more of a disappointment. (19 ratings/very mixed)

Carnegie's
American $$

Reserv: Accepted
Dress: Informal
Pay: AE, MC, V, DC, CB, Disc.
Parking: Yes
Map Reference: M-10
Area: Mark Center
Handicap Access: Yes
Nonsmoking Area: Yes
Bar: Full/separate
Hours: M-Th 11:30am-2:30pm, 5-10pm (F&Sa 11pm); Su brunch 10:30am-2:30pm, dinner 4-9pm

1700 N. Beauregard St
Alexandria, VA (703) 820-4432

A popular place for business-day lunch and a local gathering place in evenings. Contemporary menu—seafood, pasta, prime rib, Cajun-style dishes. Sun. brunch buffet and twilight dinner specials are good values and popular with families. Reputation for great Cobb salad and breads. Service can be slow during busy times. (60 ratings/very mixed)

73 68 70 73

Casa Maria
Mexican $

Reserv: Suggested
Dress: Informal
Pay: AE, MC, V, DC, CB, Disc.
Parking: Yes
Map Reference: M-10
Area: Landmark
Handicap Access: No
Nonsmoking Area: Yes
Bar: Full/separate
Hours: M-Th 11:30am-10:30pm; F 11am-11:30pm; Sa noon-11:30pm; Su 10am-10pm

5951 Stevenson Ave
Alexandria, VA (703) 370-9681

If Mexican fast food is what you're after, the tacos, fajitas, and burritos served by this restaurant chain will fill the bill. Sun. brunch (10am-3pm) and all-you-can-eat lunch buffet (weekdays) are popular. Two other locations; see ratings for Tysons Corner, Va. (893-2443) location. El Torito and 700 Water Street Grill (see below) are part of chain. (31 ratings/mixed)

73 73 76 71

Caspian Tea Room
Persian $$

Reserv: Suggested
Dress: Informal
Pay: AE, MC, V, DC, Checks
Parking: Yes
Map Reference: I-10
Area: Spring Valley Center
Handicap Access: Yes
Nonsmoking Area: No
Bar: Full/separate
Hours: M-F 8am-9:30pm; Sa 11am-10pm

4801 Massachusetts Ave, NW
Washington, DC (202) 244-6363

Old World charm and elegance in an uptown shopping center. The quiet, uncrowded dining room is adorned with Persian rugs and other treasures of the Samiy family. Phyllis Richman found the "European dishes range from dull to fine and the Iranian dishes are invariably delicious." Be sure to try the fessenjan—chicken with a walnut and pomegranate sauce. **Honors:** Richman's 50 Favorites. (16 ratings/consistent)

Food | Service | Ambience | Value

69 69 66 70

Chadwicks $
American

Reserv: Not accepted
Dress: Informal
Pay: AE, MC, V
Parking: No
Metro: Friendship Heights
Map Reference: H-11
Handicap Access: Ltd.
Nonsmoking Area: Yes
Bar: Full/separate
Hours: M-Th 11:30am-midnight; F&Sa 11:30am-1am; Su 10am-midnight, brunch til 4pm

5247 Wisconsin Ave, NW
Washington, DC (202) 362-8040

Basic, unassuming contemporary food—soups, salads, sandwiches, limited number of entrees, and homemade desserts. Pleasant atmosphere, but noisy and crowded at times; more of a singles bar than a place for serious dining. Two other locations; all have same menu. See ratings for Alexandria, Va. (836-4442) location, which is more of a neighborhood restaurant. (24 ratings/consistent)

80 74 71 69

Charley's Crab $$$
Seafood

Reserv: Suggested; lunch required
Dress: Informal
Pay: AE, MC, V, DC, CB, Disc.
Parking: No
Metro: Farragut North
Map Reference: J-12
Area: Downtown
Handicap Access: Ltd.
Nonsmoking Area: Yes
Bar: Full/separate
Hours: M-F 11:30am-3pm, 5-10pm; Sa 11:30am-10pm

1101 Conn. Ave, NW; Conn. Connection
Washington, DC (202) 785-4505

Charley's still serves good fresh fish and other seafood (not whole crabs, though), but the prices and the bustle are getting to be too much for some raters, especially at lunch. The dining room is attractive and might be more relaxing than the lounge area. You'll find this upscale restaurant in numerous other cities, too. (19 ratings/consistent)

69 68 72 67

Charley's Place $$
American

Reserv: Suggested
Dress: Informal
Pay: AE, MC, V, DC, CB, Disc.
Parking: Yes
Map Reference: I-9
Handicap Access: Ltd.
Nonsmoking Area: Yes
Bar: Full/separate
Hours: M-Sa 11:30am-10pm (Sa 11pm); Su 10:30am-9pm, brunch til 2:30pm

6930 Old Dominion Dr
McLean, VA (703) 893-1034

Part of restaurant group that includes Carnegie's, Ribsters, Fedora Cafe, and Devon Grills. Assembly-line food preparation in evidence here. Comfortable surroundings; service slow, particularly at lunch. Early bird dinners nightly. Kids under 10 eat for only $1 at Sun. brunch. Live jazz on Fri. nights. See ratings for other location, Springfield, Va. (451-0662). (40 ratings/mixed)

84 77 74 79

Charlie Chiang's
Chinese **$**

Reserv: Accepted weekdays
Dress: Informal
Pay: AE, MC, V, DC
Parking: Yes
Map Reference: M-10
Handicap Access: Ltd.
Nonsmoking Area: Yes
Bar: Full/separate
Hours: Daily 11:30am-3pm, 5-9pm; Su brunch noon-3pm

660 S. Pickett St
Alexandria, VA (703) 751-8888

Exterior doesn't reflect how good food inside can be—some say the best Chinese in Alexandria. Ads boast that only fresh vegetables are used. Varied menu includes hot and spicy dishes. Sun. brunch buffet is popular. Peking duck was criticized in ***Washingtonian's*** search for best duck in area. Three other locations; menu varies somewhat by location. (21 ratings/mixed)

77 74 65 83

Chef Theo's
Continental **$$**

Reserv: Accepted
Dress: Informal
Pay: AE, MC, V, Disc.
Parking: Yes
Map Reference: G-12
Area: White Oaks Shopping Center
Handicap Access: No
Nonsmoking Area: Yes
Bar: Full
Hours: M-F 9am-10pm; Sa 7am-10pm; Su 7am-9pm, brunch 10am-3pm

11271 New Hampshire Ave
Silver Spring, MD (301) 593-5350

Small, family-type restaurant known for its large servings of good food and reasonable prices. Try the lamb shish kebab, spinach pie, or the owner-chef's favorite, flounder stuffed with crabmeat. ***Washington Post*** said you can have "a very pleasant dinner here." Salad bar, Sat. breakfast bar, and Sun. brunch. (13 ratings/mixed)

83 72 73 74

Chef's Secret
Continental **$$**

Reserv: Required
Dress: Informal
Pay: AE, MC, V, DC, CB, Disc.
Parking: Yes
Map Reference: D-6
Handicap Access: Yes
Nonsmoking Area: Yes
Bar: Full
Hours: M-F 11:30am-10:30pm; Sa&Su 4:30-9:30pm

5810 Greenbelt Rd
Greenbelt, MD (301) 345-6101

The secret is that beyond the drab exterior there is plenty of good, fresh seafood. The swordfish, red snapper, and lobster are popular selections. The ***Washingtonian*** advises you to order your fish "plain rather than fancy," but the ***Washington Post*** found seafood in general to be "superlative." Good pasta, meat dishes, and homemade desserts also available. Crowded; service erratic. (38 ratings/mixed)

Food	Service	Ambience	Value

---

69 77 65 77

Chesapeake Bay Seafood House $$
Seafood

Reserv: Not accepted
Dress: Informal
Pay: Checks
Parking: Yes
Map Reference: D-2
Area: Herndon Centre
Handicap Access: Yes
Nonsmoking Area: Yes
Bar: Full
Hours: M-F 11:30am-2pm, 5-9pm (F 9:30pm); Sa 11:30am-9:30pm; Su noon-9pm

428 Elden St
Herndon, VA (703) 435-4225

All-you-can-eat feature at this chain of seafood houses can be considered a good deal or an invitation to stuff yourself, particularly on fried foods. French fries, cole slaw, and hush puppies go with the seafood. Special prices for kids, so it's popular with families. Some selections not all that inexpensive, e.g., the crab legs. Numerous locations in area; see ratings for Springfield, Va. (451-7405) location. (11 ratings/mixed)

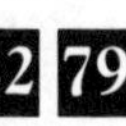

84 82 79 76

Chez Nous $$
French

Reserv: Req. weekends
Dress: Informal
Pay: AE, MC, V, DC
Parking: Yes
Map Reference: G-10
Area: Wildwood Shopping Center
Handicap Access: Yes
Nonsmoking Area: Yes
Bar: Full
Hours: M-Sa 11:30am-2:30pm, 5:30-10:30pm; Su 5-9:30pm

10223 Old Georgetown Rd
Bethesda, MD (301) 564-4910

Another good restaurant tucked into a suburban shopping center. Regular menu of salmon steak, duck with raspberry sauce, rack of lamb, and other standards. Daily specials emphasize fresh ingredients, including seafood. Early bird dinners Mon.-Thurs., 5:30-7pm. Good desserts. Small, art deco dining room; seating is tight. (43 ratings/mixed)

67 67 68 70

Chi-Chi's $
Mexican

Reserv: Not accepted
Dress: Informal
Pay: AE, MC, V, DC
Parking: Yes
Map Reference: F-3
Handicap Access: Yes
Nonsmoking Area: Yes
Bar: Full/separate
Hours: M-Th 11am-11pm; F&Sa 11am-midnight; Su 11am-10pm

7010 Old Keene Mill Rd
Springfield, VA (703) 569-9400

Some say Chi-Chi's serves the best Mexican fast food in the area. If so, not here; the Russell Ave., Gaithersburg location got the best food rating. Nonetheless, this one is crowded most of the time. Features the "subtle spicing" of Mexico's Sonora region. See table for ratings on five of the seven other locations. There were complaints about the cleanliness of this one. All have a lunch buffet Mon.-Sat. (38 ratings/very mixed)

Food	Service	Ambience	Value

Chili's
American — $

Food	Service	Ambience	Value
72	70	70	73

Reserv: Not accepted
Dress: Informal
Pay: MC, V
Parking: Yes
Map Reference: L-9
Handicap Access: Yes
Nonsmoking Area: Yes
Bar: Full/separate
Hours: M-Th 11am-11pm; F&Sa 11am-midnight; Su noon-10pm

5501 Leesburg Pike
Baileys Crossroads, VA (703) 379-2035

Texas-based chain specializing in burgers, chili, ribs, fajitas, and all the fixin's. Tex-Mex atmosphere; can be fun, but does get crowded. Menu is heavy on burgers. ***Washington Post*** called it "average chuck-wagon fare." Three other locations; see ratings for Springfield, Va. (451-0222) location. (27 ratings/consistent)

China Coral
Chinese — $$

Food	Service	Ambience	Value
78	72	69	77

Reserv: Accepted
Dress: Informal
Pay: AE, MC, V
Parking: Yes
Metro: Bethesda
Map Reference: G-10
Handicap Access: Ltd.
Nonsmoking Area: Yes
Bar: Full
Hours: M-F 11:30am-10:30pm (F 11:30pm); Sa 11am-11:30pm; Su 11am-10pm; Sa&Su brunch til 3pm

6900 Wisconsin Ave
Bethesda, MD (301) 656-1203

Seafood in the Hong Kong tradition, not just the usual shrimp and lobster, but conch, squid, sea cucumber, abalone, and seasonal specialties. "Every dish is an artwork" (***Washington Times***). Nonseafood selections, too. Dim sum daily. Dining room is large, and service suffers when crowded. **Honors:** Richman's Best of Best and 50 Favorites, ***Washingtonian*** 50 Best★★. (64 ratings/mixed)

China D'Lite
Chinese — $

Food	Service	Ambience	Value
81	81	75	80

Reserv: Required
Dress: Informal
Pay: MC, V
Parking: Yes
Map Reference: C-6
Area: Laurel Lakes Ctr
Handicap Access: Yes
Nonsmoking Area: Yes
Bar: Full/separate
Hours: Su-Th 11:30am-10pm; F&Sa 11:30am-10:30pm

14252 Baltimore Ave
Laurel, MD (301) 490-8111

Popular local restaurant with extensive selection of Hunan and Szechuan dishes. Courteous, helpful staff. Atmosphere "fairly romantic" when not crowded. Hot towel presented at end of meal is a nice touch. Branches in Chantilly and Centreville, Va. (10 ratings/consistent)

Food	Service	Ambience	Value
77	71	67	80

China Harbor $$
Chinese

Reserv: Suggested
Dress: Informal
Pay: AE, MC, V
Parking: Yes
Map Reference: C-4
Area: Wintergreen Plaza
Handicap Access: Yes
Nonsmoking Area: Yes
Bar: Full
Hours: Su-Th 11:30am-10:30pm; F&Sa 11:30am-11:30pm

865-B Rockville Pike
Rockville, MD (301) 340-8778

Reasonably priced Chinese seafood restaurant. Steamed or braised fish and lobster with ginger are the chef's favorites. Nonseafood dishes also on menu, including Peking duck. Lunch buffet Mon.-Fri. until 2pm. "One of the better Chinese restaurants specializing in fruits of the sea" (***Washington Business Journal***). (18 ratings/consistent)

Food	Service	Ambience	Value
77	65	62	77

China Inn $$
Chinese

Reserv: Accepted
Dress: Informal
Pay: AE, MC, V
Parking: No
Metro: Gallery Place
Map Reference: J-12
Area: Chinatown
Handicap Access: Yes
Nonsmoking Area: No
Bar: Full
Hours: M-Th 11am-3am; F&Sa 11am-4am; Su 11am-1:30am

631 H St, NW
Washington, DC (202) 842-0909

This place, which the ***Washingtonian*** called "the city's best source of authentic Cantonese cooking," has been refurbished since our ratings began coming in. Perhaps that explains the ratings for service and ambience. Seafood is a high point of the extensive menu. **Honors:** ***Washingtonian*** 50 Best ★★★ and Cheap Eats. (16 ratings/mixed)

Food	Service	Ambience	Value
76	78	67	79

China Village $$
Chinese

Reserv: Accepted
Dress: Informal
Pay: AE, MC, V
Parking: Yes
Metro: Bethesda
Map Reference: G-10
Handicap Access: No
Nonsmoking Area: Yes
Bar: Full
Hours: M-Th 11am-10pm; F&Sa 11am-11pm; Su 12:30-10pm

4820 Bethesda Ave
Bethesda, MD (301) 654-7787

Lively neighborhood walk-up providing quick service and good value. Friendly staff. Hunan dishes featured on menu that includes numerous old favorites, such as lemon chicken, orange beef, and Kung pao chicken. Gets crowded at times. (13 ratings/mixed)

Food	Service	Ambience	Value

78	73	71	70

City Cafe $$
New American

Reserv: Suggested
Dress: Informal
Pay: Checks
Parking: No
Metro: Foggy Bottom
Map Reference: J-11
Area: West End
Handicap Access: No
Nonsmoking Area: No
Bar: Full/separate
Hours: M-F 11:30am-11pm (F midnight); Sa 5:30-midnight; Su 5:30-11pm

2213 M St, NW
Washington, DC (202) 797-4860

Serves seasonal menu of light foods, pizza and pasta, and grilled and stir-fried meats and seafood. In the style of its parent restaurant, Nora's (see below). ***Washingtonian*** called it "slick, post-modern dining," and Phyllis Richman described it as the "soul of urbanity," but some raters were disappointed given such reviews. **Honors:** Richman's 50 Favorites. (38 ratings/mixed)

77	73	73	76

Claude's $$
French

Reserv: Suggested
Dress: Informal
Pay: AE, MC, V, DC, CB, Disc.
Parking: Yes
Map Reference: B-3
Handicap Access: Yes
Nonsmoking Area: Yes
Bar: Full/separate
Hours: M-F 11:30am-2:30pm, 5:30-10pm (F 10:30pm); Sa 5:30-10:30pm; Su brunch 11am-3pm, dinner 4-9pm

9021 Gaither Rd
Gaithersburg, MD (301) 258-0405

Attractive bistro in Shady Grove Shopping Center. Known for its fresh seafood and early bird dinner specials (before 7pm). In addition, couscous is featured on Wed. and bouillabaisse on Fri. One rater suggested kitchen hits its stride on weekends. Happy hour weekdays, 4-7pm. (15 ratings/mixed)

79	76	82	72

Clyde's $$$
American

Reserv: Suggested
Dress: Coat sugg.
Pay: AE, MC, V, DC, CB, Checks
Parking: Yes
Map Reference: D-3
Area: Tysons Corner
Handicap Access: Yes
Nonsmoking Area: Yes
Bar: Full/separate
Hours: M-Sa 11am-2am; Su 10am-2am, Su brunch til 4pm

8332 Leesburg Pike
McLean, VA (703) 734-1900

Classic fern bar/cafe/grill. Features homemade soups and chili, fresh seafood, and beef. Won ***Wine Spectator's*** 1987 Award of Excellence for its wine list. Popular with suburban singles; may have to wait for table, especially weekends. Two other locations; see ratings for Columbia, Md. (730-2828) location. (39 ratings/mixed)

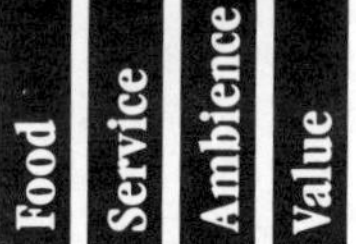

Colonel Brook's Tavern
American $

Reserv: Accepted
Dress: Informal
Pay: MC, V
Parking: Yes
Metro: Brookland
Map Reference: J-13
Handicap Access: Ltd.
Nonsmoking Area: Yes
Bar: Full/separate
Hours: M-F 11am-2am (F 3am); Sa 11:30am-3am; Su 11am-2am, brunch til 3pm

901 Monroe St, NE
Washington, DC (202) 529-4002

The menu of this neighborhood tavern lists over 10 domestic and imported draft beers and a specially priced "brew of the month." To go with that brew, there are snack platters, pizza, ribs, burgers, and seafood. Dixieland jazz Tues. nights. Draws a crowd of young people from university and hospitals in area. (15 ratings/consistent)

66 71 75 67

Comus Inn
American $$$

Reserv: Suggested
Dress: Coat/tie sugg.
Pay: AE, MC, V, DC, CB
Parking: Yes
Map Reference: A-2
Area: Rte 270, exit onto route 109
Handicap Access: No
Nonsmoking Area: Yes
Bar: Full
Hours: M-Sa 11:30am-9pm; Su brunch 11am-2pm, dinner noon-9pm

23900 Old Hundred Rd
Comus, MD (301) 428-8593

Historic (1860) inn with beautiful view of Sugarloaf Mountain. Complete luncheons and dinners served, including Maryland crab imperial, Virginia fried chicken, and Colorado prime rib. Pleasant stop on an excursion into country. Crowded in summer. Waterlily gardens at Lilypons are nearby summer attraction. (28 ratings/mixed)

76 71 67 75

Cracked Claw
Seafood $$

Reserv: Accepted
Dress: Informal
Pay: AE, MC, V, Checks
Parking: Yes
Map Reference: B-3
Handicap Access: Yes
Nonsmoking Area: Yes
Bar: Full
Hours: T-F 11:30am-10pm; Sa 5-10pm; Su 5-9pm

19815 Frederick Rd
Gaithersburg, MD (301) 428-0588

Casual crab and seafood house in the Eastern Shore mold. All-you-can-eat crab (Sun., Tues., Wed.) and crab 'n' shrimp feasts (Thurs.). Crab cakes, crab imperial, surf 'n' turf, stuffed flounder, etc., available for those who don't want to work for their food. Dining on porch in warm weather. (15 ratings/very mixed)

Food | Service | Ambience | Value

84 73 55 70

Crisfield's
Seafood **$$$**

Reserv: Not accepted
Dress: Informal
Pay: Cash only
Parking: No
Metro: Silver Spring
Map Reference: G-12
Handicap Access: No
Nonsmoking Area: Yes
Bar: Beer/wine
Hours: T-Th 11am-10pm; F&Sa 11am-11pm; Su noon-9:30pm

8012 Georgia Ave
Silver Spring, MD (301) 589-1306

Famous for its crab imperial, crab-stuffed shrimp and flounder, and Chincoteague oysters. The long lines, close quarters, and run-down appearance are part of lore, too. Phyllis Richman and the *Washingtonian* say it's the best place in area for American seafood, but some raters weren't that enthusiastic. **Honors:** Richman's Best of Best, *Washingtonian* 50 Best★★★. (55 ratings/mixed)

80 84 84 83

Csiko's
Hungarian **$$**

Reserv: Sugg. weekends
Dress: Informal
Pay: AE, MC, V, DC, CB, Disc.
Parking: Yes
Metro: Cleveland Park
Map Reference: I-11
Handicap Access: Yes
Nonsmoking Area: No
Bar: Full
Hours: M-Sa 6-10pm

3601 Conn. Ave, NW, Broadmoor Apts
Washington, DC (202) 362-5624

"Old World charm" were words used most often to describe D.C.'s only Hungarian restaurant. Hearty food at reasonable prices, including beef goulash, stuffed cabbage, and chicken, rabbit, or veal paprikash with homemade noodles. Chef's favorites are game dishes (prepared only during winter). **Honors:** *Travel-Holiday* selection. (10 ratings/consistent)

82 76 78 75

Da Domenico
Italian **$$**

Reserv: Suggested
Dress: Informal
Pay: AE, MC, V, DC, CB, Checks
Parking: Yes
Map Reference: D-3
Area: Tysons Corner
Handicap Access: Yes
Nonsmoking Area: Yes
Bar: Full/separate
Hours: M-F 11:30am-4pm, 5-11pm; Sa 5-11pm

1992 Chain Bridge Rd
McLean, VA (703) 790-9000

Family-owned and -operated neighborhood restaurant. Menu of northern Italian dishes features homemade pastas, seafoods, and milk-fed veal. Host/co-owner extends a warm welcome to all. Very attractive dining room; nice place for families. (17 ratings/mixed)

Food	Service	Ambience	Value

71	72	73	72

Dalt's
American — $

Reserv: Accepted
Dress: Informal
Pay: AE, MC, V, DC, CB
Parking: Yes
Map Reference: L-9
Handicap Access: Yes
Nonsmoking Area: Yes
Bar: Full/separate
Hours: M-F 11:30am-1am; Sa 11am-2am; Su 10:30am-2am; Sa&Su brunch til 3pm

5715 Columbia Pike
Baileys Crossroads, VA (703) 671-8443

Recaptures oldies-but-goodies atmosphere. Includes a soda fountain-grill counter, a lounge for drinks and snacks, and a dining area. Traditional and contemporary American food. A fun kind of place; good for families. Food and service uneven. The *Journal* papers found it "surprisingly good," but the *Washington Post* cautioned that the "extensive menu may strain the kitchen at times." (29 ratings/very mixed)

73	82	85	70

Dar Es Salam
Moroccan — $$

Reserv: Suggested
Dress: Informal
Pay: AE, MC, V
Parking: No
Map Reference: J-11
Area: Georgetown
Handicap Access: No
Nonsmoking Area: No
Bar: Full
Hours: Daily, 5-11pm

3056 M St, NW
Washington, DC (202) 342-1925

Relax and get into the spirit of eating with your fingers while seated on a low sofa. Most groups share a multicourse diffa, a traditional celebration dinner. Raters were as enthusiastic as critics about the elegant decor and ambience, but not about the food—or prices, which border on expensive. Entertainment in downstairs club nightly. **Honors:** Richman's 50 Favorites, *Washingtonian* 50 Best★★. (16 ratings/very mixed)

77	72	75	70

Devon Seafood Grill
Seafood — $$

Reserv: Suggested
Dress: Informal
Pay: AE, MC, V, DC, CB, Disc.
Parking: Yes
Map Reference: D-3
Area: American Center
Handicap Access: Yes
Nonsmoking Area: Yes
Bar: Full/separate
Hours: M-F 11:30am-3pm, 5:30-10pm (F 11pm); Sa 5-11pm; Su brunch 10:30am-3pm, dinner 5-9pm

8330 Boone Blvd
Vienna, VA (703) 442-0401

Lively restaurant and local watering hole. Much of the seafood and meat is cooked on mesquite grill—"with generally good results" (*Washington Post*). Bar area can be boisterous and crowded. Twilight dinner specials and Sun. brunch are good values. See ratings for downtown D.C. location (833-5660), which raters suggested is too popular for the kitchen to handle. (55 ratings/mixed)

Food	Service	Ambience	Value
82	80	82	76

Dominique's
French **$$$**

Reserv: Suggested
Dress: Coat req.
Pay: AE, MC, V, DC, CB
Parking: Valet
Metro: Farragut West
Map Reference: J-12
Area: Downtown
Handicap Access: No
Nonsmoking Area: No
Bar: Full/separate
Hours: M-Th 11:30am-2:30pm, 5:30-11:30pm; F&Sa 11am-2:30pm, 5:30pm-midnight

1900 Pennsylvania Ave, NW
Washington, DC (202) 452-1126

Great combination of food and fun. Popular with celebrities and local folks who like to get caught up in the activity and who recognize the great value in the pre- and post-theater dinners. Menu ranges from traditional to exotic. Seafoods items are popular. The maitre d', Diana Damewood, gets raves. **Honors:** AAA◆◆◆, Mobil ★★★, *Travel-Holiday* selection. (85 ratings/consistent)

Food	Service	Ambience	Value
73	71	65	67

Dona Flor
Brazilian **$$**

Reserv: Suggested
Dress: Informal
Pay: AE, MC, V, Checks
Parking: No
Metro: Tenleytown
Map Reference: I-11
Handicap Access: No
Nonsmoking Area: No
Bar: Full/separate
Hours: M-F 11:30am-3:30pm, 5-11pm (F 11:30pm); Sa 3-11:30pm; Su noon-11pm, brunch til 4pm

4615 Wisconsin Ave, NW
Washington, DC (202) 537-0404

One of the area's few Brazilian restaurants. Feijoada, a spicy national dish made with black-bean chili and pork, and seafood are highlights of the menu. Pleasant, often lively dining room. Brazilian music on piano Tues. & Wed. nights. Saturday afternoons are given over to feijoada, Brazilian beer, and the samba. (14 ratings/mixed)

Food	Service	Ambience	Value
79	71	56	72

Duck Chang's
Chinese **$**

Reserv: Accepted
Dress: Informal
Pay: AE, MC, V
Parking: Yes
Map Reference: E-3
Handicap Access: Ltd.
Nonsmoking Area: No
Bar: Full
Hours: M-Sa 11am-11pm; Su noon-10pm

4427 John Marr Dr
Annandale, VA (703) 941-9400

Like so many other neighborhood restaurants, the physical surroundings here aren't much. The attraction is a three-course Peking duck dinner, carved at tableside (no advance notice required). Szechuan, Cantonese, and other Peking dishes "well above average found in neighborhood Chinese restaurants" (***Washingtonian***). Duck is also on carryout menu. (16 ratings/consistent)

Food	Service	Ambience	Value

---

72 70 67 63

Duke Ziebert's $$$
American

Reserv: Accepted
Dress: Coat/tie sugg.
Pay: AE, MC, V, DC, CB
Parking: Yes (after 5pm)
Metro: Farragut North/West
Map Reference: J-12
Area: Downtown
Handicap Access: Yes
Nonsmoking Area: No
Bar: Full/separate
Hours: M-Sa 11:30am-11:30pm; Su 5-10pm; closed Su in summer

1050 Connecticut Ave, NW
Washington, DC (202) 466-3730

The classy new location, nostalgia for the old Duke's, and the power patrons make Duke's very popular. The majority of our raters weren't impressed, however. They said the power scene was overrated and the food mediocre and overpriced, which is about where the *Journal* papers came out. Phyllis Richman would disagree; she says "Duke's is at its prime nowadays." **Honors:** Richman's 50 Favorites. (26 ratings/mixed)

81 73 67 80

Dynasty $$
Chinese

Reserv: Suggested
Dress: Informal
Pay: AE, MC, V
Parking: No
Map Reference: C-4
Area: Triangle Bldg
Handicap Access: No
Nonsmoking Area: Yes
Bar: Full/separate
Hours: Daily, 11:30am-1am

11123 Viers Mill Rd
Wheaton, MD (301) 942-3070

Much appreciated local restaurant, particularly for its seafood and dim sum (served daily). Cantonese dishes are featured, but other regions are also represented on the extensive menu. Peking-style duck suggests "the roasters of Canton have it over their Peking counterparts" (*Washingtonian*). On the cramped side if crowded. (37 ratings/consistent)

---

85 83 85 77

East Wind $$
Vietnamese

Reserv: Sugg. weekends
Dress: Informal
Pay: AE, MC, V, DC, CB
Parking: No
Map Reference: N-11
Area: Old Town
Handicap Access: Yes
Nonsmoking Area: Yes
Bar: Full
Hours: M-F 11:30am-2:30pm, 6-10pm (F 10:30pm); Sa 6-10:30pm; Su 6-10pm

809 King St
Alexandria, VA (703) 836-1515

Excellent Vietnamese dishes tastefully presented in a relaxed atmosphere. Specialties include fried or steamed whole fish, stuffed calamari, roast quail, and bo'dun (marinated beef strips broiled on a skewer). Phyllis Richman wrote of the "subtle intricacy" of the cooking and *Frommer's* placed it high on the list of "recommendables." (21 ratings/consistent)

Food | Service | Ambience | Value

79 72 71 76

Eastport Raw Bar $$
Seafood

Reserv: Accepted
Dress: Informal
Pay: AE, MC, V
Parking: Yes
Map Reference: M-10
Handicap Access: Ltd.
Nonsmoking Area: Yes
Bar: Full/separate
Hours: M-Th 11:30am-10:30pm; F&Sa 11:30am-11:30pm; Su 11am-10pm, brunch til 3pm

4111 Duke St
Alexandria, VA (703) 823-1166

Comfortable and casual seafood house. Most raters thought seafood in general was good, but raw bar was singled out as particularly so. ***Washingtonian*** suggested diners stick to raw bar or order a hamburger, but raters also liked hush puppies, daily chalkboard specials, and bread pudding. Dining on the porch in summer. Suggestion: turn down the evening bar music. (37 ratings/consistent)

73 68 66 66

Ecco Cafe $$
New American

Reserv: Accepted
Dress: Informal
Pay: AE, MC, V
Parking: No
Metro: Ballston
Map Reference: K-10
Area: Ballston Common
Handicap Access: Ltd.
Nonsmoking Area: Yes
Bar: Full/separate
Hours: M-Sa 11am-midnight; Su 11am-10pm

4238 Wilson Blvd
Arlington, VA (703) 525-3226

New American-Italian menu features seafood and innovative pizza and pasta dishes. A haven for shoppers at the mall and a gathering place for nearby apartment dwellers. "Much of the food is worth a trip all by itself" (***Washington Post***). Sidewalk patio during warm weather, but it faces busy Wilson Blvd. Small deli for take-out. Original Ecco is in Alexandria, Va. (22 ratings/mixed)

El Bandito $
Mexican

Reserv: Accepted
Dress: Informal
Pay: AE, MC, V, DC, CB
Parking: Yes
Map Reference: F-4
Handicap Access: Yes
Nonsmoking Area: No
Bar: Beer/wine
Hours: M-F 11am-10pm (F 10:30pm); Sa noon-10:30pm

6113 Franconia Rd
Alexandria, VA (703) 922-9050

Inexpensive hideaway serving authentic, homemade Mexican food. Family operated; nothing fancy about surroundings. Efficient service and generous portions. Good for families. Margaritas served in addition to wine and beer. (12 ratings/mixed)

Food	Service	Ambience	Value

Food	Service	Ambience	Value
76	71	70	72

El Caribe
Latin American **$$**

Reserv: Suggested
Dress: Informal
Pay: AE, MC, V, DC, CB
Parking: Yes (eves)
Metro: Bethesda
Map Reference: G-10
Handicap Access: No
Nonsmoking Area: Yes
Bar: Full
Hours: M-Th 11:30am-10:30pm; F&Sa 11:30am-11pm; Su noon-10pm

8130 Wisconsin Ave
Bethesda, MD (301) 656-0888

The newest of the three El Caribes, this one has the best atmosphere. Menu is basically the same at all three—fajitas, empanadas, refried beans, and a variety of seafood dishes. "Serves superb empanadas" (Phyllis Richman). Food, overall, is tasty, but La Posada (see below), an offshoot on the next block, and Georgetown location (338-3121) got higher ratings for value. (17 ratings/mixed)

Food	Service	Ambience	Value
74	70	76	77

El Torito
Mexican **$**

Reserv: Suggested
Dress: Informal
Pay: AE, MC, V, DC, CB, Disc.
Parking: Yes
Map Reference: D-6
Handicap Access: Yes
Nonsmoking Area: Yes
Bar: Full/separate
Hours: M-F 11am-10pm (F 11pm); Sa 11:30am-11pm; Su 10am-10pm, brunch til 3pm

7607 Greenbelt Rd
Greenbelt, MD (301) 474-6122

Mass Mexican food, lacking in character according to some raters. Others thought there was good food and good value to be had here. Reviewer for *Journal* papers found food "sometimes even worthwhile." Cantina was described as both a fun place to meet and eat and a "meet" market. Five locations in area; see ratings for Rockville, Md. (984-5880) location. (30 ratings/mixed)

Food	Service	Ambience	Value
81	82	75	77

Embassy
French **$$**

Reserv: Suggested
Dress: Informal
Pay: AE, MC, V, DC, CB
Parking: Yes
Map Reference: C-4
Area: Ambassador Inn
Handicap Access: Yes
Nonsmoking Area: Yes
Bar: Full
Hours: M-F 6:30-10am, 11:30am-2:30pm, 5-10pm; Sa 7:30-10:30am, 11:30am-2:30pm, 5-10pm; Su 7:30-10:30am, 5-10pm

2715 University Blvd
Wheaton, MD (301) 946-2180

A sleeper of a neighborhood restaurant hidden away in a motel. Pleasant surroundings with a European air. Menu includes a long list of appetizers, many of them seafood, and such entrees as duck with sherry sauce, veal Calvados, and salmon steak. Early bird dinners a good value, but only available weeknights and for a short time. Same ownership as Nova Europa (see below). (15 ratings/consistent)

Food	Service	Ambience	Value

77	72	68	71

Enriqueta's $$
Mexican

Reserv: Accepted
Dress: Informal
Pay: AE, MC, V, DC, CB
Parking: No
Map Reference: J-11
Area: Georgetown
Handicap Access: Ltd.
Nonsmoking Area: Yes
Bar: Full
Hours: M-F 11:30am-2:30pm, 5-10pm (F 11pm); Sa 5-11pm; Su 5-10pm

2811 M St, NW
Washington, DC (202) 338-7772

The authentic renditions of Mexican food will tempt you to venture beyond tacos and burritos. Our raters were less effusive than critics in describing food quality, however. Cheerful setting; seating is cramped, and prices a bit high for some. There's a branch in Adams Morgan, too. **Honors:** Richman's Best of Best and *Washingtonian* 50 Best★★. (16 ratings/mixed)

82	76	71	81

Espositos Pizza 'n Pasta $$
Italian

Reserv: Accepted
Dress: Informal
Pay: AE, MC, V
Parking: Yes
Map Reference: E-3
Handicap Access: Yes
Nonsmoking Area: Yes
Bar: Beer/wine
Hours: Su-F 11am-10pm; Sa 11am-11pm

9917 Lee Hwy
Fairfax City, VA (703) 385-5912

As close to true southern Italian food as any in local area. Not fancy but well prepared and reasonably priced. Hot antipasto, homemade pastas, and pizza cooked on a wood-burning stove are specialties. Nice place for families. Buffet lunch a good value. **Honors:** Mobil specialty spot. (22 ratings/mixed)

66	72	82	63

Evans Farm Inn $$
American

Reserv: Suggested
Dress: Informal
Pay: AE, MC, V, DC, CB, Disc.
Parking: Yes
Map Reference: I-8
Handicap Access: Yes
Nonsmoking Area: Yes
Bar: Full/separate
Hours: M-F 11:30am-2:30pm, 5-9pm (F 10pm); Sa 11:30am-3pm, 5-10pm; Su brunch 11am-2pm, dinner noon-9pm

1696 Chain Bridge Rd
McLean, VA (703) 356-8000

Early Americana can't make up for poorly prepared food, although a few raters detected some improvement. Lovely colonial setting, spacious grounds, gift shop, and outdoor attractions make this suburban oldtimer popular with families and tourists. Lunch buffet Mon.-Sat.; piano bar Fri. & Sat. **Honors:** *Travel-Holiday* Award. (41 ratings/very mixed)

Falls Landing
Seafood

$$$

Reserv: Suggested
Dress: Coat req.
Pay: AE, MC, V, DC, CB
Parking: Yes
Map Reference: D-3
Area: Great Falls Village Centre
Handicap Access: Yes
Nonsmoking Area: Yes
Bar: Full
Hours: M-F 11:30am-2:30pm, 5:30-10pm (F 10:30pm); Sa 5:30-10pm; Su 4-9pm

774 Walker Rd
Great Falls, VA (703) 759-4650

Dine on seasonally available seafood in inviting Early American setting. Among the traditional and nouvelle seafood selections, swordfish brochette, crab imperial, and Maine lobster are popular. Nonseafood entrees also on menu. Working fireplaces add to charm in cold weather. Same owner as Cannon Seafood, a branch of which is located in shopping center, too. **Honors:** AAA◆◆◆. (33 ratings/mixed)

84 82 84 80

Fantasy Garden
Chinese

$

Reserv: Suggested
Dress: Informal
Pay: AE, MC, V
Parking: Yes
Map Reference: F-3
Area: W. Springfield Shopping Center
Handicap Access: Yes
Nonsmoking Area: Yes
Bar: Full/separate
Hours: M-Th 11am-10pm; F&Sa 11am-11pm; Su noon-10pm

6230-66 Rolling Rd
Springfield, VA (703) 569-4800

Pleasant neighborhood restaurant. Hunan and Szechuan dishes featured. Food is good looking and tasty, but one rater thought it was better before change in management. Friendly service. Frequently busy, but you won't be rushed. (10 ratings/mixed)

Far East
Chinese

$$

Reserv: Suggested
Dress: Informal
Pay: AE, MC, V
Parking: Yes
Map Reference: C-4
Handicap Access: No
Nonsmoking Area: Yes
Bar: Full
Hours: M-Th 11am-10pm; F&Sa 11am-11pm; Su noon-10pm

5055 Nicholson Ln
Rockville, MD (301) 881-5552

Went from small storefront to more lavish surroundings, and most raters thought the food hadn't suffered in the process. In fact, many think it's tops in Rockville area. Extensive menu of Szechuan and Hunan dishes. Food well prepared; service reasonably good. Lunch is better value than dinner. (48 ratings/mixed)

78 71 76 68

Fedora Cafe
Italian — $$

Reserv: Suggested
Dress: Informal
Pay: AE, MC, V, DC, CB, Disc.
Parking: Valet
Map Reference: D-3
Area: Zenith Bldg
Handicap Access: Yes
Nonsmoking Area: Yes
Bar: Full/separate
Hours: M-F 11:30am-3pm, 5-10:30pm (F 11:30pm); Sa noon-3pm, 5-11:30pm; Sun 10:30am-2:30pm, 4:30-9:30pm

8521 Leesburg Pike
Vienna, VA (703) 556-0100

Trendy food, with emphasis on Italian, served in elegant cafe. A popular spot, but several raters complained of variable food quality, slow service, and prices. Early dinner specials and Sun. brunch buffet (10:30am-2:30pm) are good values. "A singles bar to rival Clyde's" (Phyllis Richman). Same ownership as Devon Grills, Carnegie's, Charley's Place (see write-ups). Piano music Tues.-Sat. (38 ratings/mixed)

75 73 68 79

Ferdinand's
Continental — $$

Reserv: Suggested
Dress: Informal
Pay: AE, MC, V, DC, CB
Parking: Yes
Map Reference: C-4
Handicap Access: No
Nonsmoking Area: Yes
Bar: Full/separate
Hours: M-Sa 11am-11pm; Su 1-10pm

11300 Fern St
Wheaton, MD (301) 949-1617

A good value over the years. Varied menu features homemade soups, lots of beef, seafood, and some Greek dishes. Choice of salad bar or the house's El Greco salad with all entrees. Soup and salad bar special at lunch. Comfortable, but often crowded. Separate lounge. Owner oversees dining room. (53 ratings/mixed)

84 71 74 70

Filomena
Italian — $$$

Reserv: Suggested
Dress: Informal
Pay: AE, MC, V, DC
Parking: No
Map Reference: J-11
Area: Georgetown
Handicap Access: No
Nonsmoking Area: No
Bar: Full/separate
Hours: M-F 11:30am-11:45pm; Sa&Su 5-11:45pm

1063 Wisconsin Ave, NW
Washington, DC (202) 338-8800

Dark interior may contribute to the atmosphere in this cafe, but it makes it difficult to read the menu. Fried calamari, sauces, and the homemade pastas and pastries were recommended by raters. Complimentary after-dinner cordial and other pleasant small touches. Noisy at times, and there were many complaints about service. **Honors:** Mobil★★★. (31 ratings/mixed)

Food	Service	Ambience	Value

74	61	61	81

Fio's $
Italian

Reserv: Accepted
Dress: Informal
Pay: AE, MC, V, DC, CB
Parking: No
Map Reference: I-12
Area: Mount Pleasant
Handicap Access: Ltd.
Nonsmoking Area: No
Bar: Full/separate
Hours: T-Su 5-10:45pm

3636 16th St, NW, Woodner Apts
Washington, DC (202) 667-3040

Homey, cheap, authentic Italian food—pizza, pasta, and a lot of daily specials. Food preparation varies, but can be very good. "Strengths are the hearty dishes of southern Italy" (*Washingtonian*). Art deco fifties look complete with jukebox. **Honors:** *Washingtonian* Cheap Eats. (10 ratings/consistent)

70	75	71	69

Fireside Beef House $$
American

Reserv: Suggested
Dress: Informal
Pay: MC, V
Parking: Yes
Map Reference: G-15
Handicap Access: No
Nonsmoking Area: Yes
Bar: Full/separate
Hours: M-Th 11am-10pm; F&Sa 11am-12:30am; Su 11am-10pm, brunch til 2:30pm

6011 Greenbelt Rd
Berwyn Heights, MD (301) 474-1755

Ledo pizza, other Italian dishes, and seafood are served here, but the best choices may be the steak and salad bar. "Nothing out of ordinary" sums up a number of comments, and the reviewer for *Journal* papers found food "so disappointing on so many levels" he gave the restaurant zero stars. Deejay Fri. and Sat. nights. (19 ratings/very mixed)

72	68	72	70

Fish Market $$
Seafood

Reserv: Not accepted
Dress: Informal
Pay: AE, MC, V
Parking: Yes
Map Reference: N-12
Area: Old Town
Handicap Access: Yes
Nonsmoking Area: Yes
Bar: Full/separate
Hours: Daily, 11:15am-midnight

105 King St
Alexandria, VA (703) 836-5676

A fun place with good food and good value was the majority opinion; the dissenters complained of the noisy beer joint atmosphere and mediocre-to-poor food. Menu is mostly seafood, but the *Journal* papers cautioned against being "beguiled into [expecting] seriously good seafood." Sandwiches, salads, and some nonseafood entrees also available. Piano player upstairs in evenings. (35 ratings/very mixed)

Food | Service | Ambience | Value

The Fishery
Seafood **$$$**

5511 Connecticut Ave, NW
Washington, DC (202) 363-2144

Reserv: Required
Dress: Informal
Pay: AE, MC, V, DC, CB
Parking: Yes
Map Reference: G-11
Area: Chevy Chase, DC
Handicap Access: No
Nonsmoking Area: No
Bar: Full/separate
Hours: M-Th 11:30am-2:30pm, 5-10pm; F&Sa 11:30am-2:30pm, 5-11pm; Su 1-10pm

All is not well here. The seafood is reliably fresh, but otherwise raters said they were asked to pay too much for some poorly prepared dishes, spotty service, and noisy surroundings. The ***Washingtonian***, however, sang the praises of the crab cakes and seafood gumbo. Phyllis Richman said that the fish, when "left alone to speak for itself," is the "best of The Fishery." (24 ratings/consistent)

5 and Dime Cafe
American **$$**

728 Pine St
Herndon, VA (703) 471-5108

Reserv: Accepted
Dress: Informal
Pay: AE, MC, V
Parking: Yes
Map Reference: D-2
Handicap Access: Yes
Nonsmoking Area: No
Bar: Full
Hours: M-F 11:30am-3pm, 5-10pm (F 11pm); Sa 5-11pm

Good, honest American cooking in a converted 5 and Dime store. Casual, friendly atmosphere. Jazz music is canned on weekdays, live on Fri. and Sat. Several raters thought prices were high for food offered; dinner specials are a better value. Homemade soups and desserts were special attractions for ***Washington Post*** reviewer. (12 ratings/mixed)

Flaming Pit
American **$$**

18701 N. Frederick Rd
Gaithersburg, MD (301) 977-0700

Reserv: Suggested
Dress: Informal
Pay: AE, MC, V, DC, CB
Parking: Yes
Map Reference: B-3
Handicap Access: Ltd.
Nonsmoking Area: Yes
Bar: Full/separate
Hours: M-F 11:30am-10:30pm (F 11pm); Sa 4-11pm; Su 5-10pm

Beef and seafood house that lays claim to best prime rib in Montgomery County. Veal, lamb, and poultry also served. Top of menu can get pricey. Friendly, accommodating staff. Cramped and too busy at times, but most raters thought the prime rib made it worthwhile. Daily lunch and dinner specials. Piano player and sing-along nightly in lounge. You can warm yourself by the fire in cold weather. (21 ratings/mixed)

Food | Service | Ambience | Value

82 81 77 79

Floriana
Italian
$$

Reserv: Suggested
Dress: Informal
Pay: AE, MC, V
Parking: No
Metro: Friendship Heights
Map Reference: H-11
Handicap Access: No
Nonsmoking Area: Yes
Bar: Full
Hours: Su-Th 11:30am-2:30pm, 5-10pm; F&Sa 11:30am-2:30pm, 5-11pm

4936 Wisconsin Ave, NW
Washington, DC (202) 362-9009

Small, intimate neighborhood restaurant offering some unusual Italian dishes, fresh tastes, and large portions. Impressionistic decor creates pleasant atmosphere, and Floriana herself makes a terrific hostess. Good place for a family night out. (22 ratings/consistent)

---

75 75 76 71

Foggy Bottom Cafe
American
$$

Reserv: Suggested
Dress: Informal
Pay: AE, MC, V, DC, CB
Parking: Valet
Metro: Foggy Bottom
Map Reference: J-11
Handicap Access: Yes
Nonsmoking Area: No
Bar: Full/separate
Hours: M-F 7am-2pm, 5:30-11:30pm (M 10:30pm); Sa&Su 8am-2pm, 5:30-11:30pm (Su 10:30pm); Sa&Su brunch 10:30am-2pm

924 25th St, NW, River Inn Hotel
Washington, DC (202) 338-8707

Small, pleasant cafe. One of few places to eat close to Kennedy Center. Menu ranges from hamburgers to more substantial dishes, like pasta, tempura, ribs, and seafood. Several raters noted that cafe was once a favorite but now food and prices are moving farther apart. Phyllis Richman said that "along with misses . . . there are always . . . hits." (30 ratings/mixed)

78 72 61 76

Four Rivers
Chinese
$$

Reserv: Suggested
Dress: Informal
Pay: AE, MC, V, Checks
Parking: Yes
Metro: Twinbrook
Map Reference: C-4
Handicap Access: Yes
Nonsmoking Area: Yes
Bar: Full
Hours: Su-Th 11:30am-10pm; F&Sa 11:30am-11pm

184 Rollins Ave
Rockville, MD (301) 230-2900

Ambitious Szechuan-Hunan menu with many seafood selections and some dishes not found elsewhere. Tea-smoked duck and whole fish get good marks from critics, but *Washington Post* suggested "most of the trick is choosing carefully," and raters were divided about just how good food is. Lots of family activity. (19 ratings/mixed)

Food	Service	Ambience	Value

75	71	66	75

Four Seasons $$
Continental

Reserv: Accepted
Dress: Informal
Pay: AE, MC, V, DC, CB
Parking: Yes
Map Reference: M-10
Area: Landmark
Handicap Access: Yes
Nonsmoking Area: Yes
Bar: Full
Hours: Su-Th 7am-3am; F&Sa 24 hrs

557 S. Van Dorn St
Alexandria, VA (703) 823-9767

Family-owned diner/restaurant serving generous portions of nicely prepared food late into the night and all night Fri. and Sat. Large selection of sandwiches, salads, seafood, steaks, Continental specialties, and homemade breads and desserts. Full menu available at all times. Suburban late night spot. Crowded and noisy at times. (31 ratings/very mixed)

79	77	71	77

Frascati $$
Italian

Reserv: Suggested
Dress: Informal
Pay: AE, MC, V, DC, CB, Checks
Parking: Yes
Map Reference: G-10
Handicap Access: Yes
Nonsmoking Area: Yes
Bar: Beer/wine
Hours: M-F 11:30am-2:30pm, 4:30-10:30pm; Sa&Su 4:30-10:30pm

4806 Rugby Ave
Bethesda, MD (301) 652-9514

Warm and friendly neighborhood spot, but not memorable in all respects. Large portions of homemade Italian food, including pasta with a variety of sauces, seafood, chicken, and an array of veal dishes. ***Washington Post*** called it a "place for people who take their dining seriously." (14 ratings/consistent)

75	72	66	72

Fred & Harry's $$
Seafood

Reserv: Suggested
Dress: Informal
Pay: AE, MC, V
Parking: Yes
Map Reference: G-12
Handicap Access: Yes
Nonsmoking Area: Yes
Bar: Full
Hours: M-F 11am-10pm (F midnight); Sa 11am-11pm; Su noon-10pm

10110 Colesville Rd
Silver Spring, MD (301) 593-7177

Small, homey neighborhood restaurant that dates back to 1946. Third-generation family members now prepare the oysters, scallops, clams, crab cakes, crab imperial, shore platters, and New American seafood dishes. "The betting here is that the food will get even better," said the ***Journal*** papers. "Light Fare" menu available for smaller appetites. Small tables; crowded nonsmoking area. (21 ratings/very mixed)

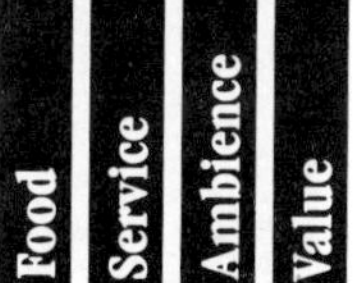

77 76 75 77

Fritzbe's
American **$$**

Reserv: Accepted
Dress: Informal
Pay: AE, MC, V
Parking: Yes
Metro: Twinbrook
Map Reference: C-4
Handicap Access: Yes
Nonsmoking Area: Yes
Bar: Full/separate
Hours: M-Th 11:30am-1am; F&Sa 11:30am-2am; Su 10:30am-1am, brunch til 3pm

1592 Rockville Pike
Rockville, MD (301) 984-8890

Saloon-type dining from the creators of Artie's, Carlyle Grand Cafe (see write-ups), and other area restaurants. Neighborhood spot for drinks, sandwiches, pasta, ribs, and seafood, but food can be uneven. Good for families, but try a weekday if you are bothered by lots of people and noisy bar. Deejay and dancing on Tues. See ratings for locations in Annandale, Va. (354-4560) and Reston, Va. (476-4400). (24 ratings/mixed)

81 71 67 79

Fuddruckers
American **$**

Reserv: Not accepted
Dress: Informal
Pay: AE, MC, V
Parking: Yes
Map Reference: E-3
Handicap Access: Yes
Nonsmoking Area: Yes
Bar: Beer/wine
Hours: Su-Th 11am-10pm; F&Sa 11am-11pm

4300 Backlick Rd
Annandale, VA (703) 642-0221

Great hamburgers and do-it-yourself fixings make this fast-food restaurant a popular stop for kids and hungry adults. Menu also includes hot dogs, tacos, steaks, and homemade rolls and pastries. Long lines and highest decibel count in area when busy. Several other locations in area. (58 ratings/mixed)

Gadsby's Tavern
American **$$**

Reserv: Suggested
Dress: Informal
Pay: AE, MC, V
Parking: No
Map Reference: N-12
Area: Old Town
Handicap Access: No
Nonsmoking Area: No
Bar: Full
Hours: M-Sa 11:30am-3pm, 5:30-10pm; Su brunch 11am-3pm, dinner 5:30-10pm

138 N. Royal St
Alexandria, VA (703) 548-1288

Dine on roast duckling and other colonial favorites in registered historic landmark (1792 City Hotel). A strolling balladeer entertains Tues. through Sat. A "serving wench" presides over Publick Table (colonial feast) and entertains guests Sun. and Mon. Nice place for families and visitors. Next door, you can visit the original tavern (1770), which is now a museum. (17 ratings/consistent)

Food | Service | Ambience | Value

---

77 72 70 58

Galileo
Italian **$$$**

Reserv: Suggested
Dress: Informal
Pay: AE, MC, V, DC, CB
Parking: Valet
Metro: Dupont Circle
Map Reference: J-12
Handicap Access: No
Nonsmoking Area: No
Bar: Full
Hours: M-F noon-2:30pm, 5:30-10pm; Sa 5:30-10:30pm

2014 P St, NW
Washington, DC (202) 293-7191

Raters and critics agree that the continuously changing menu of innovative Italian appetizers and entrees offers many a delight. But the portions, prices (the extras can add up), service, cramped quarters, noise level, and parking detract too much from the quality of the food for many. **Honors:** AAA★★★, Richman's Best of Best and 50 Favorites, *Travel-Holiday* Award, *Washingtonian* 50 Best★★. (29 ratings/very mixed)

66 66 74 62

Gangplank
Seafood **$$**

Reserv: Suggested
Dress: Informal
Pay: AE, MC, V
Parking: Yes
Metro: L'Enfant Plaza
Map Reference: K-12
Area: S.W. Waterfront
Handicap Access: No
Nonsmoking Area: No
Bar: Full/separate
Hours: M-F 11:30am-2pm, 5:30-10pm (F 11pm); Sa 11:30am-3pm, 5:30-11pm; Su 11am-3pm, 5:30-10pm

600 Water St, SW
Washington, DC (202) 554-5000

The view of the waterfront from the restaurant and the cocktail lounge at the end of the pier is the biggest attraction. Thus, it's not surprising that this traditional seafood house has been going strong for 20 years even though the food is, as the *Washington Times* put it, "merely pleasant, safe." Sun. brunch (11am-3pm) is popular. Close to Arena Stage. (19 ratings/mixed)

72 67 71 68

Geppetto
Italian **$**

Reserv: Not accepted
Dress: Informal
Pay: AE, MC, V, DC, CB
Parking: Yes
Map Reference: G-10
Area: Wildwood Shopping Center
Handicap Access: Yes
Nonsmoking Area: Yes
Bar: Full
Hours: M-Th 11:30am-10pm; F&Sa 11:30am-11:30pm; Su noon-9pm

10257 Old Georgetown Road
Bethesda, MD (301) 493-9230

Known primarily for its deep-dish, thick-crust pizza. The *Journal* papers and *Washington Post* suggest you select carefully once you get past the pizza, but there are salads, sandwiches, pasta, and a few meat and seafood entrees. Puppet decorations add to attraction for kids. Cheerful, but noisy; service slow. Other location, Georgetown (333-2602), got better ratings. (38 ratings/mixed)

82 79 77 73

Geranio

Italian

$$

Reserv: Suggested
Dress: Informal
Pay: AE, MC, V, Checks
Parking: No
Map Reference: N-11
Area: Old Town
Handicap Access: Ltd.
Nonsmoking Area: Yes
Bar: Full
Hours: M-F 11am-2:30pm, 6-10:30pm; Sa 6-10:30pm

722 King St
Alexandria, VA (703) 548-0088

Northern Italian dishes served in cheerful, unassuming setting presided over by owner. Food is getting a bit expensive, however. Pasta, veal, and seafood dominate the menu, but as Phyllis Richman said, "the delicacies in this house are soups, salads, veal, and the chef's daily whims." (21 ratings/consistent)

82 77 79 73

Germaine's

Asian

$$$

Reserv: Suggested
Dress: Informal
Pay: AE, MC, V, DC, CB
Parking: Yes
Map Reference: J-11
Area: Upper Georgetown
Handicap Access: No
Nonsmoking Area: No
Bar: Full/separate
Hours: M-F 11:30am-2:30pm, 5:30-10pm (F 11pm); Sa 5:30-11pm; Su 5:30-10pm

2400 Wisconsin Ave, NW
Washington, DC (202) 965-1185

Sample the best of the cuisines of Korea, India, Indonesia, Japan, and Thailand in this attractive Pan-Asian restaurant. Dining here can be a refreshing, pleasurable experience. Try the fish dishes. Service deteriorates when it's crowded. **Honors:** Mobil★★★, Richman's Best of Best and 50 Favorites. (22 ratings/mixed)

69 65 72 64

Glen Echo Station

American

$$

Reserv: Suggested
Dress: Informal
Pay: AE, MC, V
Parking: Yes
Map Reference: H-9
Handicap Access: Ltd.
Nonsmoking Area: Yes
Bar: Full/separate
Hours: M-Sa 11:30am-3pm, 6-10pm; Su brunch 11am-4pm, dinner 5-9pm

6119 Tulane Ave
Glen Echo, MD (301) 229-2280

Roadhouse on fringe of Glen Echo Park. Fun place to stop for a drink of an evening—and there are few along that stretch of road. Outdoor dining can be pleasant in good weather. Okay for light food to accompany that drink, but erratic quality and service mar the potential of menu for those who are more interested in the food than the action. (23 ratings/mixed)

Food | Service | Ambience | Value

82 76 71 77

Golden Bull $$

Steak House

Reserv: Suggested
Dress: Informal
Pay: AE, MC, V, DC, CB
Parking: Yes
Map Reference: G-14
Handicap Access: Ltd.
Nonsmoking Area: Yes
Bar: Full/separate
Hours: M-Sa 11am-11pm; Su noon-10pm

9107 Riggs Rd
Adelphi, MD (301) 439-4800

A traditional steak house—plenty of prime rib and steak actually cooked to order. Fresh seafood, other entrees, and daily specials also available. Additional "Lite Brite" menu offers smaller portions at reduced prices. "A restaurant for the whole family" (***Washington Times***). Happy hour (3-7pm) nightly and early bird specials. See ratings for Gaithersburg, Md. (948-3666) location. (21 ratings/consistent)

67 70 64 73

Golden Flame $$

Continental

Reserv: Suggested
Dress: Informal
Pay: AE, MC, V, DC, CB
Parking: Yes
Metro: Silver Spring
Map Reference: G-12
Area: Montgomery Ctr
Handicap Access: Yes
Nonsmoking Area: Yes
Bar: Full/separate
Hours: M-F 11am-10pm; Sa&Su 4-10pm

8630 Fenton St
Silver Spring, MD (301) 588-7250

Another neighborhood spot for prime rib, steak, and fresh seafood. Extensive salad bar of vegetables, fruits, and cheeses goes with your entree. Lunch and dinner specials. Nightly happy hour. A place to go when you can't think of any place to go. Recently renovated. (14 ratings/very mixed)

79 73 74 79

Golden Palace $$

Chinese

Reserv: Not accepted
Dress: Informal
Pay: AE, MC, V, DC, CB
Parking: No
Metro: Gallery Place
Map Reference: J-12
Area: Chinatown
Handicap Access: Ltd.
Nonsmoking Area: No
Bar: Full/separate
Hours: Su-Th 11am-10pm; F&Sa 11am-midnight

720 7th St, NW
Washington, DC (202) 783-1225

Cantonese dishes and the daily dim sum lunch (til 3pm) are the attractions here. Hunan and Szechuan dishes also prepared. Several raters suggested food and service had gone downhill. Closed for health code violations October 6-9, 1987: unsound cans of food in storage and ineffective rodent control; and May 13-15, 1987: ineffective rodent control, unsound food, and poor garbage disposal facilities. (17 ratings/very mixed)

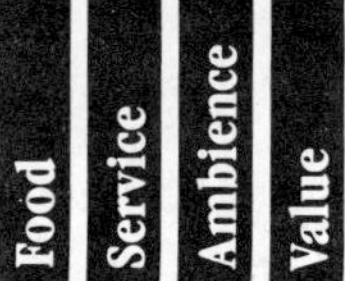

71 70 68 71

Grand Wok

Chinese

$$

Reserv: Suggested
Dress: Informal
Pay: AE, MC, V, DC, CB
Parking: Yes
Map Reference: I-8
Area: Commons Shopping Center
Handicap Access: No
Nonsmoking Area: Yes
Bar: Full/separate
Hours: Daily, 11:30am-10:30pm

7403 Colshire Dr
McLean, VA (703) 893-0830

Wide-ranging menu includes whole Peking duck carved at tableside and Hunan, Szechuan, and Mandarin dishes. Attractive setting, including pool for carp in foyer. Accommodating service; can handle large groups. But beyond the duck, our raters joined the *Washington Post* in wishing for "a menu that more consistently rises above the ordinary." (15 ratings/consistent)

77 74 66 75

H. I. Ribster's

American

$

Reserv: Not accepted
Dress: Informal
Pay: AE, MC, V, DC, CB, Disc.
Parking: Yes
Map Reference: E-3
Handicap Access: No
Nonsmoking Area: Yes
Bar: Full
Hours: M-F 11am-11pm (F midnight); Sa noon-midnight; Su noon-10pm

7243 Little River Tpke
Annandale, VA (703) 750-2751

Casual place for onion-ring loaf, spicy chicken wings, baby back ribs, barbecue chicken, prime rib, and a fish entree or two. A lot of people think the ribs can't be beat. The *Washington Post* described them as "mercifully simple . . . and incredibly tender," but the *Journal* papers were less enthusiastic. Often crowded, sometimes hurried. Rib dinner specials daily. Cigarette smoke a problem. (27 ratings/mixed)

72 67 69 70

Hamburger Hamlet

American

$

Reserv: Not accepted
Dress: Informal
Pay: AE, MC, V, DC
Parking: No
Metro: Friendship Heights
Map Reference: H-11
Handicap Access: No
Nonsmoking Area: Yes
Bar: Full/separate
Hours: Su-T 11am-10pm; W&Th 11am-11pm; F&Sa 11am-midnight; Su brunch til 3pm

5225 Wisconsin Ave, NW
Washington, DC (202) 244-2037

A place to go if you want a little atmosphere and relaxation with a thick, juicy, cooked-to-order hamburger. "This place was dishing out yuppie hamburgers before yuppies were invented" (*Washington Post*). Soups, salads, omelets, chili, and other light fare also available. Good place for families. Outdoor terrace. Two other locations; see ratings for Bethesda, Md. (897-5350) location. (37 ratings/consistent)

Food | Service | Ambience | Value

---

78 70 70 82

Hard Times Cafe
Chili

$

Reserv: Not accepted
Dress: Informal
Pay: MC, V
Parking: No
Metro: King Street
Map Reference: N-11
Handicap Access: Yes
Nonsmoking Area: No
Bar: Beer/wine
Hours: M-Th 11am-10pm; F&Sa 11am-11pm; Su 4-10pm

1404 King St
Alexandria, VA (703) 683-5340

This chili parlor got many raters' vote for the best chili in town, and the *Washingtonian* and *Frommer's* agree. Texas Red, Cincinnati, and vegetarian chili served. Rustic setting; country and western records on jukebox. Ratings weren't as good for other location, Rockville, Md. (294-9720). **Honors:** Mobil specialty spot, *Washingtonian* Cheap Eats. (27 ratings/very mixed)

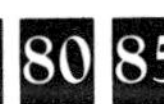

83 80 85 69

Harvey's
Seafood

$$$

Reserv: Suggested
Dress: Informal
Pay: AE, MC, V, DC, CB, Checks
Parking: Yes
Map Reference: B-3
Handicap Access: No
Nonsmoking Area: Yes
Bar: Full/separate
Hours: M-Sa 11:30am-3pm, 5:30-10pm

15201 Shady Grove Rd
Rockville, MD (301) 258-9670

The downtown Harvey's has all the lore (opened in 1858), but the offspring gets the better ratings. Traditional seafood house with all the favorites. Elegant but expensive. Phyllis Richman advises, for downtown at least, that you skip the "French elaborations and stick to plain local seafood." Guitarist/singer Fri. and Sat. See ratings for downtown D.C. (833-1858) location. (21 ratings/mixed)

83 79 87 81

Heart in Hand
American

$$

Reserv: Required
Dress: Informal
Pay: MC, V, Checks
Parking: Yes
Map Reference: F-2
Handicap Access: Ltd.
Nonsmoking Area: No
Bar: Full
Hours: T-Sa 11am-2pm, 6-9:30pm; Su 11:30am-8pm, brunch til 3pm

7145 Main St
Clifton, VA (703) 830-4111

Country dining in a quaint village that is worth the trip in itself. Generous portions of home-style food—like deep-fried chicken Suzanne—served in a converted nineteenth century store. The brunch and old-fashioned Southern supper served on Sun. are very popular. Patio dining in good weather. Phyllis Richman found food "mainly pleasant rather than admirable." (17 ratings/consistent)

58 63 60 53

Heidelberg
German

$$

Reserv: Req. weekends
Dress: Informal
Pay: AE, MC, V
Parking: No
Map Reference: N-12
Area: Old Town
Handicap Access: No
Nonsmoking Area: No
Bar: Full/separate
Hours: Daily, 11am-11pm; Su brunch til 3pm

100 King St
Alexandria, VA (703) 549-8440

The ratings pretty much say all that needs to be said about what one rater called fake, mushy German food. One rater did like the bratwurst platter, one liked the German draft beer, and another liked the location. (15 ratings/very mixed)

84 76 78 76

Helen's
New American

$$

Reserv: Suggested
Dress: Informal
Pay: AE, MC, V
Parking: No
Metro: Dupont Circle
Map Reference: J-12
Handicap Access: No
Nonsmoking Area: No
Bar: Full/separate
Hours: M-Th 6-11pm; F&Sa 6pm-midnight

1805 18th St, NW
Washington, DC (202) 483-1813

New American food that surprises and frequently delights. Intimate, candle-lit dining room. Good variety of dishes, many with Oriental influences, and all attractively presented. Phyllis Richman predicted Helen's was "likely on its way to excellence," but several raters thought it uneven. There's Helen's Too for carryout. **Honors:** Richman's Best of Best. (14 ratings/mixed)

80 79 74 68

Helga's Cafe
German

$$

Reserv: Suggested
Dress: Informal
Pay: AE, MC, V, DC, CB, Checks
Parking: Yes
Map Reference: I-9
Handicap Access: No
Nonsmoking Area: No
Bar: Full
Hours: M-F 11:30am-2:30pm, 5:30-9pm (F 10pm); Sa 5:30-10pm

6710 Old Dominion Dr
McLean, VA (703) 556-0780

Much about Helga's—the restaurant itself, the menu, the tables, the portions—is small. But small also means good here, at least most of the time. The menu is eclectic, the personal attention warm. Be sure to try the goulash soup and a dessert. Rotating fixed-price dinner special Tues.-Sat., e.g., pistachio-stuffed pork and fresh Mississippi catfish with red pepper sauce. (17 ratings/consistent)

Food | Service | Ambience | Value

78 79 84 72

Henry Africa
French

$$$

Reserv: Required
Dress: Informal
Pay: AE, MC, V, DC, CB
Parking: No
Map Reference: N-11
Area: Old Town
Handicap Access: No
Nonsmoking Area: No
Bar: Full/separate
Hours: T-Sa 11:30am-2:30pm, 6-10:30pm (F&Sa 11pm); Su brunch 11am-3pm, dinner 5:30-9:30pm

607 King St
Alexandria, VA (703) 549-4010

Traditional and nouvelle French-Continental cuisine and fresh, pleasant atmosphere. Food sometimes very good, sometimes not. Extensive but pricey wine list. Friendly bar scene with jazz trio on Tues.-Sat., starting at 9pm. The "Broker's" lunch can be a good value. Same owner as Taverna Cretekou (see below). (20 ratings/consistent)

64 62 66 59

Hogate's
Seafood

$$$

Reserv: Suggested
Dress: Informal
Pay: AE, MC, V, DC, CB, Disc.
Parking: No
Metro: L'Enfant Plaza
Map Reference: K-12
Area: S.W. Waterfront
Handicap Access: Ltd.
Nonsmoking Area: Yes
Bar: Full/separate
Hours: M-F 11am-11pm; Sa noon-midnight; Su brunch 10:30am-2:30pm, dinner noon-10pm

9th St & Maine Ave, SW
Washington, DC (202) 484-6301

Now celebrating its fiftieth anniversary, but only the name is the same. Mass production seafood platters may be okay for tour groups, but there's much better seafood available elsewhere. View of waterfront and Sunday brunch were the two bright spots raters found, and *Washington Times* reported "the view beats the food by a long shot." Near Arena Stage. (56 ratings/mixed)

74 72 76 75

Houlihan's
American

$

Reserv: Suggested
Dress: Informal
Pay: AE, MC, V, DC, CB, Disc.
Parking: Yes
Metro: Friendship Heights
Map Reference: H-11
Handicap Access: Yes
Nonsmoking Area: Yes
Bar: Full/separate
Hours: M-Th 11am-11pm; F&Sa 11am-midnight; Su 10:30am-10pm, brunch til 3pm

4444 Willard Ave
Chevy Chase, MD (301) 654-9020

Fajitas, Cajun shrimp, and chicken teriyaki at an Irishman's place? That's because the Irish theme is just packaging. Nonetheless, the menu has an interesting array of current favorites, and the atmosphere is pleasant and unhurried. Good place to take the kids or to stop for a bite after shopping or a movie. Another location in D.C. (19 ratings/mixed)

Food	Service	Ambience	Value

79	73	63	76

House of Chinese Gourmet $$
Chinese

Reserv: Suggested
Dress: Informal
Pay: AE, MC, V
Parking: Yes
Metro: Twinbrook
Map Reference: C-4
Handicap Access: Yes
Nonsmoking Area: Yes
Bar: Full
Hours: Su-Th 11:30am-10pm; F&Sa 11:30am-11pm

1485 Rockville Pike
Rockville, MD (301) 984-9440

One of the leaders along Rockville's Hong Kong strip. Extensive menu of Hunan, Szechuan, and classical Chinese vegetarian dishes. Plain surroundings. Dim sum on weekends. Some raters were disappointed given the reviews in the ***Washingtonian***; perhaps that's why it was dropped from magazine's 50 Best list for 1988. **Honors:** ***Washingtonian*** Cheap Eats. (51 ratings/mixed)

83	79	78	83

House of Dynasty $$
Chinese

Reserv: Req. weekends
Dress: Informal
Pay: AE, MC, V, DC, CB
Parking: Yes
Map Reference: F-4
Area: Hayfield Shopping Center
Handicap Access: Yes
Nonsmoking Area: Yes
Bar: Full
Hours: M-Th 11am-10pm; F&Sa 11am-10:30pm; Su 11:30am-9:30pm

7550 Telegraph Rd
Alexandria, VA (703) 922-5210

Downtown-quality restaurant in suburban shopping center. Wide variety of dishes—some say best Chinese food in No. Virginia. Generous portions and at moderate prices. Staff eager to please, but kitchen can be slow at times. (15 ratings/consistent)

79	67	69	77

House of Fortune $$
Chinese

Reserv: Suggested
Dress: Informal
Pay: AE, MC, V, DC, CB, Disc.
Parking: Yes
Map Reference: I-9
Handicap Access: No
Nonsmoking Area: No
Bar: Full
Hours: Daily, 10:30am-10pm

6715 Lowell Ave
McLean, VA (703) 821-3779

Another good Chinese restaurant in a suburban neighborhood. Szechuan, Hunan, and Mandarin dishes served in cheerful dining room. One rater suggests you skip the tepid eggrolls and go directly to the moo-shi pork. (24 ratings/mixed)

Food	Service	Ambience	Value

72	71	70	69

House of Hunan
Chinese **$$**

Reserv: Suggested
Dress: Informal
Pay: AE, MC, V, DC, CB
Parking: No
Metro: Farragut North/West
Map Reference: J-12
Area: Downtown
Handicap Access: No
Nonsmoking Area: No
Bar: Full/separate
Hours: M-Sa 11:30am-4:30pm, 5-10:15pm; Su 12:30-10:15pm

1900 K St, NW
Washington, DC (202) 293-9111

The spicy dishes many first learned to love here aren't as good as they used to be; the same is true of the service. And the attractive surroundings are lost among the crammed-together tables. Closed for health code violations Sept. 18-19, 1987: ineffective roach/fly/rodent control and unsanitary conditions. (28 ratings/very mixed)

87	86	88	77

House of Kao
Chinese **$$**

Reserv: Suggested
Dress: Coat/tie sugg.
Pay: AE, MC, V, DC, CB
Parking: Yes (eves)
Metro: Bethesda
Map Reference: G-10
Area: Clark Bldg
Handicap Access: No
Nonsmoking Area: Yes
Bar: Full
Hours: M-F 11:30am-10:30pm (F 11pm); Sa noon-11pm; Su noon-10:30pm

7500 Old Georgetown Rd
Bethesda, MD (301) 657-8868

Johnny Kao's entry for most beautiful Chinese restaurant in Bethesda. Extensive menu of Hunan and Szechuan selections, including two pages of "chef's suggestions," which are considerably more expensive than rest of menu. Perhaps that's why some raters thought the "gorgeous presentation" and "exceedingly dressy dishes" (*Washington Times*) weren't worth the cost. (30 ratings/mixed)

81	76	61	84

House of Mandarin
Chinese **$**

Reserv: Accepted
Dress: Informal
Pay: AE, MC, V
Parking: Yes
Map Reference: D-3
Handicap Access: No
Nonsmoking Area: No
Bar: Full
Hours: Daily, 11:30am-10:30pm

165 Glyndon St, SE
Vienna, VA (703) 281-9600

A local Chinese restaurant that has evoked strong neighborhood loyalty. Family-run restaurant serves generous portions of Mandarin and other regional dishes, such as chicken with cashews, Szechuan beef, and the chef's favorite, peppercorn shrimp. Food is best when grandma is in the kitchen. Closed for health code violation November 17, 1987: holding food at unsafe temperatures and unsanitary conditions. (11 ratings/consistent)

Food | Service | Ambience | Value

82 78 74 77

Houston's

American **$$**

Reserv: Not accepted
Dress: Informal
Pay: AE, MC, V
Parking: Yes
Map Reference: C-4
Handicap Access: Yes
Nonsmoking Area: Yes
Bar: Full
Hours: M-Th 11:15am-11pm; F&Sa 11:15am-midnight; Su 11:15am-10pm

12256 Rockville Pike
Rockville, MD (301) 468-3535

Gathering place for the fun side of dining. Juicy burgers, ribs, fish, and steak are grilled over wood chips while you watch. Chili, barbecue pork, and snack foods to go with a drink also served. Brings a "touch of class" to popular foods (*Washington Times*). Expect long wait for table at peak times. See ratings for Georgetown (338-7760) location. (57 ratings/consistent)

86 79 67 84

Hsian Foong

Chinese **$**

Reserv: Accepted
Dress: Informal
Pay: AE, MC, V, DC
Parking: Yes
Metro: Clarendon
Map Reference: K-10
Handicap Access: Ltd.
Nonsmoking Area: Yes
Bar: Full
Hours: M-Th 11:30am-10pm; F&Sa 11:30am-11pm; Su 4-10pm

2919 N. Washington Blvd
Arlington, VA (703) 527-6677

A strong contender for best neighborhood Chinese restaurant. Serves generous portions of Hunan and Szechuan food. All dishes are good, but some are better than others. Ask server for day's recommendations. Has some family-style dinners. Look for it behind Ollie's Trolley and next to 7-Eleven. Setting is dark, and parking is tight. Also has a Rosslyn location. (20 ratings/very consistent)

83 74 78 75

Hunan

Chinese **$$**

Reserv: Suggested
Dress: Informal
Pay: AE, MC, V, DC
Parking: Yes
Map Reference: C-4
Handicap Access: Yes
Nonsmoking Area: Yes
Bar: Full
Hours: Daily, 11am-10:30pm

1190 Rockville Pike
Rockville, MD (301) 279-2883

Hold on to your hats while we work our way through the maze of "Hunan" restaurants. We're off to an uncertain start: The food here is still better than average but not as good as it was, and the once attentive service now gets complaints. The dining room is still classy. The *Washington Post* also reported that "many of the once-distinctive dishes have slipped noticeably." (36 ratings/mixed)

Food	Service	Ambience	Value

83 77 79 82 — Hunan Chinatown — $$

Chinese

624 H St, NW
Washington, DC (202) 783-5858

Reserv: Required
Dress: Informal
Pay: AE, MC, V, DC, CB
Parking: No
Metro: Gallery Place
Map Reference: J-12
Area: Chinatown
Handicap Access: No
Nonsmoking Area: No
Bar: Full
Hours: Su-Th 11am-11pm; F&Sa 11am-1am

Hunan and Szechuan dishes that are a cut above the average. Attractive dining rooms; quiet, formal atmosphere. Some selections to consider are the Hunan shrimp, crispy fish, tea-smoked duck, and stir-fried spinach with garlic. ***Washingtonian*** reported "kitchen is consistent" and dishes are "enhanced by their attractive presentations." **Honors:** ***Washingtonian*** 50 Best★★ (18 ratings/consistent)

82 80 76 83 — Hunan Dynasty — $$

Chinese

215 Pennsylvania Ave, SE
Washington, DC (202) 546-6161

Reserv: Suggested
Dress: Informal
Pay: AE, MC, V, DC, CB
Parking: No
Metro: Capitol South
Map Reference: K-13
Area: Capitol Hill
Handicap Access: No
Nonsmoking Area: No
Bar: Full/separate
Hours: M-F 11am-10pm (F 11pm); Sa 11:30am-11pm; Su 11:30am-10pm

The type of neighborhood restaurant you return to frequently. Menu selections represent major culinary regions of China. Food is well prepared and nicely presented. "Good food, caring service and very fair prices" (Phyllis Richman). Dim sum on weekends and holidays. (18 ratings/very consistent)

86 83 76 89 — Hunan East — $$

Chinese

9546 Old Keene Mill Rd
Burke, VA (703) 569-7600

Reserv: Accepted
Dress: Informal
Pay: AE, MC, V, Checks
Parking: Yes
Map Reference: E-3
Area: Town Plaza
Handicap Access: Yes
Nonsmoking Area: No
Bar: Full
Hours: M-Th 11am-10pm; F&Sa 11:30am-10:30pm; Su 5-10pm

Gets high marks for value and food. Serves largely local clientele. Crispy shrimp with walnuts, orange beef, and the chef's specials are popular, as are the family-style dinners. (10 ratings/consistent)

Food | Service | Ambience | Value

Hunan East
Chinese **$$**

Reserv: Suggested
Dress: Informal
Pay: AE, MC, V, DC, CB
Parking: Yes
Map Reference: L-9
Area: Leesburg Pike Plaza
Handicap Access: No
Nonsmoking Area: Yes
Bar: Full/separate
Hours: Su-Th 11:30am-10:30pm; F&Sa 11:30am-11pm

3501-A S. Jefferson St
Baileys Crossroads, VA (703) 820-3900

The "Hunan" that scored highest for food and ambience—and it missed on value by only one point. Menu of traditional and new dishes includes many seafood favorites, including Szechuan soft-shell crabs. Raters liked the ginger-garlic sauces that dress many dishes. Branch in Woodlawn, Va. (18 ratings/consistent)

73 68 62 72

Hunan Gourmet
Chinese **$$**

Reserv: Suggested
Dress: Informal
Pay: AE, MC, V
Parking: Yes (after 6pm)
Metro: Gallery Place
Map Reference: J-12
Area: Chinatown
Handicap Access: No
Nonsmoking Area: No
Bar: Full
Hours: M-Th 11am-11pm; F&Sa 11am-midnight; Su 11am-10pm

726 7th St, NW
Washington, DC (202) 783-6268

The prices are lower here than at Hunan Chinatown, one block away, but so are the ratings. Some of the same Hunan standards are on the menu, along with Szechuan dishes. Hunan Gourmet soup, whole crispy fish, smoked duck, and the chef's specials were recommended. Dim sum on weekends til 3pm. Same ownership as Hunan Gallery in D.C. and Hunan Potomac in Md. (15 ratings/consistent)

Hunan Inn
Chinese **$**

Reserv: Suggested
Dress: Informal
Pay: AE, MC, V
Parking: Yes
Map Reference: G-12
Area: Briggs-Cheney Plaza
Handicap Access: No
Nonsmoking Area: Yes
Bar: Full/separate
Hours: M-Th 11:30am-10pm; F&Sa 11:30am-10:30pm; Su noon-9pm

13843 Outlet Dr
Silver Spring, MD (301) 890-3366

This Maryland "Hunan" isn't much on ambience, but the 20-30 minute wait on weekends if you don't make reservations must mean they're doing something right. Hot crispy veal, quadruple fragrance combo (mix of vegetables and seasonings), and General Tso's chicken are popular entrees. (14 ratings/mixed)

Food | Service | Ambience | Value

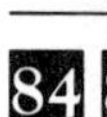

84 87 83 75

Hunan Lion
Chinese **$$**

Reserv: Suggested
Dress: Coat/tie sugg.
Pay: AE, MC, V, DC, CB
Parking: Valet (eves)
Map Reference: D-3
Area: Tycon Courthouse Bldg
Handicap Access: Yes
Nonsmoking Area: Yes
Bar: Full
Hours: Su-Th 11:30am-10:30pm; F&Sa 11:30am-11pm; Sa&Su brunch til 3pm

2070 Chain Bridge Rd
Tysons Corner, VA (703) 734-9828

Virginia outpost of the Kao restaurant group. In the mold of "new" Chinese restaurants, where elegant surroundings and attentive service are highly valued. "Most of [the food] is pleasant and expected" (*Washington Business Journal*), but as at House of Kao (see above), "chef's suggestions" can get rather expensive. **Honors:** AAA★★★. (25 ratings/consistent)

82 77 68 85

Hunan Village
Chinese

$

Reserv: Suggested
Dress: Informal
Pay: AE, MC, V, DC, CB
Parking: Yes
Map Reference: D-6
Area: Cipriano Shopping Center
Handicap Access: Yes
Nonsmoking Area: Yes
Bar: Full
Hours: Daily, 11am-10pm

8863 Greenbelt Rd
Greenbelt, MD (301) 552-9500

Solid neighborhood restaurant, but food and service can vary somewhat. Standard Hunan and Szechuan dishes—General Tso's chicken, Yu Ling duck, and the chef's favorite, orange beef. (15 ratings/consistent)

75 75 65 76

Hunan West
Chinese **$**

Reserv: Accepted
Dress: Informal
Pay: AE, MC, V
Parking: Yes
Map Reference: F-3
Area: King Park Shopping Center
Handicap Access: No
Nonsmoking Area: No
Bar: Full
Hours: M-Th 11:30am-10pm; F&Sa 11:30am-10:30pm; Su 4-10pm

8938 Burke Lake Rd
Springfield, VA (703) 425-1703

Our tour of the Hunans comes to an end with a stop at a small, inexpensive restaurant in a shopping center. Standard Hunan and Szechuan menu. Lemon chicken got the only raves. Friendly, efficient service; neighborly atmosphere. (11 ratings/consistent)

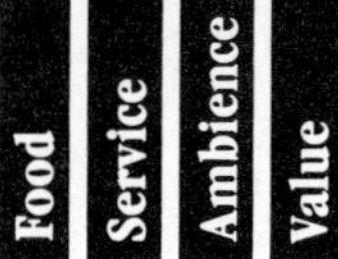

Food	Service	Ambience	Value
77	75	71	67

Ice House Cafe
New American

$$$

Reserv: Suggested
Dress: Informal
Pay: AE, MC, V, Checks
Parking: No
Map Reference: D-2
Handicap Access: Ltd.
Nonsmoking Area: No
Bar: Full/separate
Hours: M-Sa 11:30am-2:30pm, 6-10pm (F&Sa 10:30pm)

760 Elden St
Herndon, VA (703) 437-4500

Suburban restaurant with turn-of-the-century theme. Dine in oyster bar, dining room, or on back porch (seasonal). New American menu with a focus on seafood. Several raters considered it overpriced. Piano music Mon-Sat.; jazz group on weekends. (26 ratings/mixed)

Food	Service	Ambience	Value
80	76	76	78

Il Porto
Italian

$$

Reserv: Suggested
Dress: Informal
Pay: AE, MC, V
Parking: No
Map Reference: N-12
Area: Old Town
Handicap Access: Ltd.
Nonsmoking Area: Yes
Bar: Full/separate
Hours: Daily, 11:15am-midnight

121 King St
Alexandria, VA (703) 836-8833

Cozy, intimate Italian restaurant serving homemade pasta, seafood, veal, and other northern Italian dishes. Scampi is a favorite. The topper is the ragtime pianist evenings in the upstairs dining room. (19 ratings/mixed)

Food	Service	Ambience	Value
96	92	95	81

Inn at Little Washington
New American

$$$$

Reserv: Required
Dress: Informal
Pay: MC, V, Checks
Parking: Yes
Map Ref: Off map
Handicap Access: Ltd.
Nonsmoking Area: No
Bar: Full/separate
Hours: W-F 6-9:30pm; Sa 5:30-10:30pm; Su 4-9:30pm

Middle & Main Sts
Washington, VA (703) 675-3800

The accolades keep coming in from here and abroad for this elegantly appointed country inn 65 miles or so outside D.C. in Blue Ridge foothills. Superb menu of fixed-price dinners highlights locally available ingredients, many from inn's own garden. Great for romantic celebrations. **Honors:** AAA◆◆◆, Mobil★★★★, Richman's Best of Best and 50 Favorites, *Travel-Holiday* Award. (40 ratings/very consistent)

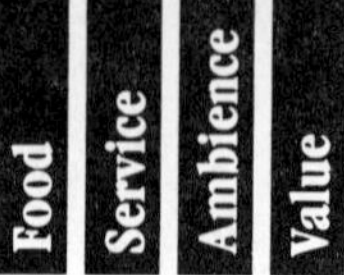

Iron Gate Inn — $$
Lebanese

Reserv: Required
Dress: Informal
Pay: AE, MC, V, DC, CB
Parking: No
Metro: Dupont Circle
Map Reference: J-12
Handicap Access: No
Nonsmoking Area: No
Bar: Full/separate
Hours: Daily, 11:30am-10pm

1734 N St, NW (rear)
Washington, DC (202) 737-1370

All the ingredients of a romantic evening—dining under the stars in the brick-walled garden in summer or by a roaring fire in the converted nineteenth century stables in winter. With that much atmosphere, you probably won't notice the flawed service or the so-so renditions of Middle Eastern favorites. ***Frommer's*** called the garden the "loveliest in Washington." (23 ratings/consistent)

Iron Skillet — $$$
French

Reserv: Suggested
Dress: Informal
Pay: AE, MC, V, DC, CB, Checks
Parking: Yes
Map Reference: L-9
Handicap Access: Ltd.
Nonsmoking Area: Yes
Bar: Full
Hours: M-Sa 11:30am-10pm

5838 Columbia Pike
Baileys Crossroads, VA (703) 820-3332

Don't be put off by the unprepossessing exterior. Inside you'll find good food and warm, friendly surroundings. Standard menu includes coq au vin, steak Diane, veal Oscar, swordfish, London broil, and the chef's favorite, frog's legs. Separate low calorie menu also available. Daily fixed-price dinner specials. (12 ratings/very mixed)

Italia Bella — $$
Italian

Reserv: Suggested
Dress: Informal
Pay: MC, V, Checks
Parking: Yes
Map Reference: K-9
Area: Westover Shopping Center
Handicap Access: No
Nonsmoking Area: No
Bar: Full
Hours: M-F 11am-2:30pm, 5-9:30pm (W-F 10:30pm); Sa 5-10:30pm; Su 5-9:30pm

5880 N. Washington Blvd
Arlington, VA (703) 534-7474

Relaxing neighborhood restaurant. The chef/co-owner prepares home-style pasta, sauces, poultry, veal, and seafood. Pasta and sauces recommended by raters. Service is friendly. Violin and accordion music Tues. and Wed., starting at 6:30pm. Going without reservations is dicey. (14 ratings/consistent)

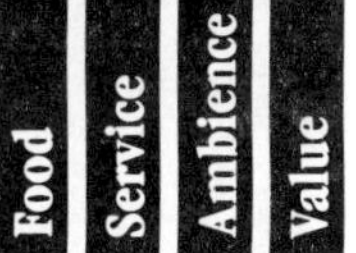

70 71 64 73

Italian Oven
Italian **$$**

Reserv: Accepted
Dress: Informal
Pay: AE, MC, V
Parking: Yes
Map Reference: I-9
Handicap Access: Yes
Nonsmoking Area: Yes
Bar: Full
Hours: M-F 11:30am-10:30pm (F midnight); Sa noon-midnight; Su noon-10pm

6852 Old Dominion Dr
McLean, VA (703) 893-7777

Neighborhood spot for homemade pasta, seafood, and pizza cooked in wood-burning oven. Friendly service and reasonable prices make it good for families. Buffet lunch Thurs. and Fri. Another location in Arlington; Espositos Pizza 'n Pasta (see above) is in family, too. (26 ratings/consistent)

82 74 54 84

Ivy's Place
Indonesian **$**

Reserv: Suggested
Dress: Informal
Pay: AE, MC, V, Checks
Parking: No
Metro: Cleveland Park
Map Reference: I-11
Handicap Access: No
Nonsmoking Area: No
Bar: Beer/wine
Hours: M-Sa 11:30am-11:30pm; Su 3:30-10:30pm

3520 Connecticut Ave, NW
Washington, DC (202) 363-7802

No frills, just generous portions of good home-style Indonesian (and some Thai) food at bargain prices. Cramped quarters inside and on sidewalk patio. "Combines simplicity with warmth" (***Washingtonian***). Try the warm vegetable salad, chicken satay, or the chef's favorite, stir-fried green peppers in garlic sauce. **Honors:** ***Washingtonian*** Cheap Eats. (23 ratings/consistent)

84 81 77 80

J. J. Muldoon's
Continental **$$**

Reserv: Accepted
Dress: Informal
Pay: AE, MC, V, DC, CB
Parking: Yes
Map Reference: B-3
Handicap Access: Yes
Nonsmoking Area: Yes
Bar: Full/separate
Hours: Daily, 11:30am-2am; Su brunch 10am-2pm

16143 Shady Grove Rd
Gaithersburg, MD (301) 258-8866

Combination local watering hole and restaurant. Menu of steaks, lots of seafood, burgers, and light fare. Daily lunch specials. Deejay and dancing Tues.-Sat. (13 ratings/consistent)

Food	Service	Ambience	Value
84	80	75	71

J.R.'s Steak House
Steak House **$$**

Reserv: Suggested
Dress: Coat/tie sugg.
Pay: AE, MC, V
Parking: Yes
Map Reference: E-3
Area: Circle Towers Bldg
Handicap Access: No
Nonsmoking Area: Yes
Bar: Full/separate
Hours: T-Th 6-10pm; F&Sa 6-11pm; Su 5-9pm

9401 Lee Hwy
Fairfax, VA (703) 591-8447

One of the best suburban steak houses, but a bit pricey. Menu features 16 selections of prime, aged, corn-fed Iowa beef, seafood, and a large salad bar. Good place for business lunches and dinners. See ratings for other location, J.R.'s Stockyards Inn, Tysons Corner, Va. (893-3390); menu essentially the same at both places. (19 ratings/mixed)

Food	Service	Ambience	Value
81	73	66	79

Jacques' Cafe
French **$$**

Reserv: Not accepted
Dress: Informal
Pay: MC, V
Parking: No
Metro: Clarendon
Map Reference: K-10
Handicap Access: Ltd.
Nonsmoking Area: No
Bar: Full/separate
Hours: T-F 11:30am-2:30pm, 5-10pm (F 11pm); Sa 5-11pm; Su 5-10pm

3012 Wilson Blvd
Arlington, VA (703) 528-8500

This neighborhood cafe may be lacking in decor and polished service, but then there are good bistro food and prices. The bouillabaisse and couscous are the chef's favorites. Nightly fixed-price dinners. Live Dixieland jazz Tues.-Sat.; jam session on Sun. *Washingtonian* said it "continues to dominate the category of French bargain restaurant." **Honors:** *Washingtonian* Cheap Eats. (13 ratings/mixed)

Food	Service	Ambience	Value
72	68	68	72

Jake's on the Pike
Italian **$$**

Reserv: Not accepted
Dress: Informal
Pay: AE, MC, V
Parking: Yes
Map Reference: C-4
Handicap Access: Yes
Nonsmoking Area: Yes
Bar: Full/separate
Hours: M-Th 11am-1am; F&Sa 11am-2am; Su 10:30am-1am, brunch til 2pm

1300 Rockville Pike
Rockville, MD (301) 770-2650

A large, colorful, somewhat noisy place to stop for a light bite: snacks, burgers, pizza, pasta, and salads. Food is a combination of Italian and American favorites. A place to relax with friends. TV in lounge and dining room; deejay in lounge nightly. Good for kids; they eat for half-price at Sun. brunch. Lunch buffet weekdays; happy hour. Also at Tysons Station, Va. (19 ratings/mixed)

Food | Service | Ambience | Value

Japan Inn
Japanese **$$**

1715 Wisconsin Ave, NW
Washington, DC (202) 337-3400

Reserv: Suggested
Dress: Informal
Pay: AE, MC, V, DC, CB
Parking: Yes
Map Reference: J-11
Area: Upper Georgetown
Handicap Access: No
Nonsmoking Area: No
Bar: Full/separate
Hours: M-F noon-2pm, 6-10pm; Sa 6-10pm; Su 5:30-9:30pm

Three ways to have Japanese food: at the sushi bar; sitting on cushions in a tatami-covered room while your food is prepared at tableside; or sitting at the teppanyaki while the chef cooks your dinner on the sizzling grill and dazzles you with his knife work. The food can be very good, but raters say it's not always up to standard. **Honors:** *Washingtonian* 50 Best★. (10 ratings/consistent)

76 72 74 73

Jasper's
American **$$**

7401 Greenbelt Rd
Greenbelt, MD (301) 441-8030

Reserv: Not accepted
Dress: Informal
Pay: AE, MC, V, DC, CB, Disc.
Parking: Yes
Map Reference: D-6
Area: Greenway Shopping Center
Handicap Access: Yes
Nonsmoking Area: Yes
Bar: Full/separate
Hours: M-Sa 11:30am-3am; Su 11am-11pm, brunch til 3pm

Jasper's invites you in "in the spirit of fun" for lunch, happy hour, and evenings of music and dancing (9:30pm). Book-length menu of snacks and light food: homemade loaded potato skins, burgers, pasta, salads, and stir-fries. Expensive for essentially fast food, but portions are generous. Long wait to get in at peak times. Outdoor cafe. Piano at Sun. brunch. (28 ratings/mixed)

Jean Louis
French **$$$$**

2650 Virginia Ave, NW
Washington, DC (202) 298-4488

Reserv: Required
Dress: Coat/tie req.
Pay: AE, MC, V, DC
Parking: Valet
Metro: Foggy Bottom
Map Reference: J-11
Area: Watergate Hotel
Handicap Access: Yes
Nonsmoking Area: No
Bar: Full
Hours: M-Sa 5:30-9:30pm

Everything here is excellent. But excellence commands a high price, too high for many. And formal French service strikes some as overbearing. Good choice if you want to experience truly fine dining and are willing to pay the price. " . . . may have peers . . . has no superiors" (Phyllis Richman). **Honors:** AAA◆◆◆◆, Mobil★★★★, Richman's Best of Best and 50 Favorites, *Travel-Holiday* Award. (24 ratings/mixed)

70 74 62 74

Jenny's
Chinese

$$

Reserv: Suggested
Dress: Informal
Pay: AE, MC, V, DC, CB
Parking: No
Map Reference: K-12
Area: Waterside Mall
Handicap Access: Ltd.
Nonsmoking Area: No
Bar: Full
Hours: M-F 11am-11pm (F midnight); Sa noon-midnight; Su noon-10pm

401 M St, SW
Washington, DC (202) 554-2202

Neighborhood restaurant where you'll find good humor and friendly service. Frequented by government workers at lunch and by diners headed for an evening at nearby Arena Stage. Szechuan and Hunan dishes featured. (24 ratings/mixed)

67 68 67 67

Joe Theismann's
American

$$

Reserv: Not accepted
Dress: Informal
Pay: AE, MC, V, DC, CB
Parking: Yes
Map Reference: D-3
Handicap Access: Yes
Nonsmoking Area: Yes
Bar: Full/separate
Hours: Su-Th 11:30am-midnight; F&Sa 11:30am-1am; Su brunch til 2:30pm

150 Branch Rd, SE
Vienna, VA (703) 281-7770

Brass and fern bar permeated with the aura of Redskins football. More for sports fans than for gourmets. The menu of beef, seafood, pasta, soup, and sandwiches is basically the same for all three of Joe's restaurants, but the execution varies. All are geared to watching sports on TV. See ratings for Baileys Crossroads, Va. (379-7777) and Alexandria, Va. (739-0777) locations. (35 ratings/mixed)

74 72 64 80

Joe's Place Pizza & Pasta
Italian

$

Reserv: Accepted
Dress: Informal
Pay: AE, MC, V, Checks
Parking: Yes
Map Reference: J-9
Handicap Access: Yes
Nonsmoking Area: Yes
Bar: Full
Hours: M-Th 10:30am-11pm; F&Sa 10:30am-midnight; Su 11am-11pm

5555 Lee Hwy
Arlington, VA (703) 532-0990

Casual neighborhood spot for pizza, pasta, calzones, and subs. Features 26 pizza toppings. All-you-can-eat lunch buffet. Good for families. Joe has a place in Falls Church, too. (10 ratings/mixed)

Food	Service	Ambience	Value

80	76	83	65

Johnny's $$$
New American

Reserv: Suggested
Dress: Informal
Pay: AE, MC, V, DC, CB
Parking: Yes
Map Reference: D-3
Area: Greensboro Bldg
Handicap Access: Ltd.
Nonsmoking Area: No
Bar: Full/separate
Hours: M-F 11:30am-3pm, 5-10:30pm; Sa 5-10:30pm; Su brunch 11am-3pm, dinner 5-10:30pm

8280 Greensboro Dr
McLean, VA (703) 847-8899

The critics' early assessment was that Johnny Kao's "great American cuisine" was great only some of the time. Our raters liked the food, but not the prices. This may be a special-occasion place for most, unless you try it for Sun. brunch or a fixed-price lunch or dinner. Piano music in lounge Wed.-Fri. An "island of tranquility" in Tysons Corner area (*Washington Times*). Also in Bethesda, Md. **Honors:** Mobil★★★. (19 ratings/mixed)

81	77	76	81

Kabul Caravan $$
Afghan

Reserv: Suggested
Dress: Coat/tie req.
Pay: MC, V
Parking: Yes
Metro: Court House
Map Reference: K-10
Area: Colonial Village Shopping Center
Handicap Access: Yes
Nonsmoking Area: No
Bar: Full
Hours: M-F 11:30am-2:30pm, 5:30-11pm; Sa&Su 5:30-11pm

1725 Wilson Blvd
Arlington, VA (703) 522-8394

The traditional Afghan dishes may have gained some Western influences since this restaurant was opened in 1979, but the food and service are good, and the prices are reasonable. One of several ethnic restaurants in a small strip of old storefronts just above Rosslyn. Inside, candles, white tablecloths, and authentic handicrafts create a very pleasant atmosphere. (16 ratings/consistent)

81	71	71	79

Kabul West $$
Afghan

Reserv: Suggested
Dress: Informal
Pay: MC, V, Checks
Parking: Yes (after 6pm)
Metro: Bethesda
Map Reference: G-10
Area: Woodmont Tri.
Handicap Access: No
Nonsmoking Area: Yes
Bar: Beer/wine
Hours: M-F 11:30am-2pm, 5:30-10pm (F 11pm); Sa 5:30-11pm; Su 5:30-10pm

4871 Cordell Ave
Bethesda, MD (301) 986-8566

The Afghan representative in an area of Bethesda teeming with good restaurants. Menu is limited, but it is "food of delicacy and modest prices" (Phyllis Richman), and it provides "an occasion to savor something very different" (*Journal* papers). Has a number of vegetarian dishes. Attitude of servers frequently criticized. **Honors:** Richman's Best of Best, *Washingtonian* Cheap Eats. (53 ratings/consistent)

Food | Service | Ambience | Value

76 74 76 72

Kaiserhof $$
German

Reserv: Suggested
Dress: Informal
Pay: AE, MC, V, DC, CB
Parking: Valet
Map Reference: E-3
Handicap Access: No
Nonsmoking Area: No
Bar: Full/separate
Hours: T-Sa 5-10pm

10418 Main St
Fairfax City, VA (703) 352-0059

This rathskeller-gausthaus claims to have the longest bar in Virginia. You'll certainly find plenty of gemutlichkeit to go along with the schnitzel, bratwurst, sauerbraten, and apple strudel. Entertainment nightly in the Austrian-Bavarian tradition: accordion, tuba, songs, dancing. In same building as Heinrich Hoffman's other restaurant, the Alibi (see above). Early bird dinners midweek. (10 ratings/mixed)

69 70 69 68

Kangaroo Katie's $$
American

Reserv: Suggested
Dress: Informal
Pay: AE, MC, V, DC, CB
Parking: Yes
Map Reference: D-6
Handicap Access: Yes
Nonsmoking Area: Yes
Bar: Full/separate
Hours: M-Th 11am-2am; F&Sa 11am-3am; Su noon-2am

7511 Greenbelt Rd
Greenbelt, MD (301) 474-9011

Young singles hangout with an Aussie theme. The food is basically contemporary saloon fare. There are a few Australian items on menu, like alligator Dundee, but the *Washingtonian* advises you avoid them. Two TV-equipped bars; deejay and dancing nightly (9:30pm). "A fun place throughout" (*Washington Times*). (15 ratings/mixed)

78 68 68 72

Katmandu $$
Indian

Reserv: Suggested
Dress: Informal
Pay: AE, MC, V
Parking: No
Metro: Dupont Circle
Map Reference: J-12
Handicap Access: Yes
Nonsmoking Area: Yes
Bar: Full
Hours: M-F 11:30am-2:30pm, 5:30-10:30pm; Sa&Su 5:30-10:30pm

1800-B Connecticut Ave, NW
Washington, DC (202) 483-6470

You'll find Indian curries and pilaf here, but it was the Nepalese dishes and the appetizers that generated the most enthusiasm among raters. The *Washington Post* called it a "fair-priced introduction to food that is as filling as it is unusual." Small, quiet rooms. **Honors:** *Washingtonian* 50 Best★. (10 ratings/consistent)

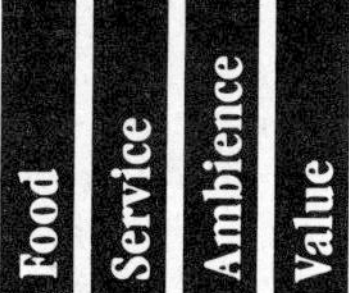

87 86 82 79

Kazan **$$**

Turkish

Reserv: Suggested
Dress: Coat sugg.
Pay: AE, MC, V, DC, Checks
Parking: Yes
Map Reference: I-9
Area: McLean Shopping Center
Handicap Access: Yes
Nonsmoking Area: Yes
Bar: Full
Hours: M-F 11am-3pm, 5-10pm; Sa 5-10pm

6813 Redmond Dr
McLean, VA (703) 734-1960

Beautifully appointed Turkish oasis in a shopping center. Presided over by congenial host/co-owner. Lamb, veal, and fish dishes all get raves. The doner kebab (served Wed., Fri., and Sat.) was particularly recommended by raters. (40 ratings/consistent)

80 74 65 80

Khyber Pass **$$**

Afghan

Reserv: Required
Dress: Informal
Pay: AE, MC, V
Parking: Yes
Metro: Woodley Park
Map Reference: I-11
Handicap Access: No
Nonsmoking Area: No
Bar: Full/separate
Hours: Daily, 5:30-11pm

2309 Calvert St, NW
Washington, DC (202) 234-4632

At this small restaurant, be sure to try the aushak, described on menu as leek-filled dumplings topped with yogurt and meat sauce. Rest of menu consists largely of lamb, beef, and chicken dishes with a variety of seasonings and accompaniments. The "best offerings can be delectable" (Phyllis Richman). Fixed-price dinners for two provide a way to sample several dishes. (14 ratings/consistent)

79 75 75 82

Kilroy's **$$**

American

Reserv: Not accepted
Dress: Informal
Pay: AE, MC, V
Parking: Yes
Map Reference: F-3
Area: Ravensworth Shopping Center
Handicap Access: Yes
Nonsmoking Area: Yes
Bar: Full/separate
Hours: M-F 11am-2am; Sa 11:30pm-2am; Su 5pm-2am

5250 Port Royal Rd
Springfield, VA (703) 321-7733

Informal food and fun at reasonable prices. Appeals to both families and singles. Deejay in lounge makes for spirited crowd in evenings. The prime rib is the main attraction on the all-American menu. Also in Woodbridge, Va. (31 ratings/consistent)

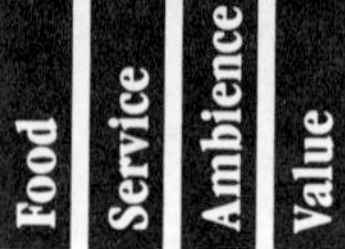

86 76 83 73

King's Contrivance $$$
French

Reserv: Required
Dress: Coat/tie sugg.
Pay: AE, MC, V, Checks
Parking: Valet
Map Reference: B-6
Handicap Access: No
Nonsmoking Area: Yes
Bar: Full/separate
Hours: M-F 11:30am-2pm, 5:30-9:30pm; Sa 5:30-9:30pm; Su 4-9pm

10150 Shaker Dr
Columbia, MD (301) 596-3455

Elegant dining in a country inn reminiscent of the Federal Period. Off the beaten path for most, but worth the drive. Rack of lamb, poached salmon with a cucumber dill sauce, fresh sauteed rainbow trout or Dover sole, sauteed veal with shrimp and mustard sauce, and daily specials to awaken your tastebuds. Nearby Christ Church is of historical interest. **Honors:** AAA◆◆◆. (20 ratings/consistent)

80 69 73 78

Kohinoor $$
Indian

Reserv: Req. weekends
Dress: Informal
Pay: AE, MC, V, DC, CB, Disc.
Parking: Yes
Map Reference: M-10
Area: Brighton Mall
Handicap Access: Yes
Nonsmoking Area: Yes
Bar: Full
Hours: M-F 11:30am-2:30pm, 5:30-10pm (F 11pm); Sa&Su noon-3:30pm, 5:30-11pm (Su 10pm)

6243 Little River Tpke
Alexandria, VA (703) 256-6080

The food here is only medium hot; the really hot sauce is served separately. Lunch at Kohinoor, which is served buffet-style, is a good way to sample the fried samosas (appetizers), tandoori-cooked meats, curries, kebabs, and vegetarian dishes that are on dinner menu. Lunch or dinner, the tandoori-baked bread, naan, is not to be missed. Kohinoor II is in downtown D.C. (13 ratings/mixed)

82 74 88 75

Kona Kai $$$
Polynesian

Reserv: Suggested
Dress: Informal
Pay: AE, MC, V, DC, CB, Disc.
Parking: Yes
Map Reference: G-10
Area: Pooks Hill Marriott
Handicap Access: Yes
Nonsmoking Area: Yes
Bar: Full/separate
Hours: M-Th 6-10pm; F&Sa 5:30-10:30pm; Su 10:30am-2:30pm (brunch only)

5151 Pooks Hill Rd
Bethesda, MD (301) 897-9191

If you feel Bali Ha'i calling you, a relaxing evening in this South Pacific setting may be the answer. Exotic Polynesian drinks and a menu of Polynesian, Chinese, and American dishes await. Pleasant view of garden area and 225-gallon fish tank. After dinner, you can linger and listen to music in the hotel's cocktail lounge. (21 ratings/mixed)

Food	Service	Ambience	Value
88	83	87	79

La Bergerie $$$
French

Reserv: Req. weekends
Dress: Coat req.
Pay: AE, MC, V, DC, CB, Disc.
Parking: No
Map Reference: M-12
Area: Old Town
Handicap Access: Yes
Nonsmoking Area: Yes
Bar: Full
Hours: M-Sa 11:30am-2:30pm, 6-10:30pm

218 N. Lee St
Alexandria, VA (703) 683-1007

A long-time favorite of Alexandrians. Traditional French menu includes a number of Basque specialties, like the filet mignon with goose liver and Madeira sauce. "The food is downright exciting" (*Washington Times*). Fixed-price lunches and dinners and daily specials available. **Honors:** AAA◆◆◆, Mobil★★★, *Washington Times*★★★. (28 ratings/consistent)

Food	Service	Ambience	Value
81	75	74	72

La Brasserie $$$
French

Reserv: Suggested
Dress: Coat/tie sugg.
Pay: AE, MC, V, DC, CB
Parking: Valet
Metro: Union Station
Map Reference: J-13
Area: Capitol Hill
Handicap Access: No
Nonsmoking Area: Yes
Bar: Full/separate
Hours: M-Sa 11:30am-11:30pm; Su brunch 11am-4pm, dinner 4-10pm

239 Massachusetts Ave, NE
Washington, DC (202) 546-9154

Small restaurant with an accomplished chef in the kitchen. Menu of traditional and nouvelle French dishes—veal stuffed with crabmeat, salmon with orange sauce, or baked crab cakes with a pepper coulis. Phyllis Richman called restaurant "gracious, reliable, and inventive." Fixed-price menu and special creations of the day also available. Outdoor cafe. **Honors:** Richman's Best of Best and 50 Favorites. (35 ratings/consistent)

Food	Service	Ambience	Value
80	75	73	77

La Chaumiere $$
French

Reserv: Required
Dress: Informal
Pay: AE, MC, V, DC, CB
Parking: Yes (2 hrs)
Map Reference: J-11
Area: Georgetown
Handicap Access: No
Nonsmoking Area: No
Bar: Full
Hours: M-F 11:30am-2:30pm, 5:30-11pm; Sa 5:30-11pm

2813 M St, NW
Washington, DC (202) 338-1784

Cozy, country-inn atmosphere, complete with toasty fire in winter. Country-style food—cassoulet, couscous, bouillabaisse—and newer treatments of seasonal ingredients. Fixed daily special for each day of week. Ratings span a change in chefs. Has become "one of this city's best dining values" (*Washingtonian*). **Honors:** *Washingtonian* 50 Best★★★. (29 ratings/consistent)

Food | Service | Ambience | Value

82 77 76 78

La Colline
French

$$

Reserv: Suggested
Dress: Informal
Pay: AE, MC, V, DC, CB
Parking: Yes (after 5pm)
Metro: Union Station
Map Reference: J-13
Area: Capitol Hill
Handicap Access: Ltd.
Nonsmoking Area: No
Bar: Full/separate
Hours: M-F 7-10am, 11:30am-3pm, 6-10pm; Sa 6-10pm

400 N. Capitol St, NW
Washington, DC (202) 737-0400

Chef/owner Robert Greault's mastery and creativity in the kitchen are commonly acknowledged by critics and diners alike. Already there are signs, though, that the ambience and service—not the food—are being affected by the "power" at lunch. Raters found pre-theater dinner specials to be one of best values in town. **Honors:** AAA◆◆◆, Richman's 50 Favorites, *Washingtonian* 50 Best★★★★. (93 ratings/mixed)

86   79

80 88

La Ferme
French

$$$

Reserv: Suggested
Dress: Informal
Pay: AE, MC, V, DC, CB
Parking: Valet
Map Reference: G-11
Handicap Access: No
Nonsmoking Area: Yes
Bar: Full/separate
Hours: T-F noon-2pm, 6-10pm; Sa 6-10pm; Su 5-9pm

7101 Brookville Rd
Chevy Chase, MD (301) 986-5255

The old farmhouse is now a comfy country inn. The carefully prepared food—rack of lamb, steak au poivre, seafood fricassee—is pleasing to the eye and palate. Piano music in evenings contributes to relaxed atmosphere. Ratings consistent for food but very mixed for service, and prices seem to be inching up. (52 ratings/consistent)

72 67 67 76

La Fonda
Mexican

$

Reserv: Not accepted
Dress: Informal
Pay: AE, MC, V, DC, CB, Disc.
Parking: No
Metro: Dupont Circle
Map Reference: J-12
Handicap Access: No
Nonsmoking Area: Yes
Bar: Full/separate
Hours: M-Sa 11:30am-3pm, 5-11pm (F&Sa midnight); Su brunch 11:30am-3pm, dinner 5-10pm

1639 R St, NW
Washington, DC (202) 232-6965

Oldtimer serving authentic regional Mexican food. Sample dishes seasoned with Mayan spices, shrimp and baby cactus, fish Veracruz-style, and chicken with mole sauce. Great sidewalk cafe. Deejay in lounge on weekend; mariachi band occasionally. (15 ratings/mixed)

Food | Service | Ambience | Value

83 78 77 82

La Fourchette $$
French

Reserv: Req. weekends
Dress: Informal
Pay: AE, MC, V, DC, CB
Parking: No
Map Reference: J-12
Area: Adams Morgan
Handicap Access: Ltd.
Nonsmoking Area: No
Bar: Full
Hours: M-F 11:30am-10:30pm (F midnight); Sa 4pm-midnight; Su 4-10pm

2429 18th St, NW
Washington, DC (202) 332-3077

A bastion of the neighborhood for good, honest, simple French food. The country French menu, which is strong on fresh seafood, changes continually. Friendly, unassuming attention from staff. Lots of activity in evenings. Patio for outdoor dining. Open for lunch on Sat. in summer. "Never flashy, usually reliable, the menu is as good as it sounds" (***Washington Post***). (14 ratings/consistent)

82 82 80 71

La Guinguette $$$
French

Reserv: Required
Dress: Coat/tie req.
Pay: AE, MC, V, DC, CB
Parking: Yes
Map Reference: E-3
Area: Merrifield Plaza
Handicap Access: Ltd.
Nonsmoking Area: Yes
Bar: Full
Hours: M-Th 11am-11pm; F&Sa 11am-midnight; Su 5-11pm

8111 Lee Hwy
Merrifield, VA (703) 560-3220

Small shopping centers take a lot of knocks these days, but in the Merrifield Plaza intimate French dining has been available for over 10 years. Garden atmosphere. Well-suited to special occasions. Best if not crowded, when special attention of the owner can be delightful. Guitarist Tues.-Sat.; trio for dancing Fri. and Sat. **Honors:** AAA◆◆◆, Mobil★★★. (26 ratings/mixed)

75 71 75 68

La Luna $$
Italian

Reserv: Suggested
Dress: Informal
Pay: AE, MC, V
Parking: Yes (after 6pm)
Metro: Bethesda
Map Reference: G-10
Area: Woodmont Tri.
Handicap Access: Ltd.
Nonsmoking Area: Yes
Bar: Full/separate
Hours: M-F 11:30am-2:30pm, 5:30-10pm (F 11pm); Sa 5:30-11pm; Su 5:30-10pm

4846 Cordell Ave
Bethesda, MD (301) 654-4600

Formerly called Mezzaluna. Menu features dishes from northern Italy and southern France, but you'll find the likes of curried scallops and blackened mahi mahi along with the pizza, pasta, and seafood. Some raters thought restaurant didn't live up to its reputation, others that it was good but not outstanding. Lunch and dinner specials. Early reviews by critics found food uneven but promising. (24 ratings/mixed)

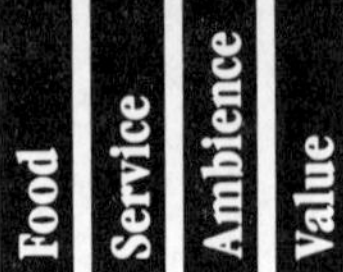

 87 83 84 83

La Maree
Seafood

$$$

Reserv: Suggested
Dress: Coat/tie req.
Pay: AE, MC, V, DC
Parking: Yes (after 5:30pm)
Metro: Farragut West
Map Reference: J-12
Area: Downtown
Handicap Access: Ltd.
Nonsmoking Area: No
Bar: Full
Hours: M-F 11:30am-2:30pm, 5:30-10:30pm; Sa 5:30-10:30pm

1919 I St, NW
Washington, DC (202) 659-4447

The menu will please many a seafood fancier. *Washington Business Journal* says "expect to be well fed—and to pay for it." Phyllis Richman advises that "the prices reflect the complexity of the food." Small dining area, tight seating; service can't always cope with full house. Fixed-price dinners a good value. (24 ratings/consistent)

85 79 79 75

La Miche
French

$$$

Reserv: Suggested
Dress: Informal
Pay: MC, V, DC, Checks
Parking: Valet
Metro: Bethesda
Map Reference: G-10
Area: Woodmont Triangle
Handicap Access: Ltd.
Nonsmoking Area: Yes
Bar: Full/separate
Hours: M-F 11:30am-2:30pm, 6-10pm; Sa 6-10pm

7905 Norfolk Ave
Bethesda, MD (301) 986-0707

Small dining room with the look of a French country inn. Menu, which changes daily, might include breast of duck, lobster fricassee, and Norwegian salmon. Phyllis Richman found that "in all, a meal at La Miche is a treat, except for occasional lapses," but our raters didn't think that the food matched the prices. Too busy at times. Piano music Fri. and Sat. (42 ratings/consistent)

75  77 77 70

La Mirabelle
French

$$

Reserv: Suggested
Dress: Coat/tie sugg.
Pay: AE, MC, V, DC, CB, Checks
Parking: Yes
Map Reference: I-9
Area: McLean Square
Handicap Access: Ltd.
Nonsmoking Area: Yes
Bar: Full/separate
Hours: M-F 11:30am-2:30pm, 5:30-9:30pm; Sa 5:30-9:30pm

6645 Old Dominion Dr
McLean, VA (703) 893-8484

Opinions varied sharply—from "bad, expensive, and annoying" to "magnificent food, prices high but worth it." Traditional French menu of seasonal specialties, many of them seafood. Early bird dinner specials. If you manage to get an agreeable server and select wisely from the menu, you could have a pleasant experience. **Honors:** AAA◆◆◆, Mobil★★★. (16 ratings/very mixed)

Food | Service | Ambience | Value

75 | 71 | 69 | 75

La Panetteria $$
Italian

Reserv: Req. weekends
Dress: Informal
Pay: AE, MC, V
Parking: Yes (after 6pm)
Metro: Bethesda
Map Reference: G-10
Area: Woodmont Triangle
Handicap Access: Ltd.
Nonsmoking Area: Yes
Bar: Full
Hours: M-F 11am-10pm; Sa 1-11pm; Su 1-10pm

4921 Cordell Ave
Bethesda, MD (301) 951-6433

A good place for pizza or a weekday lunch when you're in the Bethesda business district. Homemade pasta, salads, and more substantial northern Italian entrees also on menu. Has its ups and downs, but you won't leave hungry. Very attractive setting. (18 ratings/very mixed)

80 | 78 | 75 | 80

La Posada $
Mexican

Reserv: Suggested
Dress: Informal
Pay: AE, MC, V, DC, CB
Parking: Yes (after 6pm)
Metro: Bethesda
Map Reference: G-10
Area: Woodmont Triangle
Handicap Access: No
Nonsmoking Area: Yes
Bar: Full
Hours: M-Th 11am-10:30pm; F&Sa 11am-11pm; Su noon-10pm

8117 Woodmont Ave
Bethesda, MD (301) 656-9588

La Posada and its richer Latin American relative, El Caribe (see above), may share the same kitchen, but the ratings are higher for this, the Mexican side of it. There are the customary platters of tacos, enchiladas, fajitas, and burritos, as well as steak, some seafood, and Mexican beer and margaritas to wash it down. "The food is not adventuresome, but sound and plentiful" (***Washingtonian***). (11 ratings/mixed)

L'Alouette $$
French

Reserv: Suggested
Dress: Informal
Pay: AE, MC, V, DC, CB
Parking: Yes
Metro: Court House
Map Reference: K-10
Handicap Access: No
Nonsmoking Area: No
Bar: Full
Hours: M-F 11:30am-2:30pm, 6-10pm (F 10:30pm); Sa 6-10:30pm

2045 Wilson Blvd
Arlington, VA (703) 525-1750

What looks like yet another storefront is a highly regarded neighborhood cafe that provides good French food and a quiet setting. The chef/co-owner was at the old Company Inkwell and Rive Gauche, which says a lot about the cooking. Country-style food. The chef recommends the veal, seafood, and fresh venison (seasonal). Fixed-price dinners available. (17 ratings/consistent)

Food	Service	Ambience	Value

81	78	75	74

Landini Brothers $$
Italian

Reserv: Suggested
Dress: Coat/tie sugg.
Pay: AE, MC, V
Parking: No
Map Reference: N-12
Area: Old Town
Handicap Access: Ltd.
Nonsmoking Area: No
Bar: Full/separate
Hours: M-Sa 11:30am-11pm; Su 4-10pm

115 King St
Alexandria, VA (703) 836-8404

The seafood, meat, and pasta dishes served here are prepared in the tradition of Italy's Tuscany region. Breads, pasta, and pastries are made on the premises. The pleasant, rustic setting is "especially charming at night by candlelight" (***Frommer's***). Friendly service. Some find the chairs very uncomfortable, and two raters were so disappointed they won't return. (18 ratings/very mixed)

81	78	77	73

Laporta's $$$
New American

Reserv: Suggested
Dress: Informal
Pay: AE, MC, V
Parking: Yes (after 6pm)
Metro: King Street
Map Reference: N-11
Handicap Access: Yes
Nonsmoking Area: Yes
Bar: Full/separate
Hours: M-W 11:30am-2:30pm, 6-9:30pm; Th-F 11:30am-2:30pm, 6-10:30pm; Sa 6-10:30pm

1600 Duke St
Alexandria, VA (703) 683-6313

A bright addition to the King Street metro area. New American-Continental menu includes fresh seafood, roast duckling with wild berry sauce, and individual racks of lamb. Comfortable surroundings and friendly service. Piano music in lounge Fri. & Sat. Trifle expensive. Evidences "signs of competence, good taste, and attention to detail" (***Washington Post***). (12 ratings/mixed)

93	89	93	86

L'Auberge Chez Francois $$$$
French

Reserv: Required
Dress: Coat/tie req.
Pay: AE, MC, V
Parking: Yes
Map Reference: D-3
Handicap Access: Ltd.
Nonsmoking Area: Yes
Bar: Full
Hours: T-Sa 5:30-9pm; Su 2:30-8pm

332 Springvale Rd
Great Falls, VA (703) 759-3800

Unsurpassed French country cuisine in authentic setting in Virginia countryside. An area favorite for special occasions. Fixed-price dining in a range of prices. A "perfect union of food and setting" (***Washingtonian***). **Honors:** AAA◆◆◆, Mobil★★★, Richman's Best of Best and 50 Favorites, ***Travel-Holiday*** selection, ***Washingtonian*** 50 Best★★★. (173 ratings/consistent)

Food | Service | Ambience | Value

Lauriol Plaza
Mexican $$

1801 18th St, NW
Washington, DC (202) 387-0035

Reserv: Accepted
Dress: Informal
Pay: AE, MC, V, DC, CB
Parking: No
Metro: Dupont Circle
Map Reference: J-12
Handicap Access: Ltd.
Nonsmoking Area: No
Bar: Full/separate
Hours: M-Sa noon-midnight; Su 11am-midnight, brunch til 3pm

Offers a good selection of Mexican, Spanish, and Cuban dishes. Good when it's good. Raters liked the paella and other seafood dishes the best. The tacos are tops with Phyllis Richman. Pleasant, relaxed atmosphere; service can be slow, especially at lunch. Outdoor dining in warm weather. Same owner as nearby La Plaza. **Honors:** Richman's Best of Best and 50 Favorites. (23 ratings/consistent)

Le Canard
French $$$

132 Branch Rd, SE
Vienna, VA (703) 281-0070

Reserv: Req. weekends
Dress: Coat/tie sugg.
Pay: AE, MC, V, DC, CB, Checks
Parking: Yes
Map Reference: D-3
Handicap Access: Yes
Nonsmoking Area: Yes
Bar: Full/separate
Hours: M-F 11:30am-2:30pm, 6-11pm; Sa 6-11pm

Classical French food served in cozy, uncrowded setting. Menu includes, not unexpectedly, an assortment of duck dishes (try the one with fresh raspberries), game, fresh seafood, and veal. You could follow pre-theater dinner with performance at Wolf Trap Farm Park or linger after dinner in lounge, which has piano music Tues.-Sat.. **Honors:** Mobil★★★. (22 ratings/mixed)

79 70 72 73

Le Caprice
French $$

2348 Wisconsin Ave, NW
Washington, DC (202) 337-3394

Reserv: Suggested
Dress: Coat/tie sugg.
Pay: AE, MC, V, DC, CB
Parking: No
Map Reference: J-11
Area: Upper Georgetown
Handicap Access: Ltd.
Nonsmoking Area: No
Bar: Full
Hours: M and W-F 11:45am-2pm, 6:30-10pm; Sa&Su 6-10pm

Tiny, quaint bistro in a storefront north of Georgetown specializing in cuisine courante—updated classical French cooking. Given reviews, some raters were disappointed; they thought it cramped, slow, and a bit expensive. Fixed-price lunch and dinner available daily. Small outdoor cafe. **Honors:** *Journal* papers★★★, *Washingtonian* 50 Best ★★★. (24 ratings/mixed)

Food | Service | Ambience | Value

90 84 86 70

Le Chardon d'Or $$$$

French

Reserv: Suggested
Dress: Coat/tie req.
Pay: AE, MC, V, DC, CB, Checks
Parking: Valet
Map Reference: N-12
Area: Old Town
Handicap Access: Yes
Nonsmoking Area: Yes
Bar: Full
Hours: Daily 7-9:30am (Sa 8-10am), 11:45am-2pm, 6-9:30pm (F&Sa 10pm); Su brunch 10:30am-2:30pm

116 S. Alfred St
Alexandria, VA (703) 838-8008

Award-winning nouvelle cuisine and luxurious service in splendid Louis XIV dining rooms. A la carte and fixed-price menus change daily. "In Northern Virginia there is no other . . . quite so urbane" (Phyllis Richman); "handles seafood with obvious eclat" (***Washington Times***). Portions fit for a hummingbird and the prices diminished the value for some raters. **Honors**: Mobil★★★, Richman's 50 Favorites. (12 ratings/mixed)

83 83 83 74

Le Couvert $$$

French

Reserv: Accepted
Dress: Informal
Pay: AE, MC, V, DC, CB
Parking: Yes
Map Reference: F-3
Area: Springfield Plaza
Handicap Access: Yes
Nonsmoking Area: Yes
Bar: Full
Hours: M-Sa 11:30am-3:30pm, 5-10pm

6805 Springfield Plaza
Springfield, VA (703) 569-6323

The veal and seafood dishes at this country-style French restaurant get good marks, but some raters suggested that the food in general and service are not getting the attention they once did. Extensive dinner menu of "authentic" French dishes, some of which are flambeed tableside. The chef's favorites are the sauces. Very friendly host and hostess. (15 ratings/mixed)

86 74 63 83

Le Gaulois $$

French

Reserv: Required
Dress: Informal
Pay: AE, MC, V
Parking: No
Metro: Foggy Bottom
Map Reference: J-11
Area: West End
Handicap Access: No
Nonsmoking Area: No
Bar: Full
Hours: M-Sa 11:30am-2:30pm, 5:30-11pm (F&Sa midnight)

2133 Pennsylvania Ave, NW
Washington, DC (202) 466-3232

Noisy, cramped bistro, but you forget it when your food arrives. The reverse of restaurants that appease the eye but not the stomach. Standard menu and long list of daily specials to choose from. "Not cheap but a lot of talent for the money" (Phyllis Richman). The ***Washingtonian*** says the pot-au-feu is worth a visit in itself. **Honors:** ***Washingtonian*** 50 Best★★★. (42 ratings/mixed)

Le Jardin

75 71 78 74

French **$$**

Reserv: Suggested
Dress: Informal
Pay: AE, MC, V, DC, CB
Parking: No
Metro: Foggy Bottom
Map Reference: J-11
Area: West End
Handicap Access: No
Nonsmoking Area: No
Bar: Full/separate
Hours: M-Sa 11:30am (Sa 11am)-3pm, 5:30pm-mid. (F&Sa 12:30am); Su 10:30am-3:30pm, 5pm-mid.

1113 23rd St, NW
Washington, DC (202) 457-0057

Cheerful, sunny restaurant with lots of greenery. French-Continental menu composed primarily of fresh seafood, veal, beef, and salads. Three-course, fixed-price dinner is a good value, as is Sat. and Sun. brunch (10:30am-3pm). A few raters thought it overpriced and noisy, and a few complained about service. "The food is usually good, only infrequently dismal" (Phyllis Richman). (34 ratings/mixed)

Le Lion d'Or

90 84 82 72

French **$$$$**

Reserv: Required
Dress: Coat/tie required
Pay: AE, MC, V, DC, CB
Parking: Yes (eves)
Metro: Farragut North
Map Reference: J-12
Area: Downtown
Handicap Access: Ltd.
Nonsmoking Area: No
Bar: Full/separate
Hours: M-F noon-2pm, 6-10pm; Sa 6-10pm

1150 Connecticut Ave, NW
Washington, DC (202) 296-7972

One of area's very best French restaurants. Menu is rooted in classical French cooking. Critics praise chef for his breath of menu and the "beauty of the primal flavors" (*Washingtonian*). Raters were divided about whether it is overpriced. **Honors:** AAA, Mobil, Richman's Best of Best and 50 Favorites, *Travel-Holiday* Award, *Washingtonian* 50 Best. (40 ratings/mixed)

Le Manouche

83 84 82 79

French **$$**

Reserv: Suggested
Dress: Informal
Pay: AE, MC, V, DC, CB
Parking: Yes
Metro: Twinbrook
Map Reference: C-4
Area: Congressional Plaza area
Handicap Access: Yes
Nonsmoking Area: Yes
Bar: Full/separate
Hours: M-F 11:30am-2:30pm, 5:30-10pm; Sa 5:30-10pm

121 Congressional Lane
Rockville, MD (301) 468-2633

Said to be named after fortune teller who recommended adding a Central European twist to the nouvelle and country French cuisine. Salmon in puff pastry, filet mignon with lobster, boneless filet of duck, or more humble stuffed cabbage among entrees you might try. Small, somewhat colorless dining room presided over by owner. Early bird dinner. (24 ratings/mixed)

Food | Service | Ambience | Value

86 82 81 73

Le Marmiton
French **$$$**

Reserv: Suggested
Dress: Informal
Pay: AE, MC, V, DC, CB
Parking: Yes (after 6pm)
Metro: Bethesda
Map Reference: G-10
Area: Woodmont Triangle
Handicap Access: Yes
Nonsmoking Area: Yes
Bar: Full
Hours: M-F 11:30am-2:30pm, 6-10pm (F 10:30pm); Sa 6-10:30pm

4931 Cordell Ave
Bethesda, MD (301) 986-5188

The imaginative French menu changes daily here, but you're sure to find a variety of seafood, pasta, and meat entrees to please, including game in season. "Uncommonly charming French food" (Phyllis Richman) beautifully presented in relaxed, intimate setting. **Honors:** Mobil★★★. (19 ratings/consistent)

90 87 88 65

Le Pavillon
French **$$$$**

Reserv: Required
Dress: Coat/tie req.
Pay: AE, MC, V, DC, CB
Parking: No
Metro: Farragut North/West
Map Reference: J-12
Area: Downtown
Handicap Access: No
Nonsmoking Area: No
Bar: Full/separate
Hours: M-F 11:45am-2pm, 6:45-10pm; Sa 6:45-10pm

1050 Connecticut Ave, NW
Washington, DC (202) 833-3846

"A degree of perfection that almost requires . . . a heightened esthetic/spiritual nature to appreciate" (*Frommer's*), but the price of perfection is too dear for many raters. A la carte and fixed-price dining. Received *Wine Spectator's* 1987 Grand Award. **Honors:** AAA◆◆◆◆, Mobil★★★★, Richman's Best of Best and 50 Favorites, *Travel-Holiday* Award, *Washingtonian* 50 Best★★★★. (16 ratings/consistent)

81 79 72 77

Le Refuge
French **$$**

Reserv: Suggested
Dress: Informal
Pay: AE, MC, V, DC, CB
Parking: No
Map Reference: N-12
Area: Old Town
Handicap Access: No
Nonsmoking Area: No
Bar: Full
Hours: M-Sa 11:30am-2:30pm, 5:30-10pm

127 N. Washington St
Alexandria, VA (703) 548-4661

Charming French country setting. Regular entrees and daily specials include both hearty traditional and nouvelle dishes. Most raters thought dining here was an enjoyable experience; *Journal* papers called it a "true refuge for the mind as well as the body." Tight seating and sometimes noisy. **Honors:** *Journal* papers ★★★. (16 ratings/mixed)

Le Rivage — $$
French

1000 Water St, SW
Washington, DC (202) 488-8111

Reserv: Suggested
Dress: Coat sugg.
Pay: AE, MC, V, DC, CB
Parking: Valet
Metro: L'Enfant Plaza
Map Reference: K-12
Area: S.W. Waterfront
Handicap Access: No
Nonsmoking Area: No
Bar: Full/separate
Hours: M-Sa 11:30am-2:30pm, 5:30-11pm (F&Sa 11:30pm); Su 5-9pm

Enjoy the cozy dining area, the view of the harbor and the monuments, and some classical French cooking, much of it centering around fresh seafood. Combination of food and setting makes this a very pleasant place to linger over lunch or to while away an evening. "A jewel on the waterfront" (***Washingtonian***). Outdoor deck. Fixed-price dinner til 6:30pm; close to Arena Stage. (40 ratings/consistent)

Le Vieux Logis — $$
French

7925 Old Georgetown Rd
Bethesda, MD (301) 652-6816

Reserv: Suggested
Dress: Coat/tie sugg.
Pay: AE, MC, V, DC
Parking: Yes
Metro: Bethesda
Map Reference: G-10
Handicap Access: Yes
Nonsmoking Area: Yes
Bar: Full
Hours: M-F 11:30am-2pm, 5:30-10pm; Sa 5:30-10pm

Inside the "old lodge," you'll find an attractive interior, unpretentious atmosphere, and classic French food. Owner/chef Michel Vallet was previously at Le Lion d'Or; perhaps that's why his baked salmon in pastry, bouillabaisse, veal in Roquefort sauce, red snapper, and other dishes are well received. Good selection of wines, too. (20 ratings/mixed)

Lebanese Taverna — $$
Lebanese

5900 N. Washington Blvd
Arlington, VA (703) 241-8681

Reserv: Not accepted
Dress: Informal
Pay: MC, V
Parking: Yes
Map Reference: K-10
Area: Westover Shopping Center
Handicap Access: Yes
Nonsmoking Area: No
Bar: Full
Hours: M-Sa 11:30am-10pm

The appetizers, lamb and sausage dishes, and pizza are popular in this family-run neighborhood restaurant. Atmosphere is friendly, homey, often bustling. The ***Washington Post*** reported the "Middle Eastern dishes . . . are mainly excellent," and the ***Journal*** papers recommended the Lebanese specialties. Try during off times if you mind waiting for a table. (30 ratings/mixed)

Food | Service | Ambience | Value

84 73 58 84

Ledo $
Italian

Reserv: Not accepted
Dress: Informal
Pay: MC, V
Parking: Yes
Map Reference: H-14
Handicap Access: Yes
Nonsmoking Area: Yes
Bar: Full/separate
Hours: Su-Th 11am-4pm, 5pm-midnight; F&Sa 11am-4pm, 5pm-1am

2420 University Blvd, E
Hyattsville, MD (301) 422-8622

Pizza is what that long line of college students, families, and singles is all about—the best in Hyattsville, in the area, in the world to hear tell. The *Washington Post* and *Washington Times* share the enthusiasm, but not the *Journal* papers. Crowded, noisy, fun place; efficient, friendly service. Variety of other food on menu—if anyone cares. **Honors:** Richman's 50 Favorites. (31 ratings/mixed)

64 71 63 68

Les Champs $$
Continental

Reserv: Suggested
Dress: Informal
Pay: AE, MC, V, DC, CB
Parking: Valet
Metro: Foggy Bottom
Map Reference: J-11
Handicap Access: No
Nonsmoking Area: No
Bar: Full/separate
Hours: M-Sa 11:30am-2pm, 5:30-10:30pm (F&Sa 11:30pm)

600 New Hampshire Ave, NW
Washington, DC (202) 298-4477

Handy for dinner before going to Kennedy Center, but raters didn't find much else to say about it. Service is quick and friendly. Menu of fresh fish, veal, curry, and kebabs doesn't change much. Salad bar. View of Potomac River from cocktail lounge. (20 ratings/mixed)

76 73 74 79

L'Escargot $$
French

Reserv: Suggested
Dress: Informal
Pay: AE, MC, V
Parking: Yes
Metro: Cleveland Park
Map Reference: I-11
Handicap Access: Yes
Nonsmoking Area: Yes
Bar: Full
Hours: M-Sa 11:30am-2:30pm, 5:30-10pm

3309 Connecticut Ave, NW
Washington, DC (202) 966-7510

Cozy neighborhood restaurant with a loyal following. French country food, including coq au vin, veal Normande, calf's liver, red snapper, and filet of sole. Fixed-price dining only, including dinner specials. Service sometimes erratic. (40 ratings/mixed)

Luigi's
Italian **$$**

Reserv: Accepted
Dress: Informal
Pay: AE, MC, V, DC, CB
Parking: No
Metro: Farragut North
Map Reference: J-12
Area: Downtown
Handicap Access: No
Nonsmoking Area: No
Bar: Full
Hours: M-Sa 11am-2am; Su noon-midnight

1132 19th St, NW
Washington, DC (202) 331-7574

Hasn't changed in years—lots of pizza and pasta and mugs of beer to wash it all down. Crowded noontime scene. *Washington Times* calls pizza "among best in the area," but it does get a bit expensive as you add toppings. (13 ratings/mixed)

70 72 68 72

Machiavelli's
Italian **$**

Reserv: Not accepted
Dress: Informal
Pay: MC, V
Parking: Yes
Metro: Eastern Market
Map Reference: K-13
Area: Capitol Hill
Handicap Access: Yes
Nonsmoking Area: No
Bar: Full/separate
Hours: T-F 11:30am-2:30pm, 5-11pm; Sa&Su 5-11pm

613 Pennsylvania Ave, SE
Washington, DC (202) 543-1930

A popular stop for pizza and pasta. Raters favored the white pizza. Relaxation is the hallmark rather than the "reliable if average" menu (*Washington Post*). Ample portions and reasonable prices contribute to popularity. Same ownership as Mr. Henry's and Zapata's. (16 ratings/consistent)

Maharaja
Indian **$**

Reserv: Accepted
Dress: Informal
Pay: AE, MC, V, DC, CB
Parking: Yes
Map Reference: D-6
Area: Cipriano Square
Handicap Access: Yes
Nonsmoking Area: No
Bar: Beer
Hours: Tu-F 11am-2pm, 5-10pm; Sa-M 5-10pm

8825 Greenbelt Rd
Greenbelt, MD (301) 552-1600

Most raters liked the food, but not everyone thought it was the value the *Washington Post* and *Washingtonian* said it was. Lunch buffet (Tues.-Fri.) and sampler dishes in evenings provide opportunity to try the curries, tandoor chicken, vegetarian dishes, and the tandoori-baked bread. Attentive owner on hand to explain dishes and make recommendations. **Honors:** *Washingtonian* Cheap Eats. (10 ratings/consistent)

Food | Service | Ambience | Value

89 86 88 80

Maison Blanche $$$$
French

Reserv: Suggested
Dress: Coat req.
Pay: AE, MC, V, DC, CB, Disc.
Parking: Valet (after 5pm)
Metro: Farragut West
Map Reference: J-12
Area: Downtown
Handicap Access: Yes
Nonsmoking Area: No
Bar: Full/separate
Hours: M-F 11:45am-11pm; Sa 6-11pm

1725 F St, NW
Washington, DC (202) 842-0070

Classic French restaurant popular with Washington's politically and socially "in" group. First class in all respects. Try the daily specials and house specialties. The pre-theater (6-7pm) and post-theater (10-11pm) menus are excellent values. Fixed-price dining available; happy hour. Dissenters thought it pompous and overrated. **Honors:** AAA◆◆◆◆, Mobil★★★★. (34 ratings/consistent)

77 75 68 78

Mama's Italian $$
Italian

Reserv: Accepted
Dress: Informal
Pay: AE, MC, V, DC, CB
Parking: Yes
Map Reference: E-3
Area: Off Fairfax Circle
Handicap Access: Yes
Nonsmoking Area: Yes
Bar: Full/separate
Hours: M-Sa 11am-11pm; Su noon-10pm

9715 Lee Hwy
Fairfax City, VA (703) 385-2646

Family-run restaurant featuring pizza and home-style Italian food. Salad bar of make-your-own and made-up salads got high marks from raters. Friendly service; generous portions. Thur. special of soup, pizza, and salad bar is a good value. "Rating meter . . . hovers at the midway mark for quality" (*Washington Post*). Lounge area has fireplace, TV, and dart board. (29 ratings/very mixed)

87 84 79 77

Mamma Regina $$
Italian

Reserv: Suggested
Dress: Informal
Pay: AE, MC, V, DC, CB
Parking: Yes
Metro: Silver Spring
Map Reference: G-12
Area: Sheraton Silver Spring
Handicap Access: Yes
Nonsmoking Area: Yes
Bar: Full
Hours: M-F 11:30am-2pm, 5-10pm (M 9pm); Sa 5-10pm; Su 5-9pm

8727 Colesville Rd
Silver Spring, MD (301) 585-1040

Many people have yet to discover that this small, cozy dining room is just the place to enjoy home-made pasta and a large selection of other Italian dishes. "Perhaps the most underrated in area . . . aim for the excellent pastas, veal dishes, and fish" (*Washington Post*). Friendly staff; a bit pricey. (15 ratings/consistent)

Food	Service	Ambience	Value
87	80	75	84

Mandarin Inn $$
Chinese

Reserv: Suggested
Dress: Informal
Pay: AE, MC, V, DC, CB
Parking: Yes
Metro: Twinbrook
Map Reference: C-4
Area: Congressional Plaza
Handicap Access: Yes
Nonsmoking Area: Yes
Bar: Full/separate
Hours: M-Th 11am-10pm; F&Sa 11am-11pm; Su noon-9:30pm

1687 Rockville Pike
Rockville, MD (301) 231-0868

Another good suburban Chinese restaurant. The host, George, will help you make your choice from among the 200-odd Mandarin and Szechuan dishes on menu. You can even create a dish to your liking. Early ***Washington Post*** review found fault with sauces, but ratings indicate that that may have changed. (16 ratings/mixed)

Food	Service	Ambience	Value
81	78	77	76

Marco Polo $$
Italian

Reserv: Accepted
Dress: Informal
Pay: AE, MC, V, DC, CB
Parking: Yes
Map Reference: D-3
Handicap Access: Yes
Nonsmoking Area: Yes
Bar: Full
Hours: M-Th 11:30am-10:30pm; F&Sa 11:30am-11pm

245 Maple Ave, W
Vienna, VA (703) 281-3922

Suburban restaurant that generally gets good marks for its renditions of northern Italian, French, and American dishes. Several raters suggested it as a place to dine with friends or to celebrate a special occasion. One rater thought the food was beginning to taste microwaved, however, and that banquet rooms generate too much noise. Dancing and entertainment nightly in upstairs lounge. (22 ratings/mixed)

Food	Service	Ambience	Value
70	64	76	69

Marie Callendar's $$
American

Reserv: Accepted
Dress: Informal
Pay: AE, MC, V
Parking: No
Metro: Twinbrook
Map Reference: C-4
Handicap Access: Yes
Nonsmoking Area: Yes
Bar: Full/separate
Hours: M-Th 11am-10pm; F&Sa 11am-11pm; Su 9am-10pm

1801 Rockville Pike
Rockville, MD (301) 881-0770

Raters and critics alike have greeted the arrival of this West Coast chain with mixed, often uncomplimentary reactions. Pot pies and dessert pies are prominent features of trendy, but limited menu, and even they get mixed reviews. Frequent complaints about poor food preparation, menu items not being available, the clatter, and inattentive service. Only the decor escapes unscathed. (43 ratings/very mixed)

73 70 69 69

Market Inn $$
Seafood

Reserv: Suggested
Dress: Coat/tie sugg.
Pay: AE, MC, V, DC, CB
Parking: Valet
Metro: Fed. Center SW
Map Reference: K-12
Handicap Access: Ltd.
Nonsmoking Area: Yes
Bar: Full/separate
Hours: M-F 11am-midnight; Sa&Su 10:30am-midnight, brunch til 2:30pm

200 E St, SW
Washington, DC (202) 554-2100

Traditional seafood house dating back to late 1950s. You can get almost any kind of seafood any way you like it. The results are sometimes good, sometimes bad. "Even the quantity doesn't compensate for sheer ordinariness . . . of the fare" (Phyllis Richman). Tables are very close, and service is slow. Entertainment daily in Antique Bar starting at noon. (40 ratings/mixed)

72 78 84 74

Marrakesh $$
Moroccan

Reserv: Required
Dress: Coat/tie sugg.
Pay: Checks
Parking: Valet
Metro: Gallery Place
Map Reference: J-12
Area: Mount Vernon Square
Handicap Access: Yes
Nonsmoking Area: No
Bar: Full
Hours: M-Sa 6-11pm; Su 5-11pm

617 New York Ave, NW
Washington, DC (202) 393-9393

You'll have to knock to be admitted to this dimly lit, richly decorated casbah. There is no menu; everyone in party shares a fixed-price communal dinner using fingers or pieces of bread to pick up food. Moroccan musicians and belly dancer entertain. May not become one of your haunts, but dining here is to experience "a masterpiece of atmospheric achievement" (*Washingtonian*). (28 ratings/mixed)

75 80 77 76

Marrocco's $$
Italian

Reserv: Accepted
Dress: Informal
Pay: AE, MC, V, DC, CB
Parking: Yes
Metro: Farragut North
Map Reference: J-12
Area: Lafayette Centre
Handicap Access: Yes
Nonsmoking Area: No
Bar: Full/separate
Hours: M-F 11:30am-10pm (F 11pm); Sa 5-11pm

1120 20th St, NW
Washington, DC (202) 331-9664

The third generation of Marroccos is now overseeing the preparation of regional Italian dishes. Homemade pastas, veal, chicken, and seafood, some in subtle cream sauces and others in hearty tomato-based sauces. Pleasant surroundings and friendly staff. Happy hour 5-7pm nightly; background music for dining Thurs.-Sat. (12 ratings/consistent)

Food | Service | Ambience | Value

81 77 66 79

Matuba
Japanese
\$\$

Reserv: Accepted
Dress: Informal
Pay: AE, MC, V, DC, CB
Parking: Yes (eves)
Metro: Bethesda
Map Reference: G-10
Area: Woodmont Triangle
Handicap Access: No
Nonsmoking Area: Yes
Bar: Beer/wine
Hours: M-F 11:30am-2pm, 5:30-10pm (F 10:30pm); Sa 5:30-10:30pm

4918 Cordell Ave
Bethesda, MD (301) 652-7449

Neighborhood sushi bar and restaurant. Quality of food and reasonable prices offset cramped seating and plain, open setting. Remodeling may alleviate space problems. Tempura, teriyaki, and soups also served, plus daily specials "it would be a shame to miss" (***Washingtonian***). See ratings for Arlington, Va. (521-2811) location. **Honors:** ***Washingtonian*** Cheap Eats. (37 ratings/consistent)

80   86

79 79

Meadowlark Inn
American
\$\$

Reserv: Suggested
Dress: Informal
Pay: MC, V, Checks
Parking: Yes
Map Reference: B-2
Handicap Access: Yes
Nonsmoking Area: No
Bar: Full
Hours: Tu-Sa 11:30am-2:30pm, 5-9pm (F&Sa 10pm); Su noon-9pm

White's Ferry Rd
Poolesville, MD (301) 428-8937

Home-style American food in country inn setting. Serves complete dinners. Pleasant, relaxed atmosphere; nice place for families. Lunch buffet weekdays. If you're headed there from No. Virginia, you could take the ferry that crosses the Potomac from Leesburg to historic White's Ferry, and then drive on to the inn. (16 ratings/mixed)

73   64

73 68

Mel Krupin's
American
\$\$\$\$

Reserv: Suggested
Dress: Coat sugg.
Pay: AE, MC, V, DC, CB
Parking: Valet (after 6pm)
Metro: Farragut North
Map Reference: J-12
Area: Downtown
Handicap Access: Ltd.
Nonsmoking Area: No
Bar: Full/separate
Hours: M-Sa 11:30am-11pm

1120 Connecticut Ave, NW
Washington, DC (202) 331-7000

The critics like Mel's for the New York-style chopped liver, matzo-ball soup, crab cakes, and pickles, but most of our raters weren't carried away about any of the food—or the prices. Serving one-half the food at two-thirds the price would be an improvement. Happy hour; piano music in lounge Fri.-Sat. **Honors:** Richman's 50 Favorites, ***Washingtonian*** 50 Best★★★. (22 ratings/very mixed)

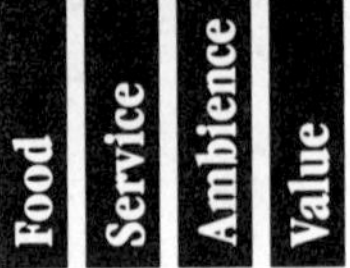

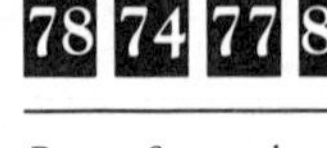

Meskerem $

Ethiopian

Reserv: Suggested
Dress: Informal
Pay: AE, MC, V, DC, CB
Parking: No
Map Reference: J-12
Area: Adams Morgan
Handicap Access: Ltd.
Nonsmoking Area: No
Bar: Full/separate
Hours: M-Th 5pm-midnight; F-Su noon-12:30am

2434 18th St, NW
Washington, DC (202) 462-4100

The most attractive of the Ethiopian restaurants in Adams Morgan. Chili peppers and a variety of spices are used to season the stews (wats and alechas), which are the focal point of the menu, and other dishes. Pieces of Ethiopian bread and fingers take the place of utensils. The dining loft is more intimate and traditional in decor than main floor. **Honors:** *Washingtonian* 50 Best★ and Cheap Eats. (22 ratings/consistent)

Michel's $$

French

Reserv: Accepted
Dress: Informal
Pay: MC, V
Parking: Yes (after 6pm)
Metro: Bethesda
Map Reference: G-10
Area: Woodmont Triangle
Handicap Access: No
Nonsmoking Area: Yes
Bar: Full
Hours: M-F 11am-10pm; Sa 4-10pm; Su 4-9pm

7904 Woodmont Ave
Bethesda, MD (301) 656-0720

Neighborhood restaurant with warm, homey atmosphere and reasonable prices. Not fancy and not too French. Menu is a bit limited but includes such favorites as veal Oscar, roast duck a l'orange, steak Diane, and stuffed flounder. Nice place for lunch. Nightly fixed-price dinners are a good value. Tables a bit close. (38 ratings/mixed)

Mikado $$

Japanese

Reserv: Accepted
Dress: Informal
Pay: AE, MC, V, DC, CB, Checks
Parking: No
Metro: Tenleytown
Map Reference: I-11
Handicap Access: No
Nonsmoking Area: No
Bar: Full
Hours: Tu-Sa 11:30am-2pm, 5:30-10pm; Su 5:30-10pm

4707 Wisconsin Ave, NW
Washington, DC (202) 244-1740

Washington's second oldest Japanese restaurant continues to please. You can order from the sushi bar, which raters gave high marks, or choose tempura, teriyaki, sukiyaki, or shabu shabu. "The cooked foods are, like the sushi, highly competent" (Phyllis Richman). Impeccable service in a simple, homey atmosphere. **Honors:** Richman's 50 Favorites. (16 ratings/consistent)

Food	Service	Ambience	Value

84 75 69 75

Mike's Italian Restaurant $$
Italian

Reserv: Suggested
Dress: Coat/tie req.
Pay: AE, MC, V, DC, CB
Parking: Yes
Map Reference: F-4
Handicap Access: No
Nonsmoking Area: Yes
Bar: Full
Hours: M-F 11:30am-11pm; Sa noon-11pm; Su 4-10pm

8368 Richmond Hwy
Alexandria, VA (703) 780-5966

Another neighborhood restaurant whose exterior belies the quality inside. Among the many northern Italian dishes, the calamari and veal dishes were singled out as excellent. The *Washington Post* described the food as "comparable in quality to that served in fancy Washington establishments." Friendly, accommodating staff, but two raters seem to have had bad experiences. (25 ratings/mixed)

71 66 59 69

Misty Harbor $$
Seafood

Reserv: Not accepted
Dress: Informal
Pay: AE, MC, V
Parking: Yes
Metro: Twinbrook
Map Reference: C-4
Area: 1776 Plaza
Handicap Access: Yes
Nonsmoking Area: Yes
Bar: Full/separate
Hours: M-F 11am-9:30pm (F 10pm); Sa 4-10pm; Su 4-9:30pm

1776 E. Jefferson St
Rockville, MD (301) 230-0320

You can still get generous portions of moderately priced fresh seafood here—crab imperial, flounder stuffed with crab, lobster Norfolk or Newburg, and seafood platters, but the treatment isn't memorable. "The quality of the food seems strangely variable" (*Washington Post*). Trick seems to be to order a dish that requires little fixing and to ignore vegetables. (31 ratings/very mixed)

76 65 61 71

Mixtec $
Mexican

Reserv: Not accepted
Dress: Informal
Pay: Cash only
Parking: No
Map Reference: J-12
Area: Adams Morgan
Handicap Access: Ltd.
Nonsmoking Area: No
Bar: Full
Hours: Su-Th 11am-9pm; F&Sa 11am-11pm

1792 Columbia Rd, NW
Washington, DC (202) 332-1011

Very small, very simple, but one of few Mexican restaurants that serve real tacos. "Mixtec is indeed authentic" (Phyllis Richman). Spicy, sauteed beef dishes, burritos, and enchiladas also on limited menu. A bit seedy, perhaps, but a great bargain. Same owner as Enriqueta's (see above). **Honors:** Richman's 50 Favorites, *Washingtonian* 50 Best★ and Cheap Eats. (10 ratings/consistent)

90 83 76 73

Morton's of Chicago $$$
Steak House

Reserv: Until 7pm
Dress: Coat/tie sugg.
Pay: AE, MC, V, DC, CB
Parking: No
Map Reference: J-11
Area: Georgetown
Handicap Access: Yes
Nonsmoking Area: No
Bar: Full/separate
Hours: M-Sa 5:30-11pm

3251 Prospect St, NW
Washington, DC (202) 342-6258

The best steaks in town—so the critics say. Thick, juicy cuts of prime, dry-aged beef cooked exactly to order. Energetic servers recite (yell) menu for you: lamb and veal chops, poultry, seafood, and all the cuts of beef. Humongous portions, noise, line for tables, and tab. Popular with notables. **Honors:** Mobil★★★, Richman's Best of Best and 50 Favorites, *Washingtonian* 50 Best★★★. (20 ratings/very consistent)

80 84 87 72

Mount Vernon Inn $$
American

Reserv: Suggested; none at lunch
Dress: Informal
Pay: AE, MC, V
Parking: Yes
Map Reference: F-4
Area: Mount Vernon
Handicap Access: Yes
Nonsmoking Area: No
Bar: Full/separate
Hours: M-Sa 11am-3pm, 5-9:30pm; Su 11am-3pm

End of George Washington Pky
Mt Vernon, VA (703) 780-0011

Cap off a scenic drive and tour of Mount Vernon with lunch or dinner at the inn just outside the gates. Menu of traditional and New American dishes, much of it cooked on mesquite grill. Bit expensive, but fixed-price dinners are offered. *Journal* papers raved about lamb chops and honey nut pastry. Candlelight dining and working fireplaces add authentic touch to the colonial setting. (15 ratings/consistent)

83 84 83 80

Mountain Jack's $$
Steak House

Reserv: Suggested
Dress: Informal
Pay: AE, MC, V, DC, CB, Disc., Checks
Parking: Yes
Map Reference: K-8
Handicap Access: Yes
Nonsmoking Area: Yes
Bar: Full/separate
Hours: M-F 11:30am-2pm, 5-10pm (F 11pm); Sa 5-11pm; Su noon-10pm

127 E. Broad St
Falls Church, VA (703) 532-6500

Definitely not in the same league (or price bracket) as Morton's, but this local representative of a national chain serves moderately priced prime rib (USDA Choice), steaks, and seafood, some of which is "quite good" (*Journal* papers). *Washington Post* thought fresh fish was especially done well. Lazy-Susan salad bar is brought to your table. Live, easy listening music Tues.-Sat. (16 ratings/consistent)

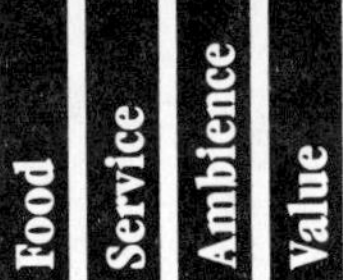

Mr. K's
Chinese **$$$$**

Reserv: Suggested
Dress: Coat req.
Pay: AE, MC, V, DC, CB
Parking: Valet (after 6pm)
Metro: Farragut North/West
Map Reference: J-12
Area: Downtown
Handicap Access: No
Nonsmoking Area: No
Bar: Full
Hours: Daily, 11:30am-11pm

2121 K St, NW
Washington, DC (202) 331-8868

Delicious food, elegant decor, excellent service, and expense account prices. Menu includes such taste tantalizers as beef mimosa, gunpowder lobster, and macadamian chicken. "Food is good, and in some cases . . . wonderful" (Phyllis Richman). Several raters complained of small portions and uneven execution. **Honors:** Mobil★★★★. (36 ratings/mixed)

Mr. L's and Sun
Chinese-Jewish **$**

Reserv: Not accepted
Dress: Informal
Pay: MC, V, Checks
Parking: No
Map Reference: I-11
Area: Van Ness
Handicap Access: Yes
Nonsmoking Area: No
Bar: Full
Hours: M-Th 9am-10pm; F&Sa 8am-11pm; Su 8am-10pm; Sa&Su brunch all day

5018 Connecticut Ave, NW
Washington, DC (202) 244-4343

Moo goo gai pan and corned beef brisket on the same menu? That's right. This is a combination Jewish deli and Chinese dining room. Some consider it a real neighborhood find; others think it's only okay for breakfast and sandwiches. **Honors:** Mobil specialty spot. (13 ratings/mixed)

Mrs. K's Toll House
American **$$**

Reserv: Suggested
Dress: Informal
Pay: AE, MC, V
Parking: Yes
Map Reference: G-12
Handicap Access: No
Nonsmoking Area: Yes
Bar: Full
Hours: T-Sa 11:30am-2:30pm, 5-8:30pm; Su noon-8:30pm

9201 Colesville Rd
Silver Spring, MD (301) 589-3500

The historic Toll House, lovely garden, and antique glass and china are the big attractions here. Menu of traditional American dishes is limited and lackluster; more attuned to older life-styles and tastes. Complete dinners centering around steak, lamb, duck, roast beef, turkey, and seafood are served. "Quantity is all" (Phyllis Richman). (42 ratings/very mixed)

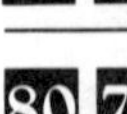

Mrs. Simpson's $$
New American

Reserv: Suggested
Dress: Informal
Pay: AE, MC, V, DC, CB
Parking: No
Metro: Woodley Park
Map Reference: I-11
Handicap Access: Yes
Nonsmoking Area: No
Bar: Full
Hours: M-Su 5:30-10:30pm; Su brunch 11am-2pm

2915 Connecticut Ave, NW
Washington, DC (202) 332-8300

Memorabilia of the Duke and Duchess of Windsor provide the theme for this lovely, small restaurant. New American menu changes frequently to take advantage of seasonal ingredients. Service tends to be leisurely. "Worth an occasion as well as an everyday visit" (Phyllis Richman). **Honors:** Richman's 50 Favorites. (25 ratings/consistent)

Mustache Cafe $$
American

Reserv: Accepted
Dress: Informal
Pay: AE, MC, V, DC, CB, Disc.
Parking: Yes
Metro: Huntington Station
Map Reference: N-11
Handicap Access: No
Nonsmoking Area: Yes
Bar: Full/separate
Hours: M-Sa 11:30am-3pm, 5-10pm; Su brunch 10:30am-3pm, dinner 5-10pm

6723 Richmond Hwy
Alexandria, VA (703) 765-0932

The friendly, relaxed atmosphere, salad and fruit bar, and Sun. champagne brunch are the hits of the show. Menu has a Continental flair to it. Lunch and dinner buffets, early bird dinners, and daily champagne dinner provide lots of fixed-price dining opportunities. Piano player/singer entertains nightly (except Mon. and Thurs.) and all day Sun. Another location at Tysons Corner. (29 ratings/mixed)

My An $
Vietnamese

Reserv: Sugg. weekends
Dress: Informal
Pay: Cash only
Parking: No
Metro: Clarendon
Map Reference: K-10
Handicap Access: No
Nonsmoking Area: No
Bar: Beer/wine
Hours: Daily, 9am-10pm

3101 Wilson Blvd
Arlington, VA (703) 276-7110

A tiny, bare bones restaurant serving authentic Vietnamese food at bargain prices. Crispy, deep-fried cha gio (not just another tired eggroll), a variety of noodle soups, grilled meat and fish, and daily specials are served. Hue noodle soup rated as one of 12 hottest dishes in area restaurants by *Washingtonian*. **Honors:** Richman's 50 Favorites. (24 ratings/consistent)

78 75 71 80

Nam Viet
Vietnamese $

Reserv: Accepted
Dress: Informal
Pay: MC, V
Parking: Yes (after 5pm)
Metro: Clarendon
Map Reference: K-10
Handicap Access: Ltd.
Nonsmoking Area: Yes
Bar: Full
Hours: Su-Th 10am-10pm; F&Sa 10am-11pm

1127 N. Hudson St
Arlington, VA (703) 522-7110

Provides more in the way of ambience and smoother service than its nearby sister restaurant, My An (see above). Raters recommended noodle soups, shrimp balls, and lemon grass chicken. ***Washington Business Journal*** found "many palate teasers" on menu, but ***Washingtonian*** thought dishes were "toned-down versions" of those available elsewhere in Arlington's Little Saigon. (16 ratings/consistent)

79 78 81 69

New Heights
New American $$

Reserv: Suggested
Dress: Informal
Pay: AE, MC, V, DC, CB, Checks
Parking: No
Metro: Woodley Park
Map Reference: I-11
Handicap Access: No
Nonsmoking Area: No
Bar: Full/separate
Hours: M-F 11:30am-2:30pm, 5:30-11pm (F mid.); Sa 5:30pm-mid.; Su brunch 11am-3pm, dinner 5:30-11pm

2317 Calvert St, NW
Washington, DC (202) 234-4110

Imaginative combinations of food colorfully presented. Some raters found dining here an enjoyable experience; others thought it precious and overpriced given the quality and quantity. The ***Washingtonian*** said "modern American cooking attains its lower depths." Dining area decorated with works of local artists. (26 ratings/mixed)

74 69 63 72

New Orleans Cafe
New Orleans $$

Reserv: Not accepted
Dress: Informal
Pay: AE, MC, V, DC, CB
Parking: No
Map Reference: J-12
Area: Adams Morgan
Handicap Access: No
Nonsmoking Area: No
Bar: Full/separate
Hours: Su-Th 8am-10pm; F&Sa 8-11pm

1790 Columbia Rd, NW
Washington, DC (202) 234-5111

Small, bustling cafe. A fun place for inexpensive Cajun food. "No pretensions . . . just good, zesty food" (Phyllis Richman); "even better now than when it opened" (***Washingtonian***). Try the cafe au lait and beignets for breakfast. Closed for health code violations May 18-19, 1988: contaminated food products; no certified food supervisor. **Honors:** Richman's 50 Favorites, ***Washingtonian*** Cheap Eats. (58 ratings/mixed)

Food	Service	Ambience	Value

85	76	64	69

New Orleans Emporium $$
Seafood

Reserv: Suggested
Dress: Informal
Pay: AE, MC, V, DC, CB
Parking: Yes
Map Reference: J-11
Area: Adams Morgan
Handicap Access: No
Nonsmoking Area: Yes
Bar: Beer/wine/separate
Hours: M-Sa 11:30am-2:30pm, 5:30-11pm (F&Sa midnight); Su brunch 11:30am-3pm, dinner 5:30-11pm

2477 18th St, NW
Washington, DC (202) 328-3421

A tonier relative of the cafe above. Raters were enthusiastic about the food, particularly the mussels with mustard sauce, the crawfish, and the "blackened" fish, but there were complaints about service, noise, and prices. Critics consider this a Cajun classic. "Tour de menu" enables you to sample popular items. **Honors:** Richman's Best of Best and 50 Favorites, *Washingtonian* 50 Best★★. (17 ratings/consistent)

71	67	71	67

New York, New York $$
American

Reserv: Suggested
Dress: Informal
Pay: AE, MC, V, DC, CB
Parking: Yes
Metro: Twinbrook
Map Reference: C-4
Area: Congressional Plaza area
Handicap Access: Yes
Nonsmoking Area: Yes
Bar: Full/separate
Hours: M-Th 11:30am-11pm; F&Sa 11:30am-midnight; Su 10:30am-10pm, brunch til 3pm

1527 Rockville Pike
Rockville, MD (301) 468-3950

Emphasis is on abundance, whether you order a gourmet burger, "outrageous" ribs, steak, seafood, whatever. Food is okay but not spectacular. *Washington Post* says "don't expect New York deli food." Many raters were put off by the noise, service, crowded tables, and glitz. Happy hour 5:30-7pm weekdays and late night buffet Mon.-Sat. See ratings for Rosslyn, Va. (243-4600) location. (43 ratings/mixed)

75	71	88	69

94th Aero Squadron $$
Continental

Reserv: Accepted
Dress: Informal
Pay: AE, MC, V, DC, CB
Parking: Yes
Map Reference: G-15
Handicap Access: Yes
Nonsmoking Area: Yes
Bar: Full/separate
Hours: M-Sa 11am-2:30pm, 5-10:30pm (F&Sa 11:30pm); Su brunch 11am-2:30pm, dinner 5-10:30pm

5240 Calvert Rd
College Park, MD (301) 699-9400

Has the look of a bombed-out WWI camp and a great view of the College Park Airport, the country's oldest operating airport. Menu of prime rib, seafood, and poultry, some of it with a trendy twist. Generous portions, but some thought prices still high. Service is slow. "Something a little different with no great culinary risks" (*Journal* papers). Happy hour and nightly deejay. (32 ratings/mixed)

Food	Service	Ambience	Value
85	83	74	81

Nizam's $$
Turkish

Reserv: Suggested
Dress: Coat/tie sugg.
Pay: AE, MC, V, DC, CB
Parking: Yes
Map Reference: D-3
Area: Village Green Center
Handicap Access: Yes
Nonsmoking Area: No
Bar: Full
Hours: T-F 11am-3pm, 5-10pm (F 11pm); Sa 5-11pm; Su 4-10pm

523 Maple Ave, W
Vienna, VA (703) 938-8948

Outstanding Turkish food. The doner kebab (served Tues. and Fri.-Sun.) and moussaka get raves from critics and raters alike, but fried eggplant with yogurt, pasta stuffed with spicy beef, grilled chicken, a little fish, and a number of other kebabs are also served. Tiny, downstairs cafe (noisy) and upstairs dining room. Tables are close. **Honors:** *Washingtonian* 50 Best★. (50 ratings/consistent)

Food	Service	Ambience	Value
88	79	81	75

Nora $$
New American

Reserv: Suggested
Dress: Informal
Pay: Checks
Parking: No
Metro: Dupont Circle
Map Reference: J-12
Handicap Access: Yes
Nonsmoking Area: No
Bar: Full/separate
Hours: M-Th 6-10pm; F&Sa 6-10:30pm

2132 Florida Ave, NW
Washington, DC (202) 462-5143

"Biodynamic" is how Nora Pouillon and co-owners describe their use of fresh, chemical- and additive-free ingredients here and at their City Cafe (see above). Small, creative menu. "Food is beautifully presented" (***Frommer's***). Excellent salads. Casual, upstairs dining room decorated with quilts. **Honors:** Richman's 50 Favorites. (18 ratings/consistent)

Food	Service	Ambience	Value
75	76	81	71

Normandie Farm Inn $$$
French

Reserv: Suggested
Dress: Coat/tie sugg.
Pay: AE, MC, V, DC, CB
Parking: Yes
Map Reference: C-3
Handicap Access: No
Nonsmoking Area: Yes
Bar: Full/separate
Hours: T-Sa 11:30am-2:30pm, 6-10pm (F&Sa 11pm); Su brunch 11am-2pm, dinner 5-9pm

10710 Falls Rd
Potomac, MD (301) 983-8838

This oldtimer (1931) is having something of a resurgence. The charming inn and spacious grounds—not the food—used to be the attraction. But new owners and a revitalized French country menu are changing that. "Better than ever" (Phyllis Richman). The popovers are still wonderful. Live entertainment in lounge Thur.-Sat.; dinner specials; outdoor dining. **Honors:** Mobil★★★. (34 ratings/consistent)

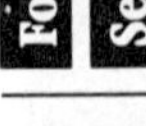

Food | Service | Ambience | Value

80 69 67 77

North China $$
Chinese

Reserv: Suggested
Dress: Informal
Pay: AE, MC, V, Checks
Parking: Yes (after 6pm)
Metro: Bethesda
Map Reference: G-10
Area: Woodmont Triangle
Handicap Access: Yes
Nonsmoking Area: Yes
Bar: Full
Hours: M-Th 11:30am-10pm; F&Sa 11:30am-10:30pm; Su noon-10pm

7814 Old Georgetown Rd
Bethesda, MD (301) 656-7922

Not as upscale as some of the "new" Chinese restaurants, but the food is good and reasonably priced. Menu features Peking and Mandarin dishes, including chicken with cashews, moo-shi pork, Peking duck, imperial shrimp, and yes, some Szechuan dishes. "Solidly good, with a few outstanding items" (***Washington Post***). Noisy. Popular with families. (29 ratings/consistent)

82 81 76 77

Nova Europa $$$
Continental

Reserv: Suggested
Dress: Informal
Pay: AE, MC, V, DC, CB, Checks
Parking: Yes
Map Reference: C-5
Area: Kemp Mill Shopping Center
Handicap Access: Yes
Nonsmoking Area: Yes
Bar: Full
Hours: M-F 11:30am-2:30pm, 5-10pm; Sa&Su 5-10pm

1311 Lamberton Dr
Wheaton, MD (301) 649-6690

Surprisingly pleasant find in small shopping center. European menu (fresh seafood, steak, and veal) features a number of Portuguese dishes, which alone made it "more than worth a visit" for the *Washington Post*. You can try the Portuguese version of paella or bouillabaisse, for example, and accompany it with a Portuguese wine. Fixed-price dinners Sun.-Thurs. (40 ratings/mixed)

78 67 57 74

O'Brien's Pit Barbecue $
Barbecue

Reserv: Accepted
Dress: Informal
Pay: AE, MC, DC
Parking: Yes
Map Reference: C-4
Handicap Access: No
Nonsmoking Area: Yes
Bar: Full/separate
Hours: Su-Th 11am-10pm; F&Sa 11am-11pm

1314 E. Gude Dr
Rockville, MD (301) 340-8596

Features Texas-style, closed-pit, hickory-smoked spare ribs, chili, and barbecued beef, chicken, and beans. A serve-yourself, serious eating kind of place. Atmosphere is Spartan. Critics liked it, but not all raters do. See ratings for other locations: Bethesda, Md. (654-9004) and Springfield, Va. (569-7801). **Honors:** ***Washingtonian*** 50 Best★ and Cheap Eats. (22 ratings/mixed)

81 79 80 72

Occidental Grill
New American

$$

Reserv: Suggested
Dress: Informal
Pay: AE, MC, V, DC, CB, Disc.
Parking: No
Metro: Metro Center
Map Reference: J-12
Area: Downtown
Handicap Access: Ltd.
Nonsmoking Area: No
Bar: Full/separate
Hours: M-Sa 11:30am-11:30pm; Su 11am-9:30pm

1475 Pennsylvania Ave, NW
Washington, DC (202) 783-1475

The critics hailed the return of the Occidental alongside the Willard Hotel not just for the nostalgia but for the food. Many raters considered it historic and succulent, a bit pricey but a real treat. Others said it was an overpriced status restaurant, more self-conscious than customer conscious. All agreed it's noisy. **Honors:** Richman's 50 Favorites, *Washingtonian* 50 Best★★. (74 ratings/mixed)

83 77 77 80

Ocean Garden

Japanese-Chinese

$$

Reserv: Suggested
Dress: Informal
Pay: AE, MC, V
Parking: Yes
Map Reference: G-12
Handicap Access: Yes
Nonsmoking Area: Yes
Bar: Full
Hours: T-Th 11:30am-10pm; F&Sa 11:30am-11pm; Su noon-10pm

8739 Flower Ave
Silver Spring, MD (301) 587-3833

Surprising combination of sushi and cooked seafood dishes of China and Japan. Raters liked the steamed fresh fish, sushi, scallops, and the Polynesian drinks. Closed for health code violation February 1-2, 1988: ineffective roach and rodent control. **Honors:** Richman's 50 Favorites. (22 ratings/consistent)

75 69 71 69

Odeon Cafe
Italian

$$

Reserv: Accepted
Dress: Informal
Pay: AE, MC, V
Parking: No
Metro: Dupont Circle
Map Reference: J-12
Handicap Access: No
Nonsmoking Area: No
Bar: Full
Hours: M-F 11:30am-4pm, 5pm-midnight (F 1am); Sa 5pm-1am; Su 4:30pm-midnight

1714 Connecticut Ave, NW
Washington, DC (202) 328-6228

Art deco cafe for pizza, pasta, and new Italian dishes. Some consider it stylish, others glitzy. One thing is certain, the noise (people and music) on the weekends is deafening. Weekday lunches are quieter. Straying from pizza and pasta dishes can be risky. The best of the "upscale pizza-and-pasta restaurants" according to the *Washingtonian*. (27 ratings/mixed)

Food	Service	Ambience	Value

81	77	75	78

O'Donnell's $$
Seafood

Reserv: Suggested
Dress: Informal
Pay: AE, MC, V, DC, CB
Parking: Yes
Map Reference: G-10
Handicap Access: Yes
Nonsmoking Area: Yes
Bar: Full/separate
Hours: M-F 11:30am-10pm (F 11pm); Sa noon-11pm; Su noon-9:30pm

8301 Wisconsin Ave
Bethesda, MD (301) 656-6200

It's not elegant or trendy, but going to this oldtimer of a seafood house (in family over 60 years) can grow on you. Good, basic food; restaurant is too large and too busy to give food much in the way of special treatment. Phyllis Richman said that "hospitality," not the food, "is the crucial quality that keeps O'Donnell's riding high." Happy hour 4:30-6pm weekdays. (118 ratings/consistent)

77	71	85	62

Old Angler's Inn $$$
French

Reserv: Req. weekends
Dress: Coat req.
Pay: AE, MC, V, DC, CB
Parking: Yes
Map Reference: D-3
Handicap Access: Ltd.
Nonsmoking Area: Yes
Bar: Full/separate
Hours: Tu-Su noon-2:30pm, 6-10:30pm

10801 MacArthur Blvd
Potomac, MD (301) 365-2425

The tree-rimmed terrace of this old inn (1860) is one of the best outdoor settings in the area; during cold weather, you can get cozy by the fire in the lounge. Atmosphere may make up for inconsistent food and service. French-style menu features seafood and grilled meats. Nearby is Great Falls Park, where you can see the falls on the Potomac. (38 ratings/very mixed)

71	70	79	66

Old Ebbitt Grill $$
American

Reserv: Suggested
Dress: Informal
Pay: AE, MC, V, DC, CB
Parking: No
Metro: McPherson Square
Map Reference: J-12
Area: Downtown
Handicap Access: Yes
Nonsmoking Area: Yes
Bar: Full/separate
Hours: M-F 7:30am-11pm; Sa 8am-11pm; Su brunch 9:30am-4pm, dinner 4-11pm

675 15th St, NW
Washington, DC (202) 347-4800

This new rendition of the history-laden original is long on well-heeled ambience. A fun place to go for the setting, history, and people watching. Raters and critics alike, however, gave the food mixed reviews—from fair, to dependably inconsistent, to quite good. Sun. brunch, hamburgers, pre-theater specials, and the bartenders got good marks. **Honors:** *Washingtonian* 50 Best★. (72 ratings/mixed)

82 76 76 77

Old Peking
Chinese

\$\$

Reserv: Suggested
Dress: Informal
Pay: AE, MC, V, Checks
Parking: Yes
Map Reference: E-3
Handicap Access: Yes
Nonsmoking Area: Yes
Bar: Full
Hours: M-Th 11:30am-10pm; F&Sa 11:30am-10:30pm

2952 Chain Bridge Rd
Oakton, VA (703) 255-9444

Small, tastefully decorated dining room. Food is a cut above average neighborhood Chinese fare. Hunan and Szechuan dishes are prepared, but the Peking specialties make for a nice change. Sampler dishes for two available. (11 ratings/mixed)

76 68 71 78

Olney Ale House
American

\$

Reserv: Not accepted
Dress: Informal
Pay: MC, V
Parking: Yes
Map Reference: B-4
Handicap Access: No
Nonsmoking Area: Yes
Bar: Beer/wine/separate
Hours: Su-Th 11:30am-10pm; F&Sa 11:30am-midnight

2000 Olney-Sandy Spring Rd
Olney, MD (301) 774-6708

The comfy down-home feeling and the rustic setting are a large part of the attraction here. Then there are the fantastic homemade breads and the imported and domestic ales and beers. Otherwise, this would be just another beer house. Outdoor dining on patio. Olney Theater is across the street. "Can't beat it for a reason to drive out of town" (Phyllis Richman). (20 ratings/mixed)

79 75 58 80

Omega
Cuban

\$\$

Reserv: Not accepted
Dress: Informal
Pay: AE, MC, V, DC, CB
Parking: No
Map Reference: J-12
Area: Adams Morgan
Handicap Access: Yes
Nonsmoking Area: Yes
Bar: Full
Hours: Tu-Th 11:30am-10pm; F&Sa 11am-11pm; Su 11:30am-10pm

1856 Columbia Rd, NW
Washington, DC (202) 462-1732

Good food in a wretched setting. Crowded, hurried, and noisy, but the faithful return for the generous portions of fluffy rice, black beans, paella, fried squid, and stews. "Good cooking and fair prices . . . make it a star" (*Washingtonian*). For the dissenters, once is enough. **Honors:** Richman's Best of Best, *Washingtonian* 50 Best★★ and Cheap Eats. (14 ratings/mixed)

Food | Service | Ambience | Value

Oscar Taylor's $$
77 71 76 67

American

11858 Rockville Pike
Rockville, MD (301) 468-6600

Reserv: Suggested
Dress: Informal
Pay: AE, MC, V, DC, CB
Parking: Yes
Metro: White Flint
Map Reference: C-4
Area: Mid-Pike Plaza
Handicap Access: Yes
Nonsmoking Area: Yes
Bar: Full/separate
Hours: M-Th 11:30am-midnight; F&Sa 11:30am-1am; Su noon-9pm

"Butcher, baker, and bar" reads the logo. Menu features mesquite-grilled beef, barbecued chicken, baby back ribs, seafood, and dinner-size "garbage salad." Desserts are from bakery up front. Lunch is a better value than dinner. Wines of the month served by the glass. Avoid Fri. nights if you don't like singles scene. Happy hour weeknights; live music in lounge Wed., Thurs., and Sat. (43 ratings/very mixed)

Oscar's $$
71 65 68 70

American

11575 Old Georgetown Rd
Rockville, MD (301) 881-6006

Reserv: Suggested
Dress: Informal
Pay: AE, MC, V
Parking: Yes
Metro: White Flint
Map Reference: C-4
Handicap Access: Yes
Nonsmoking Area: Yes
Bar: Full/separate
Hours: M-F 11:30am-3pm, 4:30-10pm (F 11pm); Sa 4:30-11pm; Su 4:30-10pm

Attractive suburban steak and seafood house. The 65-item salad bar seems to be the only real standout as far as food is concerned. Combination of soup and salad bar makes a good weekday lunch. Early bird dinner (includes salad bar) is a good value; happy hour. (16 ratings/mixed)

Otello $$

Italian

1329 Connecticut Ave, NW
Washington, DC (202) 429-0209

Reserv: Sugg. weekends
Dress: Informal
Pay: AE, MC, V, DC, CB
Parking: No
Metro: Dupont Circle
Map Reference: J-12
Handicap Access: No
Nonsmoking Area: No
Bar: Full
Hours: M-F noon-2:30pm, 6-10:30pm; Sa 6-10:30pm; Su 5:30-9:30pm

Cheery Italian-style cafe. Antipasto table and fairly standard selection of pastas, seafood, and meat dishes. One of best things about the menu is the prices. Dining room is small and busy. Some raters found service rude and pushy. *Washingtonian* found kitchen "careless" and unable "to achieve authentic Italian flavors." Needs to find way to ventilate smoke. Same ownership as Rigoletto in Falls Church, Va. (27 ratings/consistent)

80 74 71 87

P. J. Skidoos $$
American

Reserv: Not accepted
Dress: Informal
Pay: AE, MC, V
Parking: Yes
Map Reference: E-3
Area: Off Fairfax Circle
Handicap Access: Yes
Nonsmoking Area: Yes
Bar: Full/separate
Hours: M-F 11:30am-2am; Sa 5pm-2am; Su 5-10pm

9908 Lee Hwy
Fairfax, VA (703) 591-4515

Prime rib-steak house and watering hole. The lively bar scene and bargain prices draw a crowd. Noisy, but fun; not for the overly sedate. Dinner specials; happy hour weekdays; deejay in lounge nightly. ***Washingtonian*** recommends staying with the "wonderfully tender, nicely flavored" beef. **Honors:** ***Washingtonian*** Cheap Eats. (31 ratings/consistent)

84 76 76 81

Pancho Villa $$
Mexican

Reserv: Accepted
Dress: Informal
Pay: MC, V, DC, CB, Checks
Parking: Yes
Map Reference: C-4
Area: Rock Creek Village Shopping Center
Handicap Access: Yes
Nonsmoking Area: Yes
Bar: Full
Hours: M-F 11am-10pm; Sa&Su noon-10pm

5530 Norbeck Rd
Rockville, MD (301) 871-8554

Not just another fast-food operation. In addition to tacos, burritos, and fajitas, you'll find dishes that demonstrate Mexico's "innovative use of seafood and meat" (***Washington Business Journal***). Setting is casual and neighborly, and service is good if they're not too crowded. Strolling musicians nightly. (22 ratings/consistent)

84 74 71 88

Panjshir $
Afghan

Reserv: Not accepted
Dress: Informal
Pay: AE, MC, V, DC, CB
Parking: Yes
Map Reference: K-8
Handicap Access: No
Nonsmoking Area: No
Bar: Full
Hours: M-Sa 11:30am-2:30pm, 5-11pm; Su 5-11pm

924 W. Broad St
Falls Church, VA (703) 536-4566

It didn't take long for this family-run restaurant to earn a reputation for good food and good value. For appetizers, there's an assortment of dumplings and stuffed turnovers. For entrees, chicken, lamb, and beef kebabs dominate. The ***Washington Post*** called them "outstanding and generous in size." Attractive interior; leisurely service. **Honors:** ***Washingtonian*** Cheap Eats. (14 ratings/very consistent)

Food | Service | Ambience | Value

---

80 78 64 84

Parkway Deli
Delicatessen **$**

Reserv: Not accepted
Dress: Informal
Pay: Cash only
Parking: Yes
Map Reference: G-12
Handicap Access: Yes
Nonsmoking Area: Yes
Bar: Beer/wine
Hours: Su-Th 7am-9:30pm; F&Sa 7am-10pm

8317 Grubb Rd
Silver Spring, MD (301) 587-1427

Close to a New York deli: lox, sturgeon, stuffed kishke, matzo-ball soup, goulash, brisket of beef, grilled liver, london broil. Just try to walk past those deli cases "without mouthwatering anticipation" (*Journal* papers). A great place for Sun. breakfast. Lots of hustle and bustle; some like the service, some don't. Popularity could be making owner indifferent. (19 ratings/mixed)

---

68  67  65 68

Partners
American **$$**

Reserv: Accepted
Dress: Informal
Pay: Checks
Parking: Yes
Metro: Bethesda
Map Reference: G-10
Handicap Access: No
Nonsmoking Area: Yes
Bar: Full/separate
Hours: M-Sa 11:30am-2:30pm, 5:30-10:30pm

6931 Arlington Rd
Bethesda, MD (301) 654-7755

Restaurant and food emporium with a French accent picked up from its parent La Miche (see above). Offers something for everyone—lunch, after work snacks or dinner, light or hearty entrees, wine by the glass—plus deli, bakery, and carryout. With all that, raters clearly weren't as enthusiastic about the food or bargain prices as the critics have been. (31 ratings/mixed)

---

85  77  70 85

Pasta Plus
Italian **$$**

Reserv: Not accepted
Dress: Informal
Pay: MC, V
Parking: Yes
Map Reference: C-6
Handicap Access: No
Nonsmoking Area: No
Bar: Beer/wine
Hours: Tu-F 11:30am-2:30pm, 5-9:30pm (F 10pm); Sa 5-10pm; Su 4-9pm

209 Gorman Ave
Laurel, MD (301) 498-5100

Small, personal, neighborhood restaurant featuring a variety of homemade pasta and other home-cooked dishes for reasonable prices. Daily specials offer some of the best choices. Tables are small, close together, and often hard to come by. "Tomato sauces are reliably good" and the white wine sauce is "easy to love" (***Washington Post***). (17 ratings/consistent)

Peking & Hunan Gourmet — $$

80 78 66 87

Chinese

Reserv: Accepted
Dress: Informal
Pay: AE, MC, V
Parking: Yes (after 6pm)
Metro: Bethesda
Map Reference: G-10
Handicap Access: Ltd.
Nonsmoking Area: Yes
Bar: Full
Hours: M-Th 11am-10pm; F&Sa 11am-11pm; Su noon-10pm

4611 Willow Ln
Bethesda, MD (301) 951-8922

Wide selection of well-prepared, nicely seasoned dishes. Not fancy, but good. Popular dishes include crispy shrimp, Hunan chicken (the chef's favorite), crunchy, crispy beef, and the Peking duck. Friendly, helpful service. (14 ratings/mixed)

Peking Gourmet Inn — $$

86 82 72 81

Chinese

Reserv: Suggested
Dress: Informal
Pay: MC, V
Parking: Yes
Map Reference: L-9
Handicap Access: Yes
Nonsmoking Area: Yes
Bar: Full
Hours: Su-Th 11am-10:30pm; F&Sa 11am-midnight

6029 Leesburg Pike
Baileys Crossroads, VA (703) 671-8088

Large menu of Peking and Szechuan dishes, but it's the Peking duck, carved at tableside, that gets the most attention. The critics disagree about the duck, but most raters said it was excellent. Gets very crowded and noisy. Several raters thought food was getting pricey, and a few said it wasn't up to pre-expansion standards. **Honors:** Richman's 50 Favorites. (44 ratings/mixed)

Peking Imperial — $$

79 76 69 82

Chinese

Reserv: Accepted
Dress: Informal
Pay: AE, MC, V, DC, CB
Parking: Yes
Map Reference: I-9
Handicap Access: Yes
Nonsmoking Area: No
Bar: Full/separate
Hours: M-Th 11:30am-10pm; F&Sa 11:30am-11pm; Su noon-10pm

6827 Redmond Dr
McLean, VA (703) 448-0928

People in area consider this both a good family restaurant and a good place for a business lunch. Three favorites among the Peking, Szechuan, and Hunan dishes are the orange beef, imperial shrimp, and the Peking duck. Some think food quality has begun to vary, however. (14 ratings/mixed)

Food | Service | Ambience | Value

78 68 78 69

Perry's
Japanese **$$**

Reserv: Not accepted
Dress: Informal
Pay: AE, MC, V, DC, CB
Parking: No
Map Reference: J-12
Area: Adams Morgan
Handicap Access: No
Nonsmoking Area: No
Bar: Full/separate
Hours: Su-Th 6pm-midnight; F&Sa 6pm-1am

1811 Columbia Rd, NW
Washington, DC (202) 234-6218

New wave sushi bar/Japanese restaurant. Loud rock music and a lively, younger crowd go with the sushi and sashimi, cooked fish, sukiyaki, teriyaki, and tempura. Rooftop dining area/bar in summer. Very crowded. If you avoid peak hours, according to Phyllis Richman, "you can enjoy one of the most original restaurants in Washington." **Honors:** Richman's 50 Favorites. (11 ratings/mixed)

76 69 80 69

Petitto's
Italian **$$**

Reserv: Suggested
Dress: Informal
Pay: AE, MC, V, DC, CB
Parking: No
Metro: Woodley Park
Map Reference: I-11
Handicap Access: No
Nonsmoking Area: No
Bar: Full
Hours: M-F 11:30am-2:30pm, 6-10:30pm; Sa 6-10:30pm

2653 Connecticut Ave, NW
Washington, DC (202) 667-5350

Lovely, intimate dining rooms, some with a fireplace. The antipasto and the homemade pasta, dressed with a variety of sauces and other accompaniments, are the big attraction. Phyllis Richman thought "food has a fresh liveliness," and *Frommer's* predicted you'd be "blissed out" eating here, but our raters' reactions were mixed in all respects. Sidewalk cafe. (19 ratings/mixed)

67 66 69 63

Phillips Flagship
Seafood **$$$**

Reserv: Suggested
Dress: Informal
Pay: AE, MC, V, DC, CB
Parking: No
Metro: L'Enfant Plaza
Map Reference: K-12
Area: S.W. Waterfront
Handicap Access: Ltd.
Nonsmoking Area: Yes
Bar: Full/separate
Hours: M-Th 11:30am-11pm; F&Sa 11:30am-midnight; Su 11:30am-11pm, brunch til 4pm

900 Water St, SW
Washington, DC (202) 488-8515

Lots of food, fair quality, and good view. Okay if you like mobs. Serves usual array of fresh seafood—grilled swordfish, crab imperial, crab cakes, and combination platters. "Food often tastes like tourist fare" according to *Washington Times*. Service is slow. Weekday seafood buffets; live entertainment nightly. Outdoor dining area. Near Arena Stage. (48 ratings/very mixed)

75 71 71 74

Phineas
American

\$\$

Reserv: Suggested
Dress: Informal
Pay: AE, MC, V, DC, CB, Disc.
Parking: Yes
Metro: Twinbrook
Map Reference: C-4
Handicap Access: Yes
Nonsmoking Area: Yes
Bar: Full/separate
Hours: M-Th 11:30am-2:30pm, 5-10pm; F&Sa 11:30am-2:30pm, 5-11pm; Su 10:30am-9pm

1580 Rockville Pike
Rockville, MD (301) 770-5025

A lot goes on at this steak and seafood house. First, they offer four sizes of prime rib plus seafood, surf 'n' turf platters, and a huge salad bar. They also have a guaranteed quick lunch, "the world's longest happy hour," daily fixed-price dining, and a Sun. brunch (10:30am-2pm) that's free for kids under 10. Given all of that, it's a busy place, and the food sometimes reflects it. (38 ratings/mixed)

80 77 75 79

Phoenix
Greek

\$\$

Reserv: Sugg. weekends
Dress: Informal
Pay: AE, MC, V
Parking: Yes
Metro: Clarendon
Map Reference: K-10
Handicap Access: Yes
Nonsmoking Area: Yes
Bar: Full
Hours: M-F 11am-10pm (F 10:30pm); Sa 5-10:30pm

2950 Clarendon Blvd
Arlington, VA (703) 841-9494

Neighborhood restaurant with the air of a Greek country inn. Has built a loyal following based on generous portions of good food, reasonable prices, congeniality, and Greek music and dancing (Thurs.-Sat.). Menu of Greek-Continental seafood, beef, lamb, and vegetarian dishes. Early bird dinner specials. "Nothing precious, trendy, or contrived" (*Journal* papers). (17 ratings/consistent)

81 77 67 77

Piatti Pizza & Pasta
Italian

\$\$

Reserv: Not accepted
Dress: Informal
Pay: AE, MC, V
Parking: Yes
Map Reference: F-4
Handicap Access: Yes
Nonsmoking Area: No
Bar: Full
Hours: Tu-F 11:30am-10pm; Sa 5-10pm; Su 4-9pm

6125 Franconia Rd
Alexandria, VA (703) 922-6222

Homey neighborhood restaurant. The name pretty much describes the menu. Lunch buffet Tues.-Fri. (11:30am-2pm). One rater said it's great for families and lovers, and another advised you skip the clams casino. Italian music in background. (12 ratings/mixed)

Food	Service	Ambience	Value

72	70	71	71

Pier 7 $$
Seafood

Reserv: Required
Dress: Informal
Pay: AE, MC, V, DC, CB, Disc., Checks
Parking: Yes
Metro: L'Enfant Plaza
Map Reference: K-12
Area: S.W. Waterfront
Handicap Access: Yes
Nonsmoking Area: No
Bar: Full/separate
Hours: M-F 11:15am-11:15pm; Sa 4-11:15pm; Su 2-10pm

650 Water St, SW
Washington, DC (202) 554-2500

A cut above the other American seafood houses along Water St. Serves a variety of seafood (not all of it fresh) plus beef, chicken, and ribs cooked over an open hearth. "Some of the best simply prepared fresh fish in town" (***Washington Times***). Cold salmon and caper sandwich recommended for lunch. Great view. Happy hour; contemporary jazz Mon.-Sat. nights. Near Arena Stage. (56 ratings/mixed)

83	85	77	75

Pierre et Madeline $$
French

Reserv: Accepted
Dress: Coat/tie sugg.
Pay: AE, MC, V, DC, CB, Checks
Parking: Yes
Map Reference: D-3
Area: Executive Bldg
Handicap Access: Ltd.
Nonsmoking Area: Yes
Bar: Full/separate
Hours: M-F 11:30am-2:30pm, 5:30-10:30pm; Sa 5:30-10:30pm

246 Maple Ave, E
Vienna, VA (703) 938-4379

Leisurely dining in a charming setting. Menu of traditional French country dishes is small but includes such taste tempters as Dover sole amandine, salmon steak with sorrel sauce, breast of duck with marinated pears, and the chef's favorite, lobster meat in a whiskey sauce. Outstanding service; very friendly owners. Some think it a bit overpriced. (11 ratings/very mixed)

81	68	55	79

Pines of Italy $
Italian

Reserv: Not accepted
Dress: Informal
Pay: AE, MC, V, DC, CB
Parking: Yes
Map Reference: K-10
Area: Buckingham
Handicap Access: Yes
Nonsmoking Area: No
Bar: Beer/wine
Hours: Daily, 11am-11pm

237 N. Glebe Rd
Arlington, VA (703) 524-4969

This small, family-type restaurant isn't much to look at, but it serves very good southern Italian food and at bargain prices. The chef likes to prepare the roast veal, broiled flounder, white pizza, and white bean soup. "So few things to avoid and so many to enjoy" ***(Washington Post)***. **Honors:** ***Washingtonian*** Cheap Eats. (17 ratings/very mixed)

Pines of Rome $$
Italian

Reserv: Not accepted
Dress: Informal
Pay: AE, MC, V, DC, CB
Parking: No
Metro: Bethesda
Map Reference: G-10
Handicap Access: Ltd.
Nonsmoking Area: Yes
Bar: Beer/wine
Hours: M 11:30am-10pm; Tu-F 11:30am-11pm (F 11:30pm); Sa 12:30-11:30pm; Su 1-10pm

4709 Hampden Ln
Bethesda, MD (301) 657-8775

It's a noisy hole-in-the-wall and the waiting to be seated can be tiresome, but there are good red and white pizzas to be had for the waiting. Fairly priced in a pricey area. Enjoyable place; good for families. Phyllis Richman warns you "enter the higher menu ranges at your own risk." (43 ratings/consistent)

76 75 76 73

Plata Grande $$
Mexican

Reserv: Accepted
Dress: Informal
Pay: AE, MC, V, DC
Parking: Yes
Map Reference: C-6
Handicap Access: Yes
Nonsmoking Area: Yes
Bar: Full/separate
Hours: M-W 11am-3pm, 5-9pm; Th-Sa 11am-3pm, 5-11pm; Su 3-9pm

4060 Powder Mill Rd
Beltsville, MD (301) 572-7744

Mini-chain of Tex-Mex restaurants. You'll find all the popular Mexican dishes on the menu, which is more like a book than a bill of fare, plus lots of house specials. Boasts lots of fresh ingredients, limited salt, and no lard, MSG, or sulfites. Some think food isn't spicy enough and that value has dropped. Deejay and dancing nightly. Two other locations in area; see ratings for Columbia, Md. (740-5115) location. (26 ratings/mixed)

78 77 79 75

Pleasant Peasant $$
American

Reserv: Not accepted
Dress: Informal
Pay: AE, MC, V, DC, CB
Parking: Yes
Metro: Friendship Heights
Map Reference: H-11
Area: Mazza Gallerie
Handicap Access: Yes
Nonsmoking Area: No
Bar: Full/separate
Hours: Daily 11:30am-3pm, 5:30-11pm (F&Sa midnight); Su brunch til 3pm

5300 Wisconsin Ave, NW
Washington, DC (202) 364-2500

Changing menu of contemporary dishes attractively presented in overly generous portions. Friendly service and "delicious" Continental atmosphere. Those desserts make it a popular place for a shopping break or late evening sweet. Piano music Tues.-Sat. eves. Closed for health code violations May 15-19, 1987: improper storage of food and poisons; faulty refrigeration and dishwashing facilities. (61 ratings/consistent)

72 69 63 77

PoFolks
Southern — $

Reserv: Not accepted
Dress: Informal
Pay: MC, V, Checks
Parking: Yes
Map Reference: E-3
Area: Off Fairfax Circle
Handicap Access: Yes
Nonsmoking Area: Yes
Bar: None
Hours: M-Su 11am-10pm

10060 Lee Hwy
Fairfax City, VA (703) 359-2966

Part of national chain that provides generous portions of down-to-earth food at reasonable prices. Pleasant country atmosphere. Lots of kids. Service is youthful, but willing. Comments on food ranged from "horrid" to "good." Many noted fried foods were very greasy. Several locations in area. (29 ratings/very mixed)

78 76 85 74

Portner's
American — $$

Reserv: Suggested
Dress: Informal
Pay: AE, MC, V, DC, CB
Parking: No
Map Reference: M-12
Area: Old Town
Handicap Access: Ltd.
Nonsmoking Area: Yes
Bar: Full/separate
Hours: M-Sa 11:30am-2am; Su 10:30am-midnight, brunch til 3pm

109 S. St. Asaph St
Alexandria, VA (703) 683-1776

The converted 1880s Columbia Fire House has many architectural and decorative attractions. You can choose a dining room or bar to match your mood, quiet or lively. Menu includes homemade pizza and pasta, fresh seafood, and grilled meats. One rater thought children weren't very welcome, and another said forget it if you're over 50. **Honors:** *Travel-Holiday* Award. (18 ratings/mixed)

82 78 84 77

Portofino
Italian — $$$

Reserv: Required
Dress: Coat/tie req.
Pay: AE, MC, V, DC, CB, Checks
Parking: Yes
Metro: Crystal City
Map Reference: L-11
Handicap Access: No
Nonsmoking Area: Yes
Bar: Full
Hours: M-F 11am-2pm, 5-10pm; Sa&Su 5-10pm

526 S. 23rd St
Arlington, VA (703) 979-8200

One of the earliest good restaurants in Crystal City area. Several attractive dining rooms in converted home. The pasta, veal, seafood, and other dishes are handled with the lighter touch characteristic of northern Italian cooking. Also own Firenze in North Arlington, Va. (11 ratings/mixed)

Food	Service	Ambience	Value

80	76	75	71

Positano $$
Italian

Reserv: Suggested
Dress: Informal
Pay: AE, MC, V, Checks
Parking: Yes (after 6pm)
Metro: Bethesda
Map Reference: G-10
Area: Woodmont Triangle
Handicap Access: Ltd.
Nonsmoking Area: Yes
Bar: Full
Hours: M-F 11:30am-2:30pm, 5-10pm; Sa&Su 4-9pm

4940 Fairmont Ave
Bethesda, MD (301) 654-1717

Family-run restaurant serving authentic dishes from the north and south of Italy. Food can be great, but isn't always. Perhaps the kitchen can't handle the crowd. Comfortable, Italian village atmosphere and attentive service. Raters liked the pasta dishes; the *Washingtonian* singled out veal matrimoni among the entrees. (28 ratings/consistent)

71	67	78	67

Potowmack Landing $$
American

Reserv: Accepted
Dress: Informal
Pay: AE, MC, V, DC
Parking: Yes
Map Reference: F-4
Area: Washington Sailing Marina
Handicap Access: Yes
Nonsmoking Area: Yes
Bar: Full/separate
Hours: Daily, 11:30am-10pm; Su brunch til 2:30pm

Geo. Washington Memorial Pky
Alexandria, VA (703) 548-0001

Once not more than a shack where you could get a burger and a beer after sailing, it now sports a raw bar, dining room, and indoor-outdoor cafe. Menu includes lots of grilled meat and seafood. Very noisy interior. Spectacular views up, down, and across the Potomac. Phyllis Richman thought kitchen staff needed help "buying and cooking seafood," and *Journal* papers advised against "more complex dishes." (42 ratings/mixed)

83	78	80	72

Prime Plus $$$
New American

Reserv: Suggested
Dress: Coat/tie sugg.
Pay: AE, MC, V, Checks
Parking: Valet (after 6pm)
Metro: McPherson Square
Map Reference: J-12
Area: Downtown
Handicap Access: Ltd.
Nonsmoking Area: No
Bar: Full/separate
Hours: M-F 11:30am-10:30pm (F 11:30pm); Sa 5:30pm-11:30pm

727 15th St, NW
Washington, DC (202) 783-0166

A continually changing array of imaginative combinations of ingredients is what you'll find here—not a lot of prime beef. The chef's creations were generally well received by raters. Critics were more divided about whether hits outnumbered misses. Attractive art deco dining room; service has a few misses of its own. Early supper specials (5-7pm). (25 ratings/mixed)

89 87 86 75

The Prime Rib
Steak House
$$$$

Reserv: Suggested
Dress: Coat req.
Pay: AE, MC, V, DC, CB
Parking: Valet (after 6pm)
Metro: Farragut North/West
Map Reference: J-12
Area: Downtown
Handicap Access: Ltd.
Nonsmoking Area: No
Bar: Full/separate
Hours: M-F 11am-3pm, 5-11pm (F 11:30pm); Sa 5-11:30pm

2020 K St, NW
Washington, DC (202) 466-8811

First-rate but expensive. Generous portions of aged, prime beef, served amid understated elegance. Music from the baby grand at lunch and dinner. Busy, noisy cocktail bar. "Retired the trophy for best prime rib in town," said the *Washingtonian*, but Phyllis Richman was less enthusiastic. Also in Baltimore. **Honors:** AAA◆◆◆, Mobil★★★, *Travel-Holiday* selection, *Washingtonian* 50 Best★. (34 ratings/consistent)

80 73 72 70

Primi Piatti
Italian
$$

Reserv: Accepted
Dress: Informal
Pay: AE, MC, V, DC, CB, Disc.
Parking: No
Metro: Foggy Bottom
Map Reference: J-12
Area: Downtown
Handicap Access: Ltd.
Nonsmoking Area: No
Bar: Full/separate
Hours: M-F 11:30am-2:30pm, 5:30-10:30pm; Sa 5:30-11:30pm

2013 I St, NW
Washington, DC (202) 223-3600

Flashy, festive, unbearably noisy, urban Italian scene. All kinds of pizza, pasta, and grilled meats and seafood. Many said theater was more important than the food. Phyllis Richman said "the parts [are] considerably less than the whole," and *Journal* papers said food was "homogenized into blandness." Same owner as Galileo (see above). **Honors:** *Washingtonian* 50 Best★★. (29 ratings/mixed)

85 77 70 76

RT's
Seafood
$$

Reserv: Suggested
Dress: Informal
Pay: AE, MC, V, Checks
Parking: No
Map Reference: L-11
Area: Arlandria
Handicap Access: No
Nonsmoking Area: No
Bar: Full/separate
Hours: M-T 11am-10:30pm; F&Sa 11am-11pm; Su 4-9pm

3804 Mount Vernon Ave
Alexandria, VA (703) 684-6010

If you let the neighborhood keep you from stopping at this small, friendly, restaurant-lounge, you'll miss out on some good New Orleans-style seafood. Lots of seafood appetizers to go with a cold drink, plus she crab soup, crab cakes, Jack Daniels shrimp, blackened fish; nonseafood selections, too, some of them Cajun. **Honors:** Richman's 50 Favorites. (21 ratings/consistent)

Food | Service | Ambience | Value

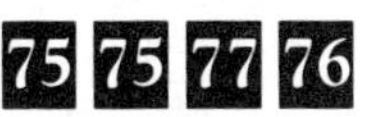

Raindancer $$
Seafood

Reserv: Suggested
Dress: Informal
Pay: AE, MC, V
Parking: Yes
Metro: Twinbrook
Map Reference: C-4
Handicap Access: Yes
Nonsmoking Area: Yes
Bar: Full/separate
Hours: Daily, 11:30am-midnight; Su brunch 10:30am-2:30pm

12224 Rockville Pike
Rockville, MD (301) 468-2300

Seafood house run by Scaggs family (see Anchor Inn above). The early bird specials (4:30-6:30pm) are a roaring success with raters. Seafood platters, Maine lobster, crab imperial, and fresh fish are popular entrees. Complaints about waiting time and nonsmoking areas, friendly but unskilled service, and consistency of food quality. (57 ratings/mixed)

79 72 67 79

Red Lobster $$
Seafood

Reserv: Not accepted
Dress: Informal
Pay: AE, MC, V, DC, CB, Disc., Checks
Parking: Yes
Map Reference: K-8
Handicap Access: Yes
Nonsmoking Area: Yes
Bar: Full/separate
Hours: M-Sa 11am-10pm; Su 4-10pm

513 W. Broad St
Falls Church, VA (703) 532-7150

National chain of seafood houses that emphasizes quantity and prices. Serves standard array of seafood, much of it fried, plus lemon sole, rainbow trout, swordfish, and fresh fish of the day. Nonseafood items also available. Setting here likened to decorated warehouse. For ratings for three of the numerous locations in area, see table at front of book; all ratings in same range. (14 ratings/consistent)

Red Sea $
Ethiopian

Reserv: Suggested
Dress: Informal
Pay: AE, MC, V, DC, CB
Parking: No
Map Reference: J-12
Area: Adams Morgan
Handicap Access: Yes
Nonsmoking Area: No
Bar: Full/separate
Hours: Daily, 11:30am-1am

2463 18th St, NW
Washington, DC (202) 483-5000

A fun place to go with a group of adventurous diners. You can order a sampler dinner or individual dishes from among the spicy wats, the more delicate alechas, and sauteed tibs (marinated meat cubes). Portions are generous. Dining is communal style, and you use fingers and pieces of bread to serve yourself. Live Ethiopian music Fri. and Sat. **Honors:** *Washingtonian* 50 Best★ and Cheap Eats. (46 ratings/mixed)

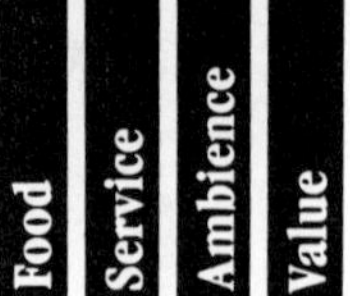

70 71 59 73

Reeves $
American

Reserv: Not accepted
Dress: Informal
Pay: Cash only
Parking: No
Metro: Metro Center
Map Reference: J-12
Area: Downtown
Handicap Access: Ltd.
Nonsmoking Area: No
Bar: None
Hours: M-Sa 6:45am-6pm

1209 F St, NW
Washington, DC (202) 347-3781

If you haven't been to this Washington landmark (opened in 1886), know that it could be "developed" out of existence very soon. The breakfast buffet bar is one of best values in town, lunch at the counter or in a booth is quick and satisfying, and the baked strawberry pie from the bakery up front is legend. (21 ratings/mixed)

87 81 76 79

The Restaurant in Bethesda $$$
French

Reserv: Sugg. weekends
Dress: Informal
Pay: AE, MC, V, DC, CB, Disc., Checks
Parking: Valet (eves)
Metro: Bethesda
Map Reference: G-10
Area: Woodmont Tri.
Handicap Access: No
Nonsmoking Area: Yes
Bar: Full
Hours: M-F 11:30am-2pm, 5:30-9:30pm (F 10pm); Sa 5:30-10pm

7820 Norfolk Ave
Bethesda, MD (301) 657-1607

May not be as well known as other restaurants in area, but raters were quite taken with the food and pleasant service. Traditional and nouvelle French dishes—with an American twist—on menu, including a 400-calorie lunch special (perhaps that's the twist). Can get crowded and noisy. Outdoor cafe. (20 ratings/consistent)

68 68 68 65

Rhiannon's $$
American

Reserv: Suggested
Dress: Informal
Pay: AE, MC, V, DC, CB, Checks
Parking: Yes
Map Reference: F-3
Area: Old Keene Mill Ctr
Handicap Access: No
Nonsmoking Area: Yes
Bar: Full/separate
Hours: Daily, 11am-11pm; Su brunch 10am-2pm

8430-B Old Keene Mill Rd
Springfield, VA (703) 644-4222

Chances are you'll either like this place or you'll hate it. Those who liked it called it an easy place to go to, a fun spot for everyone who thinks young. Others found food and service lacking. Requires "both a sense of adventure and patience" (*Washington Post*). Menu runs to steak, burgers, chicken, barbecue, and light fare with drinks. Deejay in lounge Tues.-Sat. (15 ratings/mixed)

Food | Service | Ambience | Value

69 68 61 60

The Rib $$
American

Reserv: Accepted
Dress: Informal
Pay: AE, MC, V
Parking: Yes
Metro: Twinbrook
Map Reference: C-4
Handicap Access: Yes
Nonsmoking Area: Yes
Bar: Full
Hours: Daily, 11am-10pm

128 Rollins Ave
Rockville, MD (301) 881-1970

Baby back ribs, big ribs, and lots of barbecue sauce are what this place is mainly about. You'll also find barbecued chicken, shrimp, Texas brisket, and other items on menu. Good value on early bird dinners (daily, 5-6:30pm), but otherwise prices are a bit high for the size of the platters. (14 ratings/very mixed)

70 67 66 68

Rick Walker's Scoreboard $
American

Reserv: Not accepted
Dress: Informal
Pay: AE, MC, V, Checks
Parking: Yes
Map Reference: D-2
Handicap Access: No
Nonsmoking Area: No
Bar: Full/separate
Hours: Daily, 11:30am-2am; Su brunch til 4pm

724 Pine St
Herndon, VA (703) 689-2880

Another sports-theme restaurant by a former Redskin. House specialties are baby back ribs, lots of beef—burgers, steaks, chili—and munchies during sports events. "Food fans have something to cheer about" (***Washington Post***). Lots of Redskin memorabilia and TV sets tuned to ESPN sports. Deejay nightly (except Sun.). Complaints concerned service and cramped seating. Also in Fairfax. (15 ratings/consistent)

76 76 75 77

Rips Country Inn $$
American

Reserv: Not accepted
Dress: Informal
Pay: AE, MC, V, DC, CB, Checks
Parking: Yes
Map Reference: D-6
Handicap Access: Yes
Nonsmoking Area: Yes
Bar: Full/separate
Hours: Su-Th 8am-10pm; F&Sa 8am-midnight

3809 N. Crain Hwy
Mitchellville, MD (301) 262-2963

Casual but nicer-than-usual roadside restaurant, motel, package store. Horse-racing motif; booths look like horse stalls, right to the names of horses overhead. Serves barbecued chicken and ribs, prime rib, and seafood. Comfortable and convenient; service is leisurely; may have to wait for table in nonsmoking section on weekends. Happy hour nightly. (12 ratings/very mixed)

Food | Service | Ambience | Value

63 60 66 65

Roma
Italian **$$**

Reserv: Accepted
Dress: Informal
Pay: AE, MC, V, DC, CB
Parking: Yes
Metro: Cleveland Park
Map Reference: I-11
Handicap Access: Yes
Nonsmoking Area: No
Bar: Full/separate
Hours: Daily, 11:30am-midnight

3419 Connecticut Ave, NW
Washington, DC (202) 363-6611

A focal point of neighborhood dining for almost 70 years. Dining in the grape arbor is particularly popular. Serves pizza and home-style Italian soups, pasta, and meat and seafood dishes. "Food is hearty and agreeable, if heavy-handed" (Phyllis Richman). Several raters thought setting and food quality have been deteriorating. Piano and violin music in evenings. Grape-stomping festival in fall. (12 ratings/consistent)

77 70 66 71

Roy's Place
American **$**

Reserv: Accepted
Dress: Informal
Pay: AE, MC, V, DC, CB
Parking: Yes
Map Reference: B-3
Handicap Access: No
Nonsmoking Area: Yes
Bar: Full
Hours: M-Th 11am-11pm; F&Sa 11am-midnight; Su noon-11pm

2 E. Diamond Ave
Gaithersburg, MD (301) 948-5548

Gourmet sandwiches—over 250—and something to wash them down have been the stock in trade at this jolly pub for 30 years. You might try the Song of Love, Pocohantas, or Dirty Tom Glenn. Reading descriptions on menu is a night's entertainment in itself. Local Fri. night hangout; lots of old photos on walls. Service can be slow. Roy's Place, Too is in Columbia, Md. (12 ratings/mixed)

78 72 78 75

Ruby Tuesday
American **$**

Reserv: Not accepted
Dress: Informal
Pay: AE, MC, V
Parking: Yes
Map Reference: E-2
Handicap Access: Yes
Nonsmoking Area: Yes
Bar: Full/separate
Hours: M-Th 11am-1am; F&Sa 11am-2am; Su 11am-11pm, brunch til 3pm

11724-U Fair Oaks Mall
Fairfax, VA (703) 352-3935

National chain of restaurants serving a variety of trendy food in an informal, comfortable setting. Soups, salad bar, burgers, Mexican favorites, and meat and seafood platters. Nice place for snack or lunch while shopping or for casual dinner. Fixed-price dinners on menu. Two other locations in area; see ratings for Gaithersburg, Md. (869-7740) location. (15 ratings/consistent)

Rusty Scupper $$
Seafood

Reserv: Suggested
Dress: Informal
Pay: AE, MC, V, DC, CB
Parking: Yes
Map Reference: D-3
Area: Tysons Office Ctr
Handicap Access: Yes
Nonsmoking Area: Yes
Bar: Full/separate
Hours: M-F 11:30am-2:30pm, 5:30-10:30pm (F 11pm); Sa 5-11pm; Su 4-9pm

8133 Leesburg Pike
Vienna, VA (703) 442-9590

Local representative of a national chain of restaurants-lounges serving seafood and trendy foods—Cajun dishes, pasta, grilled meats. Food and service variable. Happy hour 5-7pm nightly. Recently remodeled. (20 ratings/mixed)

Ruth's Chris Steak House $$$
Steak House

Reserv: Suggested
Dress: Informal
Pay: AE, MC, V, DC, CB
Parking: Valet
Metro: Dupont Circle
Map Reference: J-12
Handicap Access: Yes
Nonsmoking Area: Yes
Bar: Full/separate
Hours: Daily, 5-11pm

1801 Connecticut Ave, NW
Washington, DC (202) 797-0033

Some say the thick, juicy, U.S. Prime steaks served here are the best in town, and they could be right judging from the ratings. For non-beef fanciers, there are Maine lobster, Scandinavian salmon, and lamb and veal chops. Happy hour 5-7pm daily; sidewalk cafe. Other locations throughout country. (14 ratings/consistent)

Sakura Palace $$
Japanese

Reserv: Suggested
Dress: Informal
Pay: AE, MC, V
Parking: Yes
Map Reference: G-12
Handicap Access: No
Nonsmoking Area: Yes
Bar: Full
Hours: T-F 11:30am-2:30pm, 5:30-10pm; Sa&Su 5-10pm

7926 Georgia Ave
Silver Spring, MD (301) 587-7070

The first Japanese restaurant in area to serve sushi, even if it didn't have a sushi bar. Now it has a proper sushi bar; you can also have tempura, teriyaki, sukiyaki, and other dishes, plus your choice of booth, table, or tatami room. Raters liked the sushi and sashimi best. For Phyllis Richman, the beef teriyaki is "perhaps the best version" in town. Kimono-clad servers are polite, efficient, and overworked. (29 ratings/mixed)

Food	Service	Ambience	Value

Sandpiper — $$
Seafood

Reserv: Accepted
Dress: Informal
Pay: AE, MC, V
Parking: Yes
Map Reference: B-4
Area: Olney Shopping Center
Handicap Access: Yes
Nonsmoking Area: Yes
Bar: Full
Hours: M-Th 11am-9pm; F&Sa 11am-10pm; Su noon-9pm

3464 Laytonsville Rd
Olney, MD (301) 774-3777

Neighborhood seafood house with seaside decor that is carried out nicely. Menu is fairly standard—seafood bisque, broiled or fried fresh fish, crab Norfolk and imperial, stuffed shrimp. Food warrants more attention to detail for prices charged. One rater thought early bird special was of lower quality than regular menu. (13 ratings/mixed)

Sarinah Satay House — $$
Indonesian

Reserv: Suggested
Dress: Informal
Pay: AE, MC, V, DC, CB
Parking: No
Map Reference: J-11
Area: Georgetown
Handicap Access: No
Nonsmoking Area: No
Bar: Full
Hours: T-Sa noon-3pm, 6-10:30pm; Su 6-10:30pm

1338 Wisconsin Ave, NW
Washington, DC (202) 337-2955

Exotic food in an exotic setting. There are Indonesian soups, spring rolls, satays (grilled meat with peanut dipping sauce), curries, rice and vegetable dishes, and a 10-dish rijsttafel. A pleasant, reasonably priced dining experience. Some dishes are quite spicy. **Honors:** Richman's 50 Favorites. (12 ratings/consistent)

72 72 71 73

Schooner Bay Cafe — $$
Seafood

Reserv: Accepted
Dress: Informal
Pay: AE, MC, V, DC, CB
Parking: Yes
Map Reference: G-13
Area: Standard Plaza
Handicap Access: Yes
Nonsmoking Area: Yes
Bar: Full/separate
Hours: Daily, 11:30am-1am

1500 University Blvd, E
Langley Park, MD (301) 434-2233

Seafood in a quiet, relaxed, nautical setting. Regular menu—clams casino, Maryland crab soup, broiled shrimp and scallops, lobster tail, seafood platters—plus daily specials of dishes not on regular menu. Some nonseafood items. Knowledgeable service staff; won't rush you through your meal. Crowded on weekends; may have to wait for table. (13 ratings/consistent)

Food | Service | Ambience | Value

78 76 81 64

Serbian Crown
Russian

\$\$\$\$

Reserv: Required
Dress: Coat/tie req.
Pay: AE, MC, V, Checks
Parking: Yes
Map Reference: D-3
Area: Old Mill Sq Mkt
Handicap Access: Yes
Nonsmoking Area: No
Bar: Full
Hours: M-F 11:30am-2:30pm, 5:30-10:30pm; Sa 5:30-10:30pm

1141 Walker Rd
Great Falls, VA (703) 759-4150

Sit next to Hill staffers entertaining the KGB and dine on caviar, borscht, bliny, Russian salmon, rack of lamb, fresh game, and Serbian specialties. Gypsy music (Wed.-Fri.) and setting make for a pleasant, but expensive, evening. Opinions vary as to whether quality and size of portions warrant prices charged. Lunch prices, including fixed-price lunch, are better. (19 ratings/mixed)

78 78 80 75

700 Water Street Grill
American

\$\$

Reserv: Suggested
Dress: Coat/tie sugg.
Pay: AE, MC, V, DC, CB, Disc.
Parking: No
Metro: L'Enfant Plaza
Map Reference: K-12
Area: S.W. Waterfront
Handicap Access: Yes
Nonsmoking Area: Yes
Bar: Full/separate
Hours: M-F 11am-2:30pm, 5-10pm (F 11pm); Sa 5-11pm; Su 5-10pm

700 Water St, SW
Washington, DC (202) 554-7320

Several cuts above usual Water Street seafood houses. Seafood and grilled meats are given Cajun and other regional treatments. Only a few tables have waterfront view. "Excellent grilled meats . . . and honest-to-goodness fresh fish" (*Journal* papers); the food "eclipses its view" (*Washington Post*). Across from Arena Stage. Daily happy hour and pre-theater menu. **Honors:** *Journal* papers ★★★. (27 ratings/consistent)

74 73 65 71

Shooter McGee's
American

\$\$

Reserv: Accepted
Dress: Informal
Pay: AE, MC, V
Parking: Yes
Map Reference: M-10
Area: Landmark Professional Ctr
Handicap Access: No
Nonsmoking Area: Yes
Bar: Full/separate
Hours: M-Sa 11:30am-2am; Su 11am-1am

5239 Duke St
Alexandria, VA (703) 751-9266

Small, intimate restaurant serving saloon-type food. A place to stop for happy hour (Mon.-Thurs., 4-6pm), a dinner of burgers, steak, pasta, or stuffed pork chops, or a late evening drink and snack with friends. Dining on porch in good weather. Same owner as Eastport Raw Bar (see above), just down the road. (17 ratings/consistent)

Food	Service	Ambience	Value

74	58	52	82

Siddhartha
Indian
$

Reserv: Not accepted
Dress: Informal
Pay: Checks
Parking: No
Map Reference: G-12
Handicap Access: No
Nonsmoking Area: Yes
Bar: None
Hours: Daily, 11am-9pm

908 Thayer Ave
Silver Spring, MD (301) 585-0550

Vegetarian food is the entire menu here, not just a side dish or two. A bare-bones, serve-yourself dining room, complete with plastic utensils. The food is full flavored, not Americanized, and the prices are hard to beat. "You can anticipate some very good Indian cooking" (***Washington Post***)—samosas, curries, plain and stuffed dosas, and some tasty, nonalcoholic drinks. (13 ratings/mixed)

76	76	74	76

Sir Walter Raleigh
American
$$

Reserv: Not accepted
Dress: Informal
Pay: AE, MC, V, DC, CB, Disc., Checks
Parking: Yes
Map Reference: K-8
Handicap Access: No
Nonsmoking Area: Yes
Bar: Full/separate
Hours: M-F 11:15am-2pm, 5-9:30pm (F 10:30pm); Sa 5-10:30pm; Su 4-9pm

8120 Gatehouse Rd
Falls Church, VA (703) 560-6767

Area chain providing good, consistent food in a pleasant setting and for reasonable prices. The menu and the cooking are straightforward—burgers, barbecue, chicken, steak, and seafood. Salad-fruit bar is popular. Smaller portions of some dishes available. Early bird specials; happy hour. Eight other locations in area; for ratings for five other locations, see table at front of book. (34 ratings/consistent)

79	73	76	77

Squire Rockwell's
American
$$

Reserv: Not accepted
Dress: Informal
Pay: AE, MC, V, DC
Parking: Yes
Map Reference: E-3
Handicap Access: Yes
Nonsmoking Area: Yes
Bar: Full/separate
Hours: M-F 11:30am-2:30pm, 5-9:30pm (F 10:30pm); Sa 5-10:30pm; Su 5-9:30pm

8700 Little River Tpke
Annandale, VA (703) 560-3600

Energetic restaurant serving prime rib, steak, seafood, and baby back ribs. The soup-salad-fruit-bread bar is a big attraction. Most said food was good and prices reasonable. Lunch buffet weekdays. Friendly service staff tries but often can't cope with crowds. Piano music Tues.-Fri. during happy hour (4-7pm) and combo in lounge Fri. and Sat. (32 ratings/mixed)

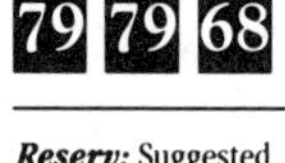

79 79 68 69

Sushi-Ko
Japanese — \$\$

Reserv: Suggested
Dress: Coat sugg.
Pay: AE, MC, V
Parking: No
Map Reference: J-11
Area: Upper Georgetown
Handicap Access: No
Nonsmoking Area: Yes
Bar: Full
Hours: T-F noon-2:30pm, 6-10:30pm; Sa 5-10:30pm; Su 5-10pm

2309 Wisconsin Ave, NW
Washington, DC (202) 333-4187

Washington's first sushi bar is still going strong despite the vigorous competition. Many raters thought the prices high in relation to the food, however. "The choice of the serious sushi crowd" (*Washingtonian*). A good time to visit is lunch. Bar service and non-sushi menu are very limited. **Honors:** *Washingtonian* 50 Best★★. (10 ratings/consistent)

73 66 69 65

Suzanne's
American — \$\$

Reserv: Accepted
Dress: Informal
Pay: MC, V, Checks
Parking: No
Metro: Dupont Circle
Map Reference: J-12
Handicap Access: No
Nonsmoking Area: No
Bar: Full/separate
Hours: M-Th 11:30am-11pm; F&Sa 11:30am-1am

1735 Connecticut Ave, NW
Washington, DC (202) 483-4633

Urban cafe above Suzanne's gourmet market and carryout. Serves cold plates, torta, pasta, seafood, lamb and veal chops. Good range of wines by the glass and excellent desserts. Cheerful, crowded, and noisy. Some said it was pricey, that food was missing something, and that it was best to go for dessert. **Honors:** Richman's 50 Favorites. (20 ratings/mixed)

71 70 67 68

Swiss Cafe
Swiss — \$\$

Reserv: Accepted
Dress: Informal
Pay: AE, MC, V, DC, CB
Parking: Yes
Map Reference: H-11
Area: Chevy Chase, DC
Handicap Access: Yes
Nonsmoking Area: No
Bar: Full/separate
Hours: Daily, 11:30am-midnight

5510 Connecticut Ave, NW
Washington, DC (202) 966-7600

Remember the fondues at the Swiss Chalet? They're available again—thick, creamy blends of cheese. Beef and chocolate fondues are prepared, too. If you're not a fondue fan, Wiener schnitzel, bratwurst, saltimbocca, and seafood are also available. Raters and critics liked the fondues, but thought menu was otherwise limited. Piano music and sing-along Tues.-Wed. and Fri.-Sat. (14 ratings/mixed)

Value

---

78 74 66 76

Sylvia's $$
Italian

14670 Southlawn Ln
Rockville, MD (301) 424-7373

Reserv: Accepted
Dress: Informal
Pay: AE, MC, V
Parking: Yes
Map Reference: C-4
Area: Industrial Park
Handicap Access: Yes
Nonsmoking Area: Yes
Bar: Full
Hours: M-F 11am-11pm; Sa 4-11pm; Su 4-10pm

Traditional Italian restaurant in the midst of an industrial park. Serves red and white pizzas and a wide selection of home-cooked food, including seafood. To some raters, the food isn't as good as it was before the expansion. "You can still eat well here, but . . . order carefully . . . simplicity is best" (***Washington Post***). (18 ratings/consistent)

73 67 59 74

Szechuan $$
Chinese

615 I St, NW
Washington, DC (202) 393-0130

Reserv: Accepted
Dress: Informal
Pay: AE, MC, V
Parking: No
Metro: Gallery Place
Map Reference: J-12
Area: Chinatown
Handicap Access: No
Nonsmoking Area: No
Bar: Full/separate
Hours: M-Th 11am-11pm; F&Sa 11am-midnight; Su 11am-10pm; Sa&Su brunch til 2:30pm

"Unchallenged as area's best source of Szechuan-Hunan cuisine" says the ***Washingtonian***, but raters say food is too variable to call it that. Service, prices, and ambience also criticized by some. Menu is enormous. Phyllis Richman said it's "old-fashioned, good, reliable," but "there are flaws." **Honors:** Richman's Best of Best, ***Washingtonian*** 50 Best★★★★ and Cheap Eats. (33 ratings/very mixed)

81 76 66 82

Szechuan Gallery $
Chinese

617 H St, NW
Washington, DC (202) 898-1180

Reserv: Accepted
Dress: Informal
Pay: AE, MC, V, DC, CB
Parking: No
Metro: Gallery Place
Map Reference: J-12
Area: Chinatown
Handicap Access: No
Nonsmoking Area: No
Bar: Full
Hours: Su-Th 11am-3am; F&Sa 11am-4am

The Szechuan and Hunan dishes are good here, and the prices even better. ***Washingtonian*** recommended the menu of Taiwanese dishes, which includes cold pork tongue, salty spareribs, fragrant crab. Ten-course special dinner for four or more. **Honors:** ***Washingtonian*** 50 Best★ and Cheap Eats. (13 ratings/consistent)

Food	Service	Ambience	Value

79	73	76	74

T.G.I. Friday's
American

$

Reserv: Not accepted
Dress: Informal
Pay: AE, MC, V, DC, CB
Parking: Yes (eves)
Map Reference: D-3
Area: Tycon Courthouse Bldg
Handicap Access: Yes
Nonsmoking Area: Yes
Bar: Full/separate
Hours: Daily, 11:30am-1am; Sa&Su brunch til 3pm

2070 Chain Bridge Rd
Tysons Corner, VA (703) 556-6173

Fun place for adults and children. The 12-page menu of traditional and trendy dishes includes everything from snacks to a full dinner and dessert. Generous portions; somewhat slow but helpful service; lots of commotion and noise. Part of national chain; also in Greenbelt, Md., and Alexandria, Va. "A formula restaurant [others] . . . can aspire to" (*Journal* papers). Happy hour. (15 ratings/consistent)

78	66	70	70

Tabard Inn
New American

$$$

Reserv: Suggested
Dress: Informal
Pay: MC, V, Checks
Parking: No
Metro: Dupont Circle
Map Reference: J-12
Handicap Access: Ltd.
Nonsmoking Area: No
Bar: Full/separate
Hours: M-F 11:30am-2:45pm, 6-10:30pm (Th&F 11pm); Sa&Su 11am-2:45pm, 6-10pm (Sa 11pm)

1739 N St, NW
Washington, DC (202) 785-1277

Charming, old urban inn. Interesting menu of New American dishes. Chef "relies on combination of flavors rather than on techniques" (Phyllis Richman). Dining room can be noisy and difficult. Courtyard is a delightful place to play hooky from the office or spend a relaxed evening. Service can be slow. **Honors:** Richman's 50 Favorites. (19 ratings/mixed)

Tachibana
Japanese

$$

Reserv: Accepted
Dress: Informal
Pay: AE, MC, V
Parking: Yes
Map Reference: J-10
Area: Cherrydale
Handicap Access: Ltd.
Nonsmoking Area: Yes
Bar: Full
Hours: M-F 11:30am-2pm, 5-10pm (F 10:30pm); Sa 5-10:30pm

4050 Lee Hwy
Arlington, VA (703) 528-1122

An exceptionally good, reasonably priced restaurant in an easy-to-miss location—just up the left fork of old and new Lee Highways coming from Rosslyn. Excellent sushi plus "many other dishes to cheer about" (*Washingtonian*). "Consistently some of the best Japanese food in area" (*Journal* papers). **Honors:** *Journal* papers★★★, *Washingtonian* Cheap Eats. (23 ratings/consistent)

72 67 66 68

Tandoor $$
Indian

Reserv: Accepted
Dress: Informal
Pay: AE, MC, V, Checks
Parking: No
Map Reference: J-11
Area: Georgetown
Handicap Access: Ltd.
Nonsmoking Area: Yes
Bar: Full
Hours: M-Su 11:30am-2:30pm, 5:30-11pm

3316 M St, NW
Washington, DC (202) 333-3376

Some thought the tandoori-baked meat and seafood and the northern Indian curries, biryanis, and vegetarian dishes served here were fine; others thought food was overcooked, underseasoned, or just mediocre. According to Phyllis Richman, "chicken dishes are best." Three other locations in area. Tandoor Express and Katmandu (see above) also in family. **Honors:** *Washingtonian* 50 Best★. (12 ratings/very mixed)

81 78 81 79

Taverna Cretekou $$
Greek

Reserv: Suggested
Dress: Informal
Pay: AE, MC, V, DC, CB
Parking: No
Map Reference: N-11
Area: Old Town
Handicap Access: Ltd.
Nonsmoking Area: Yes
Bar: Full
Hours: T-F 11:30am-2:30pm, 5-10:30pm; Sa noon-11pm; Su brunch 11am-3pm, dinner 4-11pm

818 King St
Alexandria, VA (703) 548-8688

The festive atmosphere, dining in the grape arbor, Greek music, and waiters that break into song or dance—all account as much for Taverna's popularity as the traditional Greek menu. Food is nicely presented and tasty, but variable. Crowded and noisy. "Food is . . . all decent stuff with a few highlights" (Phyllis Richman). **Honors:** Richman's 50 Favorites. (35 ratings/consistent)

Terrazza $$$
Italian

Reserv: Suggested
Dress: Coat req.
Pay: AE, MC, V, DC, CB
Parking: Valet
Map Reference: N-11
Area: Old Town
Handicap Access: Yes
Nonsmoking Area: Yes
Bar: Full/separate
Hours: M-F 11:30am-3pm, 5:30-11pm; Sa&Su 5:30-11pm

710 King St
Alexandria, VA (703) 683-6900

Northern Italian food for sophisticated tastes, but extremely slow, sometimes inept service can turn even the most remarkable food sour. Pasta is a strong point. "Has an inspired touch in both making and saucing pastas" (*Washingtonian*). Often crowded and somewhat noisy. Same ownership as Tiberio (see below) and Traggara. **Honors:** AAA◆◆◆, Mobil★★★. (21 ratings/mixed)

Food	Service	Ambience	Value

84	75	63	92

Thai Derm

Thai **$**

Reserv: Sugg. weekends
Dress: Informal
Pay: MC, V, DC, Checks
Parking: No
Metro: Silver Spring
Map Reference: G-12
Handicap Access: Ltd.
Nonsmoking Area: No
Bar: Beer/wine
Hours: M-F 11am-3pm, 5-9:30pm (F 10:30pm); Sa noon-3pm, 5-10:30pm

939 Bonifant St
Silver Spring, MD (301) 589-5341

Serves over 30 combinations of noodles with meat, fish, and vegetable accompaniments, many with or without soup. Then there are the vegetarian dishes and the chef's specials. Food is spicy, but kitchen will prepare order to your taste. Happy, family-run place, but family has trouble keeping up with customers at times. "Excels at what it is—a Thai noodle shop" (***Washingtonian***). (12 ratings/very consistent)

81	68	63	81

Thai House

Thai **$**

Reserv: Not accepted
Dress: Informal
Pay: AE, MC, V, DC, CB
Parking: Yes
Metro: Court House
Map Reference: K-10
Area: Colonial Village Shopping Center
Handicap Access: No
Nonsmoking Area: Yes
Bar: Full
Hours: Daily, 11am-10:30pm

1731 Wilson Blvd
Arlington, VA (703) 527-5772

Small, plain, inexpensive storefront restaurant. Noodle dishes dominate the menu, but there are satays, curries, and seafood dishes, too. Raters liked the crispy whole fish and the chocolate desserts in particular. One of the "better Thai restaurants we came across" (*Journal* papers). The service left one rater with a bitter aftertaste, however. (12 ratings/mixed)

85	84	85	83

Thai Kingdom

Thai **$$**

Reserv: Accepted
Dress: Informal
Pay: AE, MC, V
Parking: Yes (eves)
Metro: Farragut North/West
Map Reference: J-12
Area: Downtown
Handicap Access: Ltd.
Nonsmoking Area: No
Bar: Full/separate
Hours: M-F 11:30am-11pm; Sa noon-11pm

2021 K St, NW
Washington, DC (202) 835-1700

Offers more in the way of decor, fewer noodle dishes, and a menu with more breadth than Thai restaurants above. Many of the dishes and sauces are very spicy, so don't be afraid to ask helpful, well-informed staff for guidance. "The red curry will have you crying in your Singha beer" (***Washington Business Journal***). **Honors:** ***Washingtonian*** Cheap Eats. (15 ratings/consistent)

Food | Service | Ambience | Value

80 75 67 82

Thai Place $
Thai

Reserv: Accepted
Dress: Informal
Pay: AE, MC, V
Parking: Yes (eves)
Metro: Bethesda
Map Reference: G-10
Area: Woodmont Triangle
Handicap Access: No
Nonsmoking Area: Yes
Bar: Full
Hours: M-F 11am-3:30pm, 5-10:30pm; Sa 11am-10:30pm; Su 11am-10pm

4828 Cordell Ave
Bethesda, MD (301) 951-0535

Dining at this rather exotic, very authentic restaurant can be addictive. Raters liked the chicken with basil and green chilies, fish with green chilies, and the soups. Widely spaced tables and slow service make for long conversations. *Washington Post* called it a very good place "to learn about basic Thai sauces." Owned by Thai Derm (see above). (37 ratings/consistent)

75 67 59 78

Thai Room $
Thai

Reserv: Suggested
Dress: Informal
Pay: AE, MC, V, DC, CB
Parking: Yes
Metro: Van Ness
Map Reference: I-11
Handicap Access: Yes
Nonsmoking Area: No
Bar: Full
Hours: Su-M 11:30am-10pm; T-Sa 11:30am-10:30pm

5037 Connecticut Ave, NW
Washington, DC (202) 244-5933

Classic renditions of Thai food; some dishes very spicy. Food is good, prices even better. Atmosphere is simple. More than one chef at an area Thai restaurant did a stint here first. *Washingtonian* warns that shrimp with chili and garlic will produce "shortness of breath and great pain." (30 ratings/consistent)

85 75 65 81

Thai Taste $$
Thai

Reserv: Suggested
Dress: Informal
Pay: AE, MC, V, DC
Parking: No
Metro: Woodley Park
Map Reference: I-11
Handicap Access: Ltd.
Nonsmoking Area: No
Bar: Full
Hours: M-Th 11:30am-10:30pm; F&Sa 11:30am-11pm; Su 5-10:30pm

2606 Connecticut Ave, NW
Washington, DC (202) 387-8876

A blending of Thai and Chinese cooking helps to cool some of the fire in some of the dishes served here. Many tempting choices; deciding will be difficult. "May well be the most popular . . . on local Thai circuit" (*Washingtonian*); "delicate and intricate Thai cooking" (Phyllis Richman). Also in Georgetown and Rockville, Md. **Honors:** *Washingtonian* 50 Best★ and Cheap Eats. (26 ratings/consistent)

Food | Service | Ambience | Value

Tia Queta

76 73 69 76

Mexican **$$**

8009 Norfolk Ave
Bethesda, MD (301) 654-4443

Reserv: Accepted
Dress: Informal
Pay: AE, MC, V
Parking: Yes (after 6pm)
Metro: Bethesda
Map Reference: G-10
Area: Woodmont Triangle
Handicap Access: Ltd.
Nonsmoking Area: Yes
Bar: Full
Hours: M-Th 10am-10pm; F&Sa 10am-11pm; Su 4-10pm

Warm, friendly neighborhood spot for homemade Mexican food that exceeds repertoire of fast-food places. "A reminder of how good Mexican food can be," said *Washington Post*. Raters liked red snapper in Veracruz sauce, ceviche, guacamole, shrimp dishes, and margaritas. Sauces seem to be a strong point. Staff is accommodating, but service slows when busy. Long wait for table at peak times without reservations. (41 ratings/mixed)

Tiberio

85 80 74 60

Italian **$$$$**

1915 K St, NW
Washington, DC (202) 452-1915

Reserv: Suggested
Dress: Coat/tie req.
Pay: AE, MC, V, DC, CB
Parking: Valet
Metro: Farragut North/West
Map Reference: J-12
Area: Downtown
Handicap Access: Yes
Nonsmoking Area: No
Bar: Full/separate
Hours: M-F 11:45am-2:30pm, 6-11pm; Sa 5:30-11pm

"Classic of an expense-account meal . . . the excellence of expensive simplicity," said Phyllis Richman. Overrated and overpriced said most raters. Varied menu of pasta, veal, lamb chops, seafood, and more. For the prices, tables are very close. Helps if owner knows you. **Honors:** AAA◆◆◆, Mobil★★★, *Travel-Holiday* Award. (10 ratings/consistent)

Tivoli

82 81 83 78

Italian **$$$**

1700 N. Moore St
Rosslyn, VA (703) 524-8900

Reserv: Suggested
Dress: Coat/tie sugg.
Pay: AE, MC, V, DC, CB
Parking: Yes (eves)
Metro: Rosslyn
Map Reference: K-11
Area: Metro Bldg
Handicap Access: Yes
Nonsmoking Area: Yes
Bar: Full/separate
Hours: M-F 11:30am-2:30pm, 5:30-10pm; Sa 5:30-10pm

Elegant third-floor dining room with views of Rosslyn "cityscape." Cuisine is self-styled Italian "evolutionaire." Some found food variable, especially dinner. Pre-theater dinners (5:30-6:30pm) are an excellent value. Piano music accompanies dinner nightly. Also has an informal cafe/lounge, snack area, and a gourmet deli on lower levels. (52 ratings/mixed)

Food | Service | Ambience | Value

Tom Sarris' Orleans House — $$
American

Reserv: Not accepted
Dress: Informal
Pay: AE, MC, V, DC, CB, Checks
Parking: Yes
Metro: Rosslyn
Map Reference: K-11
Handicap Access: No
Nonsmoking Area: Yes
Bar: Full/separate
Hours: M-F 11am-11pm; Sa&Su 4-11pm

1213 Wilson Blvd
Rosslyn, VA (703) 524-2929

There was a Tom Sarris restaurant in Rosslyn long before there were any high-rises. This one has a Louisiana setting, but the food is all-American beef and seafood. The generous portions, rock bottom prices, and large salad bar both explain and help compensate for the noise, cramped seating, and long line at the door. (64 ratings/very mixed)

Tom Weston's — $$
American

Reserv: Not accepted
Dress: Informal
Pay: AE, MC, V, Checks
Parking: Yes
Map Reference: E-3
Area: K Mart Shopping Center
Handicap Access: No
Nonsmoking Area: Yes
Bar: Full/separate
Hours: M-F 11am-midnight (F 1am); Sa&Su 9am-1am, brunch til 3pm

4221 John Marr Dr
Annandale, VA (703) 750-1413

Casual neighborhood restaurant and tavern. Large menu features beef, seafood, surf 'n' turf platters, and salad bar. Dining room has relaxed, family atmosphere; good for children. Tavern has a large bar and TVs. Happy hour Mon.-Fri. 3-6pm. (21 ratings/mixed)

Tony Cheng's — $$
Mongolian

Reserv: Required
Dress: Informal
Pay: AE, MC, V
Parking: No
Metro: Gallery Place
Map Reference: J-12
Area: Chinatown
Handicap Access: Ltd.
Nonsmoking Area: No
Bar: Full
Hours: Su-Th 11am-11pm; F&Sa 11am-midnight

619 H St, NW
Washington, DC (202) 842-8669

Only two choices here: an all-you-can-eat Mongolian barbecue (you select ingredients and sauces and chef stir fries them on grill) and the Mongolian hot pot (you select ingredients and cook them at table in boiling broth). Can be a fun experience for a group of adventurous diners or like amateur night at a Japanese steak house. **Honors:** ***Washingtonian*** 50 Best★★ and Cheap Eats. (29 ratings/very mixed)

Food	Service	Ambience	Value
76	82	74	78

Tony Lin's Kitchen $

Chinese

Reserv: Suggested
Dress: Informal
Pay: AE, MC, V, Checks
Parking: Yes
Metro: White Flint
Map Reference: C-4
Handicap Access: No
Nonsmoking Area: Yes
Bar: Full
Hours: Daily, 11am-10pm; Sa&Su brunch 11am-3pm

12081-A Rockville Pike
Rockville, MD (301) 468-5858

Szechuan restaurant with an eye to healthful eating—doesn't use MSG, serves brown rice, and prepares a number of vegetarian dishes. Generous portions and reasonable prices make it a good value, but not all dishes are equally good. Dim sum brunch Sat. and Sun. Service is efficient. Piano music Sat. night. (20 ratings/very mixed)

Food	Service	Ambience	Value
78	76	67	83

Tortilla Factory $

Mexican

Reserv: Not accepted
Dress: Informal
Pay: AE, MC, V, Checks
Parking: Yes
Map Reference: D-2
Area: Pines Shopping Center
Handicap Access: Yes
Nonsmoking Area: Yes
Bar: Full
Hours: M 11:30am-9pm; T-Sa 11:30am-10pm (F&Sa 10:30pm); Su 4-9pm

648 Elden St
Herndon, VA (703) 471-1156

A long drive from D.C., but worth a side trip, perhaps from Dulles Airport. Generous portions of freshly made Mexican food at reasonable prices: quesadilla, chorizo and egg, machaca, tacos, chimichangas, Texas chili, and their original California enchilada. Make their own tortillas. Busy, friendly place. Long lines on Fri. and Sat. nights. (23 ratings/consistent)

Food	Service	Ambience	Value
80	78	76	75

Tout Va Bien $$

French

Reserv: Suggested
Dress: Informal
Pay: AE, MC, V
Parking: No
Map Reference: J-11
Area: Georgetown
Handicap Access: No
Nonsmoking Area: No
Bar: Full
Hours: M-Th 11:30am-2:30pm, 5:30-11pm; F&Sa 11:30am-3pm, 5:30-11:30pm; Su 5:30-10pm

1063 31st St, NW
Washington, DC (202) 965-1212

The sun-filled rooms are delightful at lunch, and as the light fades this quiet bistro takes on a romantic air. Imaginative French menu; The daily specials are a high point. Be sure to save room for one of their wonderful fruit tarts. (24 ratings/consistent)

Food | Service | Ambience | Value

80 73 73 77

Trattu
Italian **$$**

Reserv: Suggested
Dress: Informal
Pay: AE, MC, V
Parking: No
Metro: Dupont Circle
Map Reference: J-12
Handicap Access: No
Nonsmoking Area: No
Bar: Full
Hours: M-F 11:30am-2:30pm, 5:30-11pm; Sa 5:30-11pm

1823 Jefferson Pl, NW
Washington, DC (202) 466-4570

Small, northern Italian dining room serving primarily pasta, chicken, and veal dishes. English basement location is cramped and noisy; service is often erratic, occasionally rude. Raters' reactions to food didn't register nearly as high on enthusiasm scale as did those of ***Washington Post*** reviewer. (16 ratings/consistent)

78 66 61 75

Tung Bor
Chinese **$$**

Reserv: Not accepted
Dress: Informal
Pay: V, DC
Parking: Yes
Map Reference: C-4
Handicap Access: No
Nonsmoking Area: Yes
Bar: Full/separate
Hours: M-F 11:30am-9:30pm (F 10:30pm); Sa 11am-10:30pm; Su 11am-9:30pm

Wheaton Plaza
Wheaton, MD (301) 933-3687

Go for the dim sum—order from the menu on weekdays or from rolling carts on weekends. Don't expect much help from service staff, though. Language problems, perhaps unfriendliness, will interfere. Rest of menu is standard Cantonese-Szechuan fare. Noisy and crowded on weekends. "The pan-fried turnovers . . . are sensational" (Phyllis Richman). **Honors:** Richman's Best of Best (for dim sum). (32 ratings/mixed)

80 73 84 71

219
French Creole **$$$**

Reserv: Suggested
Dress: Coat/tie sugg.
Pay: AE, MC, V, Disc.
Parking: No
Map Reference: N-12
Area: Old Town
Handicap Access: No
Nonsmoking Area: Yes
Bar: Full/separate
Hours: M-Th 11:30am-10:30pm; F&Sa 11:30am-11pm; Su brunch 11am-4pm, dinner 5-10:30pm

219 King St
Alexandria, VA (703) 549-1141

Lots of New Orleans-style seafood, including the blackened fish of the day, barbecued shrimp, and crawfish gumbo. Received ***Wine Spectator's*** 1987 Award of Excellence for wine list. "Remains a prime Washington area source of Creole and Cajun dishes" (***Washington Times***). Some raters thought service didn't match prices and that menu was limited. Jazz band nightly in Bayou Room. **Honors:** AAA◆◆◆, Mobil★★★. (26 ratings/mixed)

Food	Service	Ambience	Value

74	70	72	72

2 Quail $$
New American

Reserv: Suggested
Dress: Informal
Pay: AE, MC, V, DC
Parking: No
Metro: Union Station
Map Reference: J-13
Area: Capitol Hill
Handicap Access: No
Nonsmoking Area: No
Bar: Full
Hours: M-F 11:30am-2:30pm, 5:30-10:30pm; Sa 5:30-11:30pm; Su brunch 10:30-3:30pm, dinner 5:30-10:30pm

320 Massachusetts Ave, NE
Washington, DC (202) 543-8030

Trying to be a cozy little place and succeeding fairly well. Popular entrees are the swordfish, chicken stuffed with cornbread and pecans, and the tortellini. Tables are very close together in these townhouse dining rooms, and service can be slow. Early bird specials. "Cozy Victorian atmosphere and imaginative cooking" (*Washington Times*). (15 ratings/very consistent)

68	70	75	66

Union Street Public House $$
American

Reserv: Not accepted
Dress: Informal
Pay: AE, MC, V
Parking: No
Map Reference: N-12
Area: Old Town
Handicap Access: No
Nonsmoking Area: Yes
Bar: Full/separate
Hours: M-Sa 11:30am-10:30pm; Su 11am-10:30pm, brunch til 3pm

121 S. Union St
Alexandria, VA (703) 548-1785

The critics like this noisy pub and its American pub food. Raters say terrific selection of beers, great atmosphere, but only okay food. Active bar scene; families will be comfortable in dining room—if they can stand the noise. Serves grilled meats and seafood, soups and stews, interesting salads, and sandwiches. *Washington Times* liked grilled calf's liver and "nifty pork fillet." **Honors:** Richman's 50 Favorites. (33 ratings/mixed)

76	69	79	75

Vagabond $$
Central European

Reserv: Suggested
Dress: Informal
Pay: AE, MC, V, DC, CB
Parking: Yes
Metro: Bethesda
Map Reference: G-10
Area: Air Rights Bldg
Handicap Access: No
Nonsmoking Area: Yes
Bar: Full/separate
Hours: M-F 11:30am-2:30pm, 5:30-10pm (F 10:30pm); Sa 6-10:30pm

7315 Wisconsin Ave
Bethesda, MD (301) 654-2575

With four or more you can share a five-course Romanian feast, complete with strolling gypsy violinists and a fortune teller (Fri.-Sat.). Menu includes lobster or shrimp Dracula, chicken paprikash, Wiener schnitzel, and veal coated with cascaval cheese. Phyllis Richman found only one "truly disappointing dish [ceroba de peste]." Happy hour (4-7pm) and dinner specials (Mon.-Thurs., 5:30-7pm). (16 ratings/mixed)

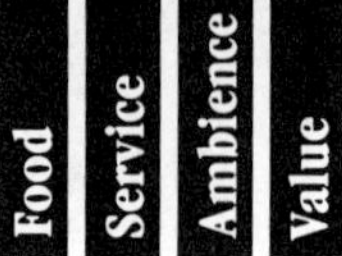

72 83

Venice
Italian

$$

Reserv: Required
Dress: Informal
Pay: AE, MC, V, DC, CB, Disc.
Parking: No
Map Reference: C-5
Handicap Access: Ltd.
Nonsmoking Area: Yes
Bar: Full/separate
Hours: Daily, 11am-11pm

2311 Price Ave
Wheaton, MD (301) 933-7070

Classic family-operated neighborhood Italian restaurant. Small, cozy, and often crowded. Northern Italian-Continental menu features pasta, veal, and prime rib. Some raters found sauces heavy and greasy. Gondola-shaped salad bar, prime rib dinner special, and early bird specials (4-6pm) provide good quality and value. (35 ratings/mixed)

Vietnam Georgetown
Vietnamese

Reserv: Not accepted
Dress: Informal
Pay: Cash only
Parking: No
Map Reference: J-11
Area: Georgetown
Handicap Access: Ltd.
Nonsmoking Area: No
Bar: Full
Hours: M-F 11am-11pm (F midnight); Sa noon-midnight; Su noon-11pm

2934 M St, NW
Washington, DC (202) 337-4536

The place where many area diners first tasted crispy deep-fried spring rolls, shrimp wrapped around a core of sugarcane, cinnamon beef, and lemongrass flavoring. Food is still quite good and reasonably priced. Has pleasant outdoor patio. Complaints focus on ambience—closeness of tables, drafts from windows, cigar butts in ashtrays, and the need to control pests. (15 ratings/consistent)

81 

61

Vincenzo
Seafood

$$$

Reserv: Suggested
Dress: Informal
Pay: AE, MC, V, DC, CB
Parking: No
Metro: Dupont Circle
Map Reference: J-12
Handicap Access: No
Nonsmoking Area: No
Bar: Full
Hours: M-F noon-2pm, 6-10pm; Sa 6-10pm

1606 20th St, NW
Washington, DC (202) 667-0047

Superb Italian seafood, marvelous pasta, but it can still disappoint. Menu is small, prices are high, and it can be crowded and noisy. Lovely side patio for dining. Service was described as indifferent, unfriendly, rude, and showing clear preference for known customers. **Honors:** Richman's Best of Best and 50 Favorites, *Washingtonian* 50 Best★★★. (36 ratings/very mixed)

Food	Service	Ambience	Value

81 77 70 80

Vinnie's

American **$$$**

Reserv: Accepted weekdays
Dress: Informal
Pay: AE, MC, V, DC, CB, Disc.
Parking: Yes
Map Reference: F-3
Area: Kings Park Shop Ctr
Handicap Access: Yes
Nonsmoking Area: Yes
Bar: Full/separate
Hours: M-F 11am-11pm (F midnight); Sa 4-midnight; Su 4-10pm

8944 Burke Lake Rd
Springfield, VA (703) 978-1212

Upscale family restaurant-pub. Adult, small dinners available for those who aren't up to the overly generous portions of steak, veal, and seafood. Salad is meal-size. Cocktail menu includes draft beers, wine by glass, and long list of exotic drinks. Happy hour; daily lunch and dinner specials. May have to wait for table. (32 ratings/mixed)

65 63 69 58

Wayfarers

Continental **$$$**

Reserv: Suggested
Dress: Informal
Pay: MC, V, DC, CB, Checks
Parking: No
Map Reference: N-12
Area: Old Town
Handicap Access: Ltd.
Nonsmoking Area: Yes
Bar: Full/separate
Hours: M-F 11:45am-2:30pm, 6-10pm (F 10:30pm); Sa 6-10:30pm

110 S. Pitt St
Alexandria, VA (703) 836-2749

Cozy English pub in nineteenth century townhouse. The small front rooms retain their Old World charm, but the addition in back has spoiled original atmosphere and decreased value for some. Serves English meat pies, prime rib, mixed grill, seafood, and English beer and ales, some on tap. Piano music Fri. and Sat. Phyllis Richman suggests you "head straight" for the savory meat pies. (13 ratings/very mixed)

72 77 69 80

Wellington's

American **$$**

Reserv: Suggested
Dress: Informal
Pay: AE, MC, V, DC, CB
Parking: Yes
Metro: Silver Spring
Map Reference: G-12
Area: Holiday Inn
Handicap Access: Yes
Nonsmoking Area: Yes
Bar: Full/separate
Hours: Daily, 6am-1am; Su brunch 11am-3pm

8777 Georgia Ave
Silver Spring, MD (301) 587-4600

The salad bars keep getting bigger—over 75 selections of fruit, vegetables, pasta, and homemade bread on this excellent example. If that's not enough, they have prime rib, steak, and seafood, which were rated only average to good. Daily dinner specials; happy hour; deejay and dancing in lounge Tues.-Sat. "One of Washington's best kept culinary secrets," according to *Washington Times.* (17 ratings/mixed)

Food | Service | Ambience | Value

78 74 79 73

West End Cafe
New American $$

Reserv: Suggested
Dress: Coat/tie sugg.
Pay: AE, MC, V, DC
Parking: Valet
Metro: Foggy Bottom
Map Reference: J-11
Area: West End
Handicap Access: Yes
Nonsmoking Area: Yes
Bar: Full/separate
Hours: M-Su 7-10am, 11:30am-2:30pm, 6-11:30pm (Sa&Su 12:30am); Su brunch 11am-3pm

One Washington Circle (NW) Hotel
Washington, DC (202) 293-5390

Sophisticated, up-to-date menu; dishes are beautifully presented and often well executed. Dine in the piano room (music Tues.-Sat. from 8pm) or the quiet, charming garden room. "Fresh local ingredients combined in exciting ways" (*Washington Times*). **Honors:** Richman's Best of Best. (32 ratings/consistent)

79 85 94 64

Willard Room
New American $$$$

Reserv: Required
Dress: Coat/tie req.
Pay: AE, MC, V, DC, CB
Parking: Valet
Metro: Metro Center
Map Reference: J-12
Area: Downtown
Handicap Access: Yes
Nonsmoking Area: No
Bar: Full
Hours: M-F 7:30-10am, 11:30am-2pm, 6:30-10pm; Sa&Su 8-10am, noon-2pm, 6:30-10pm

1401 Penn. Ave, NW, Willard Hotel
Washington, DC (202) 637-7440

The kitchen has its work cut out for it trying to compete with the opulence of the dining room, and most raters found it wanting. *Washingtonian* found that "when the kitchen was on target, it was very good," and Phyllis Richman said that although it "can dazzle, performance can be splotchy." Piano music to accompany dinner. **Honors:** *Travel-Holiday* selection. (26 ratings/very mixed)

85 80 85 66

Windows
New American $$$$

Reserv: Suggested
Dress: Coat/tie sugg.
Pay: AE, MC, V, DC, CB
Parking: Yes (eves)
Metro: Rosslyn
Map Reference: K-11
Area: USA Today Bldg
Handicap Access: Yes
Nonsmoking Area: Yes
Bar: Full/separate
Hours: M-F 11:30am-2:30pm, 5:30-10:30pm; Sa 6-11:30pm

1000 Wilson Blvd
Rosslyn, VA (703) 527-4430

New American cuisine from one of area's earliest proponents. "[Chef] Dinardo's genius makes trendiness beside the point" (*Frommer's*). Worth the price or overpriced for small portions—that's the only question. View is spectacular at night, but less so in daylight. Light fare in lounge area; happy hour (4-7:30pm). **Honors:** AAA◆◆◆◆, Mobil★★★, Richman's Best of Best and 50 Favorites, *Travel-Holiday* Award. (38 ratings/consistent)

Food | Service | Ambience | Value

70 64 67 68

Wolensky's $$

American

Reserv: Required at lunch
Dress: Informal
Pay: AE, MC, V
Parking: Yes (after 6pm)
Metro: Foggy Bottom
Map Reference: J-11
Handicap Access: Yes
Nonsmoking Area: Yes
Bar: Full/separate
Hours: M 11:30am-11pm; T-Sa 11:30am-midnight; Su 11:30am-11pm, brunch til 3pm

2000 Pennsylvania Ave, NW
Washington, DC (202) 463-0050

Bills itself as the "grazing place," food for every mood—lunch, after work snack, dinner, late night munching. Except for fantastic burgers, the varied contemporary menu, which includes sushi, tends to be spotty and unexciting. Good cocktails and draft beer. Large college crowd. Service described as indifferent, unprofessional, and affirmatively unpleasant. Jazz group Mon. eves. (27 ratings/consistent)

78 67 67 78

Woo Lae Oak $$

Korean

Reserv: Required
Dress: Informal
Pay: AE, MC, V, DC, CB, Disc.
Parking: Yes
Metro: Pentagon City
Map Reference: K-11
Handicap Access: No
Nonsmoking Area: Yes
Bar: Full
Hours: Daily, 11:30am-11pm

1500 S. Joyce St
Arlington, VA (703) 521-3706

A Korean extravaganza—if you can see through the haze from all the table-top gas grills. Large selection of grill-your-own meat dishes, plus the full array of Korean soups, entrees, and side dishes. *Washingtonian* liked the "jungsk singsun, a small, perfectly broiled fish." Large Korean clientele. Service tends to be rushed. **Honors:** *Washingtonian* Cheap Eats. (15 ratings/consistent)

80 74 73 78

Wu's Garden $$

Chinese

Reserv: Accepted
Dress: Informal
Pay: AE, MC, V, Checks
Parking: Yes
Map Reference: D-3
Area: Village Green Shopping Center
Handicap Access: Yes
Nonsmoking Area: Yes
Bar: Full
Hours: M-F 11am-10pm; Sa 11am-11pm; Su noon-10pm

418 Maple Ave, E
Vienna, VA (703) 281-4410

Better-than-average shopping center Chinese. Not fancy, but comfortable and convenient; family atmosphere. Mandarin and Peking dishes are featured, but Szechuan and Hunan cooking is also represented. Peking duck (whole or half) is carved at tableside. Lobster and garlic sauce was recommended. Fixed-price dinners available. (19 ratings/mixed)

Food | Service | Ambience | Value

73 71 68 72

Yenching Palace $$
Chinese

Reserv: Accepted
Dress: Informal
Pay: AE, MC, V, DC, CB
Parking: Yes
Metro: Cleveland Park
Map Reference: I-11
Handicap Access: Yes
Nonsmoking Area: No
Bar: Full
Hours: Su-Th 11:30am-11:30pm; F&Sa 11:30am-12:30am; Su brunch noon-2:30pm

3524 Connecticut Ave, NW
Washington, DC (202) 362-8200

After 35 years even a palace kitchen can get tired. The atmosphere is relaxed and informal, the service prompt, but food is disappointing or not much above routine. Still knows how to prepare good dim sum, though. "Not much glory remains in kitchen . . . except for eccentric moments" (Phyllis Richman). (15 ratings/mixed)

83 73 68 84

Zio's $
Italian

Reserv: Accepted
Dress: Informal
Pay: AE, MC, V, DC, CB, Checks
Parking: Yes
Map Reference: B-3
Area: Shady Grove
Handicap Access: Yes
Nonsmoking Area: Yes
Bar: Beer/wine
Hours: M-F 11am-10pm; Sa noon-10pm; Su 3-9pm

9083 Gaither Rd
Gaithersburg, MD (301) 977-6300

Red and white pizzas, pasta, calzone, subs, and build-your-own burgers, all homemade and all for eating in or carrying out. Also has salad bar. The pizza is the hands-down favorite by far. Pleasant dining room with family-type atmosphere. Another location in Olney, Md. (14 ratings/consistent)

BEST FOOD RATINGS BY CUISINE

("Food" rating in parentheses)

Afghan
Panjshir (84)
Bamiyan II (81)
Kabul Caravan (81)
Kabul West (81)

American
Inn at Little Washington (96)
Nora (88)
Artie's (87)
Windows (85)
Helen's (84)
Heart in Hand (83)
Prime Plus (83)
Flaming Pit (82)
Gadsby's Tavern (82)
Houston's (82)
Laporta's (81)
Occidental Grill (81)
Vinnie's (81)
Fuddruckers (81)

Asian
Germaine's (82)

Barbecue
Bare Bones (82)

Chinese
Hunan East-Baileys Crossroads (88)
Mandarin Inn (87)
House of Kao (87)
Hunan East--Burke (86)
Hsian Foong (86)
Peking Gourmet Inn (86)
Mr. K's (85)
Hunan Lion (84)
Charlie Chiang's (84)
Fantasy Garden (84)
House of Dynasty (83)
Hunan Chinatown (83)
Hunan (83)
Hunan Dynasty (82)
Old Peking (82)
Hunan Village (82)
Far East (81)
China D'Lite (81)
Dynasty (81)
Szechuan Gallery (81)
House of Mandarin (81)

Continental
J. J. Muldoon's (84)
Chef's Secret (83)
Black Orchid (82)
Nova Europa (82)

French
L'Auberge Chez Francois (93)
Le Lion d'Or (90)
Le Pavillon (90)
Le Chardon d'Or (90)
Maison Blanche (89)
Jean Louis (88)
La Bergerie (88)
Iron Skillet (87)
The Restaurant in Bethesda (87)

Le Rivage (87)
Le Marmiton (86)
La Ferme (86)
Le Gaulois (86)
King's Contrivance (86)
Le Vieux Logis (85)
La Miche (85)
Chez Nous (84)
L'Alouette (84)
Le Couvert (83)
Le Manouche (83)
La Fourchette (83)
Pierre et Madeline (83)
La Colline (82)
La Guinguette (82)
Dominique's (82)
Embassy (81)
Le Refuge (81)
Jacques' Cafe (81)
La Brasserie (81)
Le Canard (81)
Alibi (81)

Greek

Taverna Cretekou (81)
Ambrosia (81)

Indian

Bombay Palace (82)

Indonesian

Ivy's Place (82)
Sarinah Satay House (81)

Italian

Mamma Regina (87)
Terrazza (87)
Buon Giorno (87)
Tiberio (85)
Pasta Plus (85)
Mike's Italian Restaurant (84)
Bello Mondo (84)
Ledo (84)
Geppetto-Georgetown (84)
Filomena (84)
Alpine (83)
Italia Bella (83)
Zio's (83)
Da Domenico (82)
Espositos Pizza 'n Pasta (82)
Floriana (82)
Portofino (82)
Tivoli (82)
Geranio (82)
Bonaroti (81)
Landini Brothers (81)
Marco Polo (81)
Piatti Pizza & Pasta (81)
Pines of Italy (81)

Japanese

Tachibana (89)
Matuba-Arlington (86)
Ocean Garden (83)
Sakura Palace (83)
Mikado (81)
Matuba-Bethesda (81)

Lebanese

Bacchus (86)
Lebanese Taverna (82)

Mexican

Pancho Villa (84)
Bar J (83)
Chi-Chi's--Gaithersburg (81)

Polynesian

Kona Kai (82)

Seafood

Calvert House Inn (87)
La Maree (87)
New Orleans Emporium (85)
RT's (85)
Crisfield's (84)
Falls Landing (83)
Harvey's-Rockville (83)
Vincenzo (81)
O'Donnell's (81)

Steak House

Ruth's Chris Steak House (94)
Morton's of Chicago (90)
The Prime Rib (89)
J.R.'s Steak House (84)
Mountain Jack's (83)
Golden Bull-Adelphi (82)
J.R.'s Stockyards Inn (82)

Thai

Bangkok Gourmet (87)
Thai Kingdom (85)
Thai Taste (85)
Thai Derm (84)
Thai House (81)
Bangkok Garden (81)

Turkish

Kazan (87)
Nizam's (85)

Vietnamese

East Wind (85)
My An (81)

RESTAURANTS WITH SELECTED SPECIAL FEATURES

Sunday Brunch

(Sunday only unless Saturday is indicated with Sa)

American Cafe
Annie's Paramount Steak House (Sa)
Artie's
Bello Mondo
Bennigan's (Sa)
Bilbo Baggins Cafe
Bistro Francais (Sa)
Blue Channel Inn
Bombay Bicycle Club (Sa)
Bombay Palace (Sa)
Cafe La Ruche (Sa)
Caldwell's
Carlyle Grand Cafe
Carmack's
Carnegie's
Casa Maria
Chadwicks
Charley's Place
Charlie Chiang's
Chef Theo's
China Coral (Sa)
Claude's
Clyde's
Colonel Brook's Tavern

Comus Inn
Dalt's (Sa)
Devon Seafood Grill
Dona Flor
Eastport Raw Bar
El Torito
Evans Farm Inn
Fedora Cafe
Fireside Beef House
Foggy Bottom Cafe (Sa)
Fritzbe's
Gadsby's Tavern
Gangplank
Glen Echo Station
Hamburger Hamlet–
Wisconsin Ave., DC
Heart in Hand
Heidelberg
Henry Africa
Hogate's
Houlihan's
Hunan Lion (Sa)
J. J. Muldoon's
Jake's on the Pike
Jasper's
Joe Theismann's
Johnny's
Kona Kai
La Brasserie
La Fonda
Lauriol Plaza
Le Chardon d'Or
Le Jardin (Sa)
Market Inn (Sa)
Mr. L's and Sun (Sa)
Mrs. Simpson's
Mustache Cafe
New Heights
New Orleans Emporium
New York, New York
94th Aero Squadron
Normandie Farm Inn
Old Ebbitt Grill
Phillips Flagship
Phineas
Pleasant Peasant
Portner's
Potowmack Landing
Raindancer
Rhiannon's
Rick Walker's Scoreboard
Ruby Tuesday
Szechuan (Sa)
T.G.I. Friday's (Sa)
Taverna Cretekou
Tom Weston's (Sa)
Tony Lin's Kitchen (Sa)
219
2 Quail
Union Street Public House
Wellington's
West End Cafe
Wolensky's
Yenching Palace

Scenic View

Blue Channel Inn
Chadwicks
Clyde's–Columbia
Comus Inn
Evans Farm Inn
Gangplank
Hogate's
Le Rivage
Les Champs
Old Angler's Inn
Phillips Flagship
Pier 7
Potowmack Landing
700 Water Street Grill
Windows

Outdoor Dining

Anita's-Vienna
Armand's Chicago Pizzeria
Bangkok Gourmet
Cafe Italia II
Cafe La Ruche
Cafe Splendide
Cracked Claw
Eastport Raw Bar
Ecco Cafe
Gadsby's Tavern
Hamburger Hamlet-
  Wisconsin Ave., DC
Heart in Hand
Ice House Cafe
Iron Gate Inn
Ivy's Place
Jasper's
La Brasserie
La Fonda
La Fourchette
L'Auberge Chez Francois
Lauriol Plaza
Le Caprice
Le Rivage
Market Inn
Normandie Farm Inn
Old Angler's Inn
Olney Ale House
Phillips Flagship
Potowmack Landing
The Restaurant in Bethesda
Roma
Ruth's Chris Steak House
Shooter McGee's
Tabard Inn
Taverna Cretekou
Vietnam Georgetown
Vincenzo

Trip in Country

Comus Inn
Heart in Hand
Inn at Little Washington
King's Contrivance
L'Auberge Chez Francois
Meadowlark Inn
Mount Vernon Inn
Old Angler's Inn
Olney Ale House

Sushi

Japan Inn
Mikado
Ocean Garden
Perry's
Sakura Palace
Sushi-Ko
Tachibana
Wolensky's

Dim Sum

China Coral
Dynasty
Four Rivers
Golden Palace
House of Chinese Gourmet
Hunan Dynasty
Hunan Gourmet
Tony Lin's Kitchen
Tung Bor
Yenching Palace

Entertainment

Alamo
Alpine
Amelia's
Artie's
Asti-Roseto
Black Orchid
Cafe Mozart
Caldwell's
Charley's Place–McLean
Colonel Brook's Tavern
Dar Es Salam
Dona Flor
Evans Farm Inn
Fedora Cafe
Fireside Beef House
Fish Market
5 and Dime Cafe
Flaming Pit
Fritzbe's–Rockville
Gadsby's Tavern
Harvey's–Rockville
Henry Africa
Ice House Cafe
Il Porto
Italia Bella
J. J. Muldoon's
Jacques' Cafe
Jake's on the Pike
Jasper's
Johnny's
Kaiserhof
Kangaroo Katie's
Kilroy's
La Ferme
La Fonda
La Guinguette
La Miche
Laporta's
Le Canard
Marco Polo
Market Inn
Marrakesh
Mel Krupin's
Meskerem
Mountain Jack's
Mustache Cafe
94th Aero Squadron
Normandie Farm Inn
Oscar Taylor's
P. J. Skidoos
Pancho Villa
Phillips Flagship
Phoenix
Pier 7
Plata Grande–Beltsville
Pleasant Peasant
The Prime Rib
Red Sea
Rhiannon's
Rick Walker's Scoreboard
Roma
Serbian Crown
Squire Rockwell's
Swiss Cafe
Tivoli
Tony Lin's Kitchen
219
Vagabond
Wayfarers
Wellington's
West End Cafe
Willard Room
Wolensky's